A whole school approach

Behaviour Management

Bill Rogers

Rogers, William A. (William Arthur), 1947–.

Behaviour management: a whole–school approach.

ISBN 1 86388 356 8.

1. School discipline. 2. Teacher–student relationships.
3. Classroom management. I. Title.

371.1024

Text copyright © Bill Rogers, 1995.
Illustrations copyright © Scholastic Australia Pty limited, 1995.
Illustrated by Stephen Michael King.

First published in 1995 by Scholastic Australia Pty Limited ACN 000 614 577,
PO Box 579, Gosford 2250. Also in Sydney, Brisbane, Melbourne, Adelaide and Perth.

Reprinted in 1996 and 1997.

Typeset in Bembo 11/14 pt.

Printed by Australian Print Group, Maryborough, Vic.

9 8 7 6 5 4 3   7 8 9 / 9

'Each new generation offers
humanity a chance.'

Sir Peter Ustinov
UNICEF Goodwill Ambassador

'Any teacher who wants to,
can make a difference.'

(Anon)

Contents

Introduction

Chapter 1   **Developing a whole-school approach to behaviour management: assumptions and benefits**   **13**

Discusses the benefits of a whole-school approach to behaviour management:
- what it is and what it means
- what a whole-school approach can achieve in a school
- issues related to change in staff attitudes and behaviour
- developing a whole-school approach—a case study
- a framework is given within which a school can develop a whole-school policy and action plan. A range of fundamental questions is also given to use within the framework.

Throughout the book these concerns feature in the discussion of a wide range of behaviour management matters.

Chapter 2   **Preferred practices: student behaviour management**   **29**

Picks up a central tenet of a whole-school approach—a common set of preferred practices by which staff exercise behaviour management.

Chapter 3   **Positive discipline**   **46**

Deals with the practice of positive discipline:
- what is meant by this seemingly incongruous term?
- what does positive discipline look and sound like?

Includes discussion of:
- key teacher skills, using case examples
- parent support and use of classroom meetings.

Chapter 4   **The 'establishment' phase of the year**   **71**

Outlines:
- the crucial nature of the establishment phase of the year
- methods used to set up the 4Rs—rights, rules, responsibilities and routines.

Explores key issues such as:
- behavioural consequences
- use of withdrawal from the social group (time out).

Chapter 5   **The language of discipline**   102

Develops fully the language of discipline, giving practical, detailed examples for focused, positive, assertive behaviour management. Emphasises a management style that enables students to 'own' their behaviour in a way that actively considers others' rights.

Chapter 6   **Some problem areas in behaviour management**   124

Explores some traditional problems in managing student behaviour:
- follow-up/follow-through with students
- argumentative (backchatting) students, arguments and squabbles, especially after playtime
- put-downs by students
- swearing and 'bad' language
- maintenance of behaviour agreements (contracts)
- behaviourally disordered students
- the difficult class.

Chapter 7   **Managing playground behaviour and bullying**   163

Covers:
- playground management
- duty of care
- how to set up a management plan
- bullying in schools and a whole-school response.

Chapter 8   **Supporting colleagues in a united whole-school plan**   193

Discusses the need for unity of staff and the role of a supportive school culture in an effective whole-school approach.

Chapter 9   **Developing a behaviour management policy**   206

Discusses the development of a workable behaviour management policy which expresses:
- aims
- values
- practices
- plans.
Examples are given from school policy documents.

Conclusion   214

Appendixes   Key selections from school policy documents   217

Bibliography   229

Index   238

Acknowledgments

There are always many people to thank when releasing typed thoughts, beliefs and experiences to a publisher. First, my family. They often had to put up with a table covered in bits of transcribed thoughts, the first draft, the tenth draft, the inconveniences (deadlines!) that such a project injects into family living. Thanks Lora, Elizabeth and Sarah.

Then there are the many schools which have invited me to work with them as a consultant and allowed me to share their experiences. My special thanks go to Spring Gully Primary School (Sue Harrison and team), Mayfield Primary School (Colleen Breheney, Kelly Heathcote, Vicki Mackrill and team), Hare Street School (Louisa Sliwa, Debbie Barnes, Ros Daniels and team) and Northgate St Andrews First School (Bill Russell and team).

My thanks go to the many teachers who have asked me to take demonstration lessons in their classrooms to encourage peer modelling, team teaching and supportive peer review.

Once again, two highly skilled and patient typists have word-processed my handwriting. Thanks, Joy Draper and Jenni Shields.

Lastly, Ashton Scholastic has been patiently supportive of the project. My special thanks to Shane Armstrong and the team. I've also appreciated the goodwill and skills of a fine editor—thanks Julie Malcolm.

I hope you find the book helpful, practical and useful in your ongoing journey of whole-school behaviour management.

All the best.

Bill Rogers

Bill Rogers

Melbourne, September 1994

Introduction

QUESTIONS

The bell has just gone. Dianne has struggled with one of her Grade 5 students this morning. Craig, a student who seems to have his nose permanently out of joint, has made the morning hard work—to put it mildly. She recalls one of the exchanges when she directed Craig to sit up from his heavy chair leaning and off-task behaviour. 'Gees, you're always picking on me!' he'd grumbled. She had been drawn into an argument with him again: 'Well I wouldn't pick on you—as you call it—if you would just sit up, Craig, and not rock on your chair and turn around. That's one of the reasons you never get your work finished.' She reflects, as she heads for morning tea, that she probably argues with him too much—gives him the least helpful attention. But what else can she do?

Dianne walks past a colleague's Grade 6 class. She hears him shouting at a student in the corridor. 'How many times have I told you, Lee? Why can't you just do as I ask, eh? Is it so hard to pack up like the others?' 'Oh, no wonder! It's Lee,' Dianne thinks as she walks past, surreptitiously. She winces as she hears the tone in her colleague's voice and quickly takes in his angry body language. Yet she too, surely, has disciplined students in a similar way.

She sees a couple of boys running full pelt down the corridor. Should she say anything? She's tired. She's on playground duty in a minute. Anyway, she doesn't know their names. She had observed the deputy principal yelling at a few boys yesterday, 'Oi! This isn't a racetrack! How many times have I told you not to run in the corridor? Right, come here!' She doesn't like his yelling, especially when he corrects talkative, inattentive students during school assembly. Should she act like him to be effective? What does it mean to be effective anyway? She sighs. 'At least I've got time for a cuppa.'

Dianne quickly grabs a cuppa from the staffroom and she's off to duty. She overhears several teachers discussing behaviour problems and the upcoming review of behaviour management policy:

- 'Do you know what that little . . ., Peter, said to me in class?'
- 'They're getting noisier I'm sure, or maybe it's me getting tired at the end of term.'
- 'I'm fed up with Lisa's sulking in class.'
- 'You'd think I'd asked Sonia to fly to the moon when I asked her to pay attention! You should hear her—she's got the last-word syndrome down to a tee!' (With oblique eye contact, Dianne sees her colleague mimic Sonia, complete with whine.)
- 'I'm sure Paul has stolen money in class. I can't catch him out though. I tell you—he's an accomplished liar. Looks you straight in the eye and . . .'
- 'I just can't seem to get him to work.'
- 'What are we going to do about the teasing by the older kids?'
- 'What are we going to do about the litter problem?'
- 'What's the best punishment for . . .?'

Tune into any staff discussion, or staff meeting, stop and chat with a teacher or parent about behaviour management issues and these sorts of question and comment are common.

With the hot cuppa in hand, Dianne heads for Duty Area 3 down by the sandpit. She sees a couple of boys karate kicking, with an audience, down in that clump of trees. What should she do? She'd heard David say the other day at the staff meeting that it's just 'boys will be boys stuff' and we shouldn't get too worked up about it. Several of her female colleagues had disagreed, a few quite strongly. Is it aggressive play? If so, what should she say? How can she best approach them? She recalls a Prep teacher sharing how some Grade 6 boys had challenged her in the playground with, 'You're just a Prep teacher.'

She sees several girls sitting, eating, with litter at their feet. 'Shall I remind them to put it in the bin?' She recalls an argument she had with some senior girls last week over whose litter it was. 'Is it worth the effort?' She has watched colleagues manage students in the playground, but she hasn't always agreed with their approach. She's never had a serious discussion about how best to do playground duty. The bell goes. Dianne moves towards her class, cup in hand. She sees the keen students beginning to line up outside Building 3 in the senior school. She passes a couple of swearing boys. She is sure she heard a racist put-down. Should she stop and say something? Should she report it? What would she say? Is it worth the effort?

The principal is on his way back to the office. He's mulling over the upcoming behaviour management review. He has to raise the issues of classroom and playground discipline. How will he do it? He's partly driven by Education Department guidelines, but is also aware of staff disquiet on a number of matters such as rudeness, swearing, aggression, teasing, even bullying. There are many great things going on in 'his' school, but these behaviour problems have to be addressed. He sees one of the younger, male teachers yelling at a student in the playground. As he passes and gazes at this social vignette and sees the wagging finger, he muses, 'Doesn't look too good, does it? The student probably deserves it though. Wonder what he was doing?'

He is aware that students are more challenging today and more vocal about their rights but how can he, and his staff, challenge students to be more responsible and respectful of others' rights? 'Of course, times have changed, but the way some of these students speak! They still need discipline, guidance and instruction. In my day, I used the "strap", the cane. Was it better then? It was easier, but then we taught differently with larger groups, more teacher-directed.' He knows the authoritarian approach is ineffective and largely resisted by students today. But? And the bullying issue: 'In my day, we just lived with it. All the media attention today seems to make out it's a huge issue. We don't have many fights here.' Some of his staff have raised verbal and racial put-downs and teasing as equivalent to bullying. 'Are they right?'

Seated in his office, he takes a piece of paper and reflects on the questions raised by behaviour management. There are so many entry points into this issue of behaviour management and discipline . . .

- 'Where do I start?' (Where do *we* start?)
- 'Is there such a thing as a right way to discipline? What do we mean, anyway, by discipline? Some of the parents would be happy if I brought back corporal punishment!'
- 'What do we mean by good management practice? Who decides what is good practice?'
- 'How can I encourage my staff to reflect on their management and discipline? Some of my staff need a lot of work on their management skills. Some of my teachers need more behaviour management skills—but which skills? How? Is it all down to personality in the end?'
- 'How can I support my classroom teachers when they send Craig, Dean, Lee or Lisa to me? What am I supposed to do? I'm sure some of them expect me to bawl them out. What good does that do? Do we need a time-out policy?'

He stops writing to consider how he will address the upcoming interview with Chad's mother. The school psychologist has described Chad as 'behaviourally disordered'. 'He's that all right! What am I going to say to her—especially after the last interview? More importantly, how am I going to support Wendy? She already has that difficult Grade 2 girl.' His musings are interrupted by a knock at the door. Adam, one of his senior teachers has come to discuss the planning meeting for this staff review on behaviour management. Adam is a good listener. 'Adam, can I run these questions past you?'

Finding helpful, useful answers to these questions is not always easy. They call forth our fundamental values and beliefs, they often challenge our practices and they require reflection individually as well as with colleagues as a group.

More difficult is the fact that teachers are incredibly busy people, with little free time. The challenge of these questions occurs in the midst of their day-to-day concerns, but they have to be asked. I've sought to answer these questions in the course of my work with schools. This book sets out a range of practical answers developed by schools to address behaviour management. No answer is definitive—especially when addressing the vagaries of human behaviour when one group of people (teachers) is trying to lead, guide, direct, teach and encourage another group (students) to behave in responsible, rights-enhancing ways.

Some quite robust, human ideals are outlined in this text, especially the need for positive behaviour management practice. There is a section on how to deal with argumentative students, and the more objectionable members of the human race in our schools. A range of practical strategies is outlined for dealing with such matters as noise levels in class, calling out, teasing and dobbing. While the strategies and plans outlined here are effective, they are not easy. They require thoughtful effort and consistency in application. Clearly there are times when even the best plans, the most thoroughly considered practices and the highest ideals are frustrated by the inadequacies of others as well as our own tiredness and depleted energy reserves. We are heavily fallible—all too human. The way people behave can be frustrating and annoying enough to make us angry at times. Even our own behaviour and the slow pace of change sometimes create stress. A whole-school approach takes time and we need to accept and allow for fallibility in ourselves and others. If we focus on the school as a whole, the journey and outcomes will be more effective.

I've written this book from the conviction that schools can (and clearly do) find workable, useful and practical answers to questions of behaviour management using a whole-school approach. Things can improve when teachers:
- move from sectional self-interest to concern for the welfare of colleagues as a group, as a team
- ask, 'What do *we* believe as well as what do *I* believe?'
- ask, 'What are our aims regarding behaviour management and what practices will better fit those aims?'
- work for common plans on matters such as classroom behaviour, rules, consequences, playground management and specific issues such as calling out, put-downs, noise level, mixed ability, behaviourally disordered students, teasing, bullying, even bus duty!

Effective behaviour management is essential to the smooth running of a school and in the creation of an environment where everyone's rights and responsibilities are addressed. A balance between fundamental rights and responsibilities is at the heart of behaviour management.

This book addresses the many aspects of student and teacher behaviour which affect that balance and explores how teachers can work in practical ways towards consistent, positive and purposeful management practices school-wide.

Chapter 1

DEVELOPING A WHOLE-SCHOOL APPROACH: ASSUMPTIONS AND BENEFITS

The quality of behaviour management can be significantly improved and the social and learning environment of a school is enhanced, if a whole-school approach is developed. From extensive international experience, working and observing in schools, I have found that improvement occurs most readily when the assumptions which underpin a whole-school approach are matched with collaborative practices.

The school system and the community of people that constitute a school, need to be the focus for intervention and change. As Rutter (1979) has demonstrated, positive (and measurable) outcomes in behaviour and learning can occur apart from the socioeconomic conditions of the school's clientele. Beliefs and expectations affect teacher morale, effort and commitment to the school. Progress will be limited if the school's attitudinal stance is, 'How can we be expected to develop good learning and behaviour when we've got kids like these in this kind of environment?'

Clearly, there are many factors in the background and home environment of students that a school cannot directly affect. However, when a school applies itself, in attitude and action, to educational and social factors which it has power to change, then outcomes can be affected. Students, after all, spend at least a third of their waking day at school. Gillborn et al (1994) note, '. . . although disadvantage may manifest itself in behavioural disturbance and non-attendance, it should not be assumed it will necessarily do so. Nor should it be assumed that students who experience disadvantage cannot succeed academically' (p 114). Axworthy et al (1989) write, 'The only way [a staff] can impact a problem is by taking responsibility for those factors over which they have control. This requires an additional shift for many teachers, away from attributing blame or feeling guilt' (p 69).

Students spend at least a third of their waking day at school.

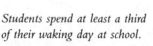

13

Significant and effective change occurs when individuals within a school system pursue a collaborative model of change with these characteristics:

- opportunities and processes are put in place for collaborative staff communication
- staff communicate collaboratively about common concerns and needs (see p 194)
- staff work on common behaviour management practices and plans
- the head teacher and senior staff have a positive commitment to change.

The Elton Report (1989, p 91) comments:

> We have identified seven aspects of school management which seem to be particularly important for students' behaviour. The head's role is central to them all. They are: staff management; establishing and maintaining internal and external communication systems; fostering a sense of community; taking the lead in setting aims and standards; encouraging collective responsibility; supporting staff; and directing overall curriculum and organisational planning. There is scope for positive action in each of these areas, but effective staff management is the key to success in them all. Senior staff need to recognise it is within their power to create a different atmosphere in the school, to initiate change through their own modelling and procedural aims. Senior staff can elicit positive responses from their staff through their own commitment such that they carry as many of the rest of their staff as possible with them.

In my experience, whole-school change is effective only when senior staff endorse and enable open communication, especially on vital aspects of behaviour management. *The Elton Report* further notes:

> Poor communication is generally recognised as a feature of bad management. Our evidence suggests that communication with and between staff is particularly important for maintaining the kind of morale and atmosphere necessary to promote good behaviour (p 93).

This commitment to effective communication needs to be reflected in a common focus for objectives from behaviour and learning through to policy and planning.

The OECD report (1989) on schools and quality noted that effective schools are marked, among other things, by collaborative planning, shared decision making and the experience of working within a framework of experimentation and evaluation.

Such a process takes time, effort, an opening up of individual and communal values and a willingness to persist in a collaborative journey. No esoteric knowledge is needed for a school to be successful. The expertise is available within the school. Active recognition of this and utilisation of teacher skills and abilities towards a common purpose will determine successful outcomes. This involves more than changing organisational structures, or even writing a policy, as important as these factors are (p 207 ff). It is essential that staff see meaning in the change process (Fullan 1991).

This process of change raises important questions.
- How much of the change process is imposed by education departments?
- What should change because current practices are ineffective, dysfunctional or incongruent with our aims or 'best practice'?
- How can we manage the change process, and implement change to avoid unnecessary stress on the school community?

Ideas and action to consider

- The reasons for change need to be explored, especially when imperatives for change are imposed from outside the school.
- Reasons for changes, such as to policy and practice, need to be clarified for staff. It is worthwhile to explore how changes might, or will, affect teaching practice and behaviour management.
- Emphasise the benefits of change. Allow for and encourage appropriate professional development and re-skilling (pp 197-8).
- Above all, give as much power as possible to those affected by the change process. The best way to do this is through effective communication and collaboration.

Most schools need to accept that imposed changes will occur as a result of the wider education system of which they are part. How individual schools manage the change process determines the degree of choice available as imposed changes are implemented.

Change can be an ally

As Fullan (1991) has noted, change is more likely to be an ally than an adversary if it is confronted. The change process takes time, effort, planning and productive failure. It is a journey from a 'here' that we believe needs review and assessment to a destination to which we are directed, a 'there' where we want and need to go. This journeying process has inbuilt natural conflict as people's beliefs, ideas and prejudices are aired, as practices are questioned, and new approaches are called for. It is relatively easy to write up aims and objectives, to create a mission statement for management policy, and quite another matter to put such statements into operation.

Wherever possible, people need time to come to terms with the processes of change. Change always requires that people reflect on their current practice. Staff need support rather than criticism as they assess comfortable, sometimes longstanding, habits and methods.

Catalysts to change

People begin to change when:
- a need or purpose for change is seen
- a framework exists within which change can operate
- models, examples and experiences for change are available
- (above all) support for change is given (Rogers 1992).

It is important that school leaders demonstrate care for their staff as individuals during this process. This can be expressed in little things such as staff morning teas, how meetings are run, laughter and humour, and celebration of birthdays. Setting up effective processes for review, feedback, ongoing communication and action planning are also important. Above all, it is necessary to actively resist the attitude that says, 'There's little or nothing we can really do. Fate is in control.' Harris (1973) puts it neatly, 'A loser believes in fate, a winner believes we make our fate by what we do or fail to do.'

The benefits of a whole-school approach

Behaviour management and discipline matters are noted in the literature as significant causes of teacher stress. Structural and professional teacher isolation is one cause of teacher stress. This results in an unwillingness to share concerns or problems about student management for fear of imputed failure. By developing a supportive culture in a school so that staff are free to address concerns within a problem-solving framework, stress levels can be significantly reduced (p 193). Such support needs to be developed at formal and informal levels across the school.

Hamilton (1986, 1989) in Axworthy et al (1989) has shown that where schools pursued a whole-school approach to managing student behaviour, the relative stress levels were lower than in control schools he had studied. Also, in schools which had embarked on a process of whole-school review, teachers attributed disruptive behaviour to factors within the school, not merely to outside factors, and the rating of disruptive behaviour was lower. Such schools also showed diminished rates of both suspension and referral of student behaviour problems to senior staff. These schools published policy statements of their beliefs and practices about behaviour management and discipline.

Schools also report a greater sense of support when needs and concerns are raised and structural reforms and plans are put in place (p 169 ff). This is especially important for managing difficulties presented by behaviourally disordered students, crises such as the removal of a student from class, the 'hard-class' syndrome, and problematic playground behaviour such as aggression, bullying and violence. There is an appropriate and proper sense of security in the knowledge that procedures are in place that will give support to teachers and students in a crisis (see Rogers 1992).

When there is a sense of 'We're in this together', staff are not left alone to cope. One of the great stressors for teachers is the anxiety created by an unsupportive environment, especially through lack of support from senior staff. Kahn and Katz (1960) in Rutter (1979) found that supervisors in highly productive working groups were generally seen by employees to be supportive, understanding of their difficulties, concerned about their problems and needs and, most importantly, interested in them as individuals. I have found the same perceptions among teachers and students (see Kyriacou 1981, 1987; Schwartz and Karasek, 1989 in Rogers 1992).

Some characteristics and effects of a whole-school approach to behaviour management

- There is an increase in effective strategies as teachers begin to share good practice, and see the results.
- Staff begin to act more consistently when the whole-school policy is the outcome of genuine, wide collaboration.
- There is an increase in staff involvement and commitment to policy imperatives.
- Staff are more confident if appropriate corrective action is spelt out.
- A shared knowledge base provides a stronger support for behaviour management.
- Staff and students better appreciate and understand why 'this school manages this way'.
- Parents begin to appreciate, and support, the values underpinning the school's policy. Any school-wide process will need to work for parent understanding, support and, wherever possible, involvement (Lowe and Istance 1989).
- 'Above all, there is renewed emphasis on preventive approaches . . . such as negotiation, problem-solving, and interpersonal and communication skills' (Nelson 1981).

A WHOLE-SCHOOL FRAMEWORK FOR A POLICY ON BEHAVIOUR MANAGEMENT

A framework for a school-wide policy on behaviour management is set out in Figure 1, showing the key elements requiring serious consideration, review, discussion by staff, professional development, application, and policy development.

The research noted earlier stresses several points.
1 It is very important for a school to:
  - clarify its values and aims (pp 29-30)
  - state its preferred management practices—how teachers act when they manage.

Clarification of preferred practice is not an imposition on teachers. They are simply assessing how their practice of management and discipline is congruent with the school's aims. This is not easy. Staff members possess a variety of personalities and a range of beliefs about what is acceptable behaviour in management, teaching/learning contexts, and in discipline and punishment. The continuum runs from authoritarian in approach through to 'take it as it comes'. Gaining a common perspective requires allowance for some creative tension within the staff. Key questions relative to this process are set out (pp 22-28).

Through the kind of leadership modelled, the outcome is not rigid conformity but encouragement of staff conviction that these practices are consistent with:
  - fundamental principles of human respect and dignity, and fair treatment
  - workable utility (They achieve the aims noted earlier. The utility of those aims is also enhanced by consistency of staff support.)
  - current educational practice and departmental guidelines on gender equity and anti-harassment.

A FRAMEWORK FOR SCHOOL POLICY ON BEHAVIOUR MANAGEMENT

Leading and supporting behaviour that is responsible in a way that acknowledges and protects mutual rights.

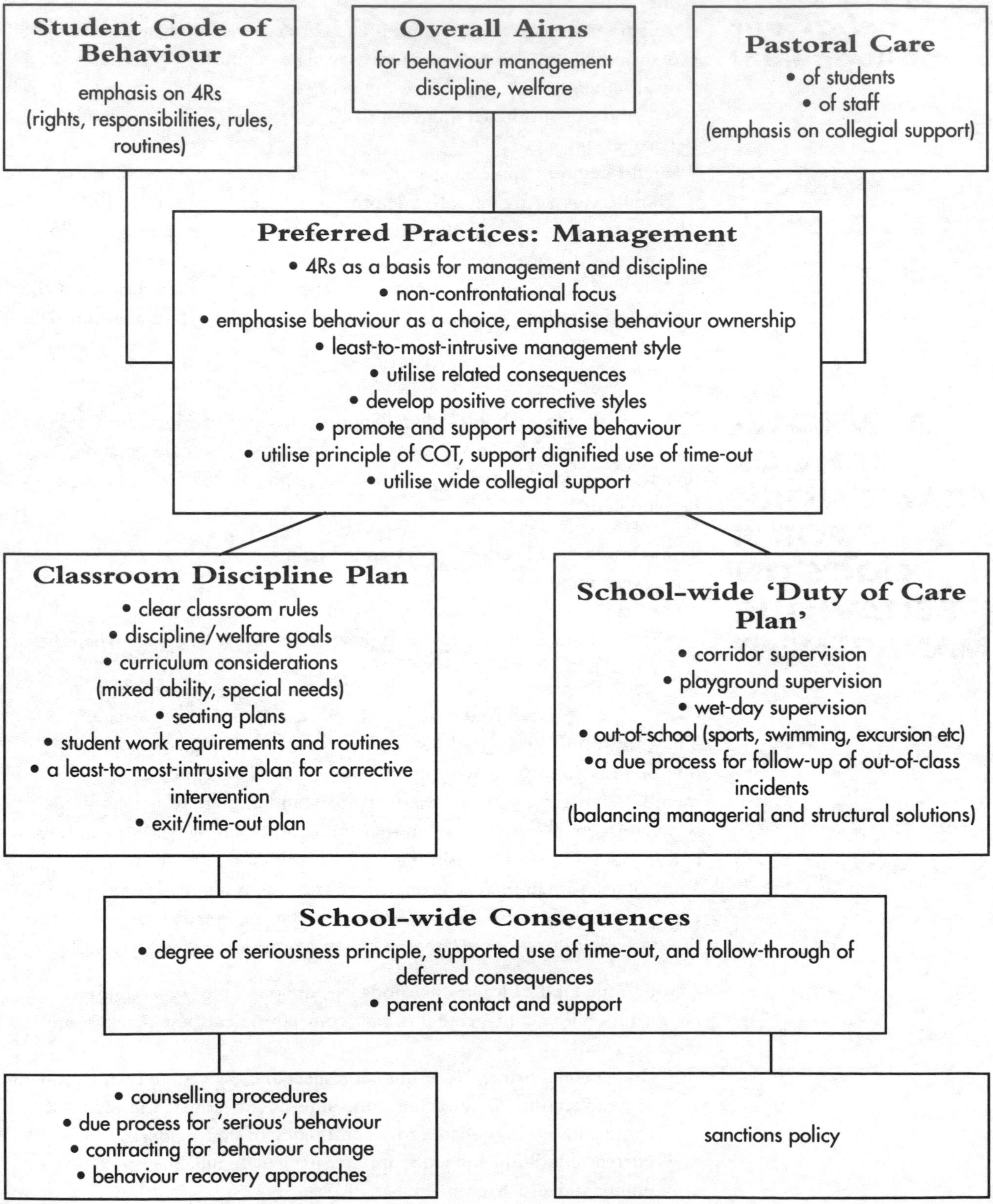

Student Code of Behaviour

emphasis on 4Rs
(rights, responsibilities, rules, routines)

Overall Aims

for behaviour management
discipline, welfare

Pastoral Care

- of students
- of staff
(emphasis on collegial support)

Preferred Practices: Management

- 4Rs as a basis for management and discipline
- non-confrontational focus
- emphasise behaviour as a choice, emphasise behaviour ownership
- least-to-most-intrusive management style
- utilise related consequences
- develop positive corrective styles
- promote and support positive behaviour
- utilise principle of COT, support dignified use of time-out
- utilise wide collegial support

Classroom Discipline Plan

- clear classroom rules
- discipline/welfare goals
- curriculum considerations
(mixed ability, special needs)
- seating plans
- student work requirements and routines
- a least-to-most-intrusive plan for corrective intervention
- exit/time-out plan

School-wide 'Duty of Care Plan'

- corridor supervision
- playground supervision
- wet-day supervision
- out-of-school (sports, swimming, excursion etc)
- a due process for follow-up of out-of-class incidents
(balancing managerial and structural solutions)

School-wide Consequences

- degree of seriousness principle, supported use of time-out, and follow-through of deferred consequences
- parent contact and support

- counselling procedures
- due process for 'serious' behaviour
- contracting for behaviour change
- behaviour recovery approaches

sanctions policy

Figure 1 © Bill Rogers

2 A school's code of conduct for students also needs to reflect the school's aims for management.

When we discipline, correct and manage, what are we trying to achieve in the immediate, emotional moment in a classroom or corridor? How do our daily corrective messages, statements and consequences teach the students about self-control and respect for others' rights? This code needs collaboration with students via the student representative council, clear explanation and discussion with students, and publication in a user-friendly form. It is also advisable to have a copy available to parents on enrolment of their child.

3 A school policy needs a parallel commitment to pastoral care of staff as well as students (p 194 ff).

4 To make the school's preferred practices meaningful, a common approach to key action plans is necessary:
(a) A classroom plan expressing how grade and specialist teachers prefer to manage behaviour has been found to be helpful with a common approach to:
  • classroom rules (to aid consistency and clarity) (pp 76-79)
  • the use of consequences
  • time-out plans (p 82 ff)
  • skills repertoire to enhance preferred practices (p 34 ff).

The skills framework is set out in some detail on page 18, outlining how staff can be appropriately assertive while remaining positive when managing students. These skills can be used in professional development to demonstrate how teachers can less stressfully fulfil their managerial and disciplinary role. For that professional development to have integrity it will be better carried out with teaching staff (who have credibility) who can model the skills in relaxed collegial settings and set up non-threatening small-group practice sessions (Rogers 1990, 1992).
(b) Duty of care plans need to consider:
  • all staff (including non-teaching personnel) who remind, encourage, direct and sometimes confront students about appropriate behaviour in corridors, canteen queues and playground
  • how best to manage students with reasonable consistency, particularly through a playground management plan. Current research has noted (p 179) that most bullying occurs in playgrounds. The usual mix of a wide age range and the freedom associated with release from classrooms contributes to problem behaviour. Schools need to emphasise, teach, and monitor safety and fair treatment outside of classrooms
  • wet-day timetabling, excursion management, school camps and, if appropriate, bus duty.

5 School-wide consequences need to be clarified for aggressive behaviour, bullying, harassment and related matters.

The 'degree of seriousness' principle needs to be considered. For management and behaviour matters, staff must clarify and make decisions about:
- what should be dealt with at classroom or playground level
- what needs to be referred to senior management for support of teaching and non-teaching staff
- time-out settings beyond the classroom or withdrawal during playground time
- how parents are contacted
- how to deal with bullying, harassment and aggressive behaviour
- the use of detention with senior grades
- how sanctions such as internal or external suspension are carried out.

6 Consistent with the school's commitment to pastoral care, it is important to:
- support behaviour management with counselling and welfare
- make provisions for and set up procedures for behaviour contracting
- introduce methods of teaching students social behaviour in one-to-one settings (see p 152 ff).

This framework is offered as a guide. Each of the elements and their interrelatedness needs serious consideration and attention. The quality of the process—the journey of reflection and development taken by the staff of a school—will determine how effective and workable the policy will be.

ONE SCHOOL'S JOURNEY

Hare Street Infant School, Harlow (UK)

Debbie Barnes and Ros Daniels write:

'Our journey towards a behaviour policy began in May 1991 after a staff training day when we focused on the behaviour observed in our playground. After analysing the unwanted behaviour, we brainstormed strategies for change and modification. This involved changing the physical layout of the playground (which was void of structure, guidelines and rules) and changing the attitudes and behaviour of students and teachers who were demoralised and in a negative spiral of low expectation.

'Our first priority was to create a structured physical environment which would enable students to be and feel safe. We negotiated positive rules with the students which were discussed publicly and were seen to be fair. The rules were jointly owned by students and adults and the responsibility for enforcing them was also shared.

'Next we looked at the playground and the activities which students enjoyed outside—running games, skipping, playing with cars, role-play, quiet reading and writing activities and many more. We set up physical zones for specific activities by painting lines on the playground so students could play appropriately and safely. Informed choices could be made about where and how they wanted to play.

'The students took responsibility for their behaviour and we introduced the idea of consequences for breaking an agreed rule. We looked at the way students came back to class after playtime and realised that a lot of inappropriate behaviour happened then. We decided that teachers would meet their students in a class circle on the playground and play a ring game before bringing them in.

'By the start of the autumn term, the new playground system was in operation. We felt it was crucial to share the reality of our vision and its practical implications with our midday supervisors. We gave them a much higher profile by showing how we valued them and their contribution to the school community. They were given a new uniform and badges to wear, their photos were displayed in the entrance hall, and a rota was made for teachers to support them in the dining hall. [Students in UK schools often have hot lunches at tables, supervised by non-teaching staff.] Students became monitors to help with sweeping up and wiping tables. We invited them to training sessions to equip them for their new roles and encouraged them to look for positive behaviour in the playground. Every week they choose two students from each class to receive a certificate for good behaviour. Stickers are given out on a daily basis.

'The playground atmosphere improved dramatically and continues to do so. However, as staff, we have had to review constantly, and occasionally change the activities within each zone due to popularity, seasonal changes or problems.

'As our attitudes to and expectations for playground behaviour changed, we began to focus our attention on the behaviour within the classroom. During the academic year, teachers gradually began to analyse their practice and to share concerns and information—everything from problem behaviour to successful strategies. Through trial and error we developed an initial system of consequences which included time-out procedures. However, we still lacked confidence and although we believed that students should take responsibility for their behaviour, we needed a practical framework on which to build. After attending a summer school at the University of Cambridge Institute of Education with Bill Rogers, we were able to work through many of the issues which had been concerning us at that time.

'In September, during several training sessions, we shared ideas and strategies for establishing a whole-school policy. This involved each class publishing their own negotiated rules, charts to show movement from the classroom, sound charts to monitor noise levels, class meetings and peer group support. We organised a system of preventive, corrective, consequential and support action which we implemented throughout the school.

'We then reviewed our use of language for disciplining students. We considered the content of what we say, its timing and the tone of voice used. We had to redress the balance of power to include mutual respect by adults and students, and we now have an expectation of positive behaviour within our school.

'The parents were invited to an open meeting where we were able to share and discuss our new and exciting behaviour policy. This involved forum theatre (dramatic presentations) which allowed parents to share their ideas about discipline in a non-threatening context. This was then followed by a presentation which explained the policy through an illustrated booklet. The evening was very well attended and the exchange of ideas enabled the parents to see the policy in practice and as a result it was very well received.

'The journey isn't yet finished. The school is still evolving as we take on new ideas and learn from our mistakes. This process of change has resulted in empowerment of the staff and students in our community. The effects of the behaviour policy in the school have been far reaching both academically and socially. We believe that the students are now beginning to realise their full potential through this positive approach.'

•   •   •

FUNDAMENTAL QUESTIONS ON BEHAVIOUR MANAGEMENT

When addressing behaviour management across a school, much of the hassle and pain can be minimised by the kinds of question we ask, and the focus we develop from those questions. Throughout this text, key questions will be referred to frequently, whether addressing classroom discipline, corridor supervision or playground management. These questions can be applied to any area of behaviour management. They focus on four fundamental facets of behaviour management that need to be balanced to ensure a comprehensive approach.

1 Prevent and minimise

How can we prevent or minimise unnecessary problems associated with behaviour in social groups?

In the establishment phase of the year, effective teachers work hard to set up classrooms with positive routines and rules which assist the smooth running of a classroom. Even before we think about corrective discipline, we need a framework in which to manage, correct and encourage.

With preventive planning, we can provide better management of:
• classroom
• corridor
• playground (the wearing of hats in summer, lining up routines at the canteen, toilet procedures, litter, teasing, play fighting)
• wet-day supervision
• bus duty.

Prevention can be exercised in how we organise the social aspects of behaviour and the characteristics of the teaching and learning environment. Consider the importance of physical aspects of the environment such as the quality of seating and its arrangement, setting up of learning centres, and appropriate heating and shade.

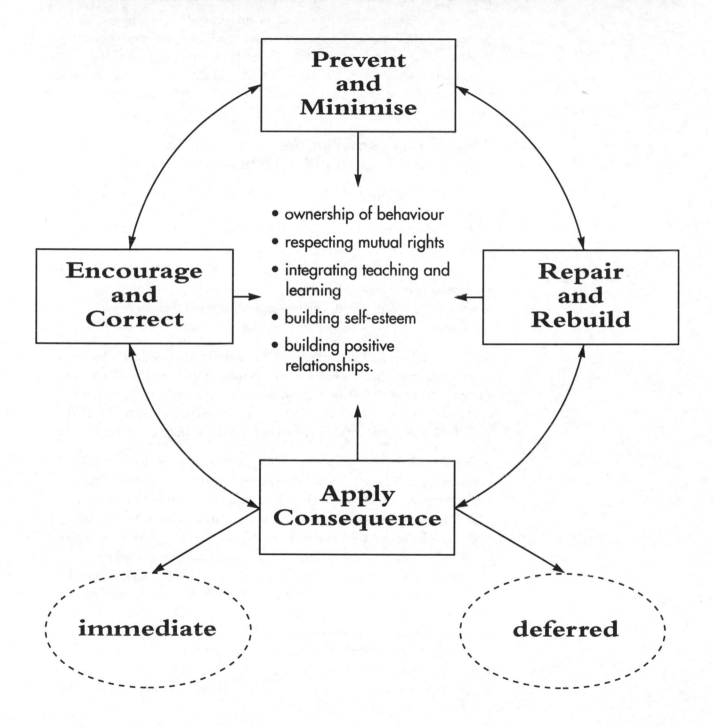

- ownership of behaviour
- respecting mutual rights
- integrating teaching and learning
- building self-esteem
- building positive relationships.

Balancing the key facets of behaviour management.

Figure 2 © B Rogers 1995,
see also *The Language of Discipline,* Rogers 1994, Northcote House.

2 Encourage and correct

How can we encourage positive and responsible behaviour and correct behaviour which infringes on rights?

How can we balance correction and encouragement? When students infringe on the rights of others, correction is necessary. By correction, I mean what teachers do to deal with behaviour, immediately as well as in the longer term. Calling out, butting in, running in the corridor, task refusal, answering back, swearing, teasing or bullying all require some form of correction.

How can we correct in the least intrusive way so that respect and dignity are kept intact?

Correction can range from something as basic and minimal as a privately understood signal (for example, a teacher might signal 'four on the floor' with extended fingers to a heavy 'chair leaner') through to assertive direction where unambiguous firmness is required.

Two key aspects of correction are explored later:
- the principle of least-to-most-intrusive correction
- balancing correction with encouragement, support and the re-establishment of working relationships.

When correcting student misbehaviour as distinct from student mistakes, it is impossible for teachers to know in every instance exactly how to correct students. What is important in a whole-school approach is a commitment to act from common values and a framework of preferred practice. This gives a shared sense of purpose and increases reasonable, workable consistency.

Although we all have our idiosyncratic personalities, we can take a common approach to behaviour management through shared practices and plans (Chapter 2). Consider this example from playground duty. Many teachers have the experience of students coming up to them, whining, 'Someone took my ball' or 'No-one will play with me, Miss' or 'Miss! Miss! Some boys are spoiling our game.' Some teachers characteristically respond by shooing the students away, saying, 'Go away and play somewhere else. I'm trying to drink my tea!' or 'Look. No wonder no-one wants to play with you, when you whine like that!' I have heard some male teachers brush off the self-styled victim with the words, 'Are you a man or what are you! You go and get the ball back yourself. Grow up!' Other teachers may seek to solve the problem for the students. These responses reflect various values which create a disparate management practice.

We also need to consider more constructive ways to help such students cope with exclusion from social play, having games interrupted, having their games equipment taken. Our playground policy (Chapter 7) will consider the main questions relative to preventive, corrective, supportive and consequential management.

3 Apply appropriate consequences

What consequences ought to follow when students refuse or abuse corrective management?

Consequences are a necessary feature of discipline and behaviour management. Apart from the natural consequences that occur in life, behaviour management requires that connections be made between behaviour and the outcomes that follow from rights, rules and responsibilities. Students need to learn that all behaviour has outcomes (positive and negative). These outcomes relate to how the rights of others are affected by one's behaviour.

Some supplementary questions about consequences

- What is the difference between consequences and simple punishment?
- What do students learn from the consequences we apply? What do they learn about the relationship between the consequence and their disruptive behaviour?
- What do we consider to be fair consequences?
- How much negotiation should students have regarding their consequences?
- What consequences should be non-negotiable?
- How do we distinguish between the certainty of consequences and the severity of application of a consequence?
- What degree of seriousness do we build into our consequences?

4 Repairing and rebuilding

How can we repair and rebuild after correction and consequences?

If we relied only on preventive, corrective and consequential discipline, the student–teacher and student–student relationships would be adversely affected. Repairing and rebuilding goes beyond correction and consequences to:

- assure students that they are still accepted as members of the class and the school
- deal with the natural bad feelings that go with facing consequences and punishment
- emphasise reconciliation (re-peace-ing) especially of teacher and student
- provide a model of reconciliation for the student concerned as well as any others involved. (It is reasonable to expect, rather than demand, reconciliation. Of course, the teacher must initiate and model the process.)

As a teacher, one of the hardest things to do is to go beyond consequences to forgiveness and reconciliation. This means we must try to take one day at a time, treat students with respect by our actions (pp 32, 38–39), avoid holding grudges, and accept students back into the group. I've seen countless examples of teachers who have behaved in ways that make reconciliation very difficult. For example, when time-out has been used as a consequence of disruptive behaviour, the teacher heralds the student's return to class with words such as, 'Right! I hope you're not going to be stupid like you were before, because if you are . . .!'

A teacher has a hard day with a noisy class. 'I've had it up to here with you lot! You're like a pack of animals. What's wrong with you? You've spoiled my day you have! Yes, you can laugh, Craig . . . you're the worst!' This lecture, arising from understandable frustration (if unhelpfully expressed), is not finished. The next morning, prior to 'morning talk', he says, 'Right, I hope you're not going to be like you were yesterday. I had a headache last night because of you lot! Yes, it was all your fault.'

Rebuilding damaged, strained and dysfunctional relationships also involves teaching better, even new, behavioural patterns. This can be carried out in a number of ways but with persistently disruptive students, the process has to be whole-school in application. We need to ask how we, as a team, can assist our colleague to help that student:
- rebuild more effective ways to solve problems
- work more effectively in class
- manage frustration and anger
- overcome dysfunctional ways of belonging to a group
- minimise the effects of poor socialisation
- adjust unacceptable patterns of play in the playground.

It is particularly annoying to hear colleagues saying things in the staffroom like, 'Do you know what *your* Jason did in the playground today?' When Jason is in the playground, corridor, at swimming, following a wet-day timetable, or in specialist classes, there is a sense in which he is everybody's Jason. If a colleague happens to be the poor person who has Jason enrolled in their class and we, as a team, are aware of Jason's recidivist behaviour, then both teacher and student need whole-school support. The student needs to be taught alternatives and also experience consistent correction, consequences and encouragement.

Problem-solving questions

As well as key planning questions there are some crucial questions that relate to problem solving. These can be applied to the widest range of behaviour issues by:
- students and teachers (as in a classroom meeting)
- staff and parents.

1 What is the problem as we see it?
   It is important to define the issue from a broad perspective, especially where the issue affects many people. It is especially important to involve students on key issues like playground behaviour such as teasing, play fighting and bullying.

2 Who is affected?
   How many students? How often? Where? (If the behaviour is occurring in the playground, are there any hot spots or trouble areas?)

3 Why do we think it is occurring?

4 What are we characteristically doing now to address problem behaviour?

This must relate to specific behaviour such as
- teasing, dobbing, play fighting, out-of-bounds play in the playground
- calling out, noise levels, answering back, task avoidance in the classroom.

5 Is our current management of such behaviour effective? Does what we're currently doing fit in with our policy? our preferred practices? our fundamental aims?

6 If it isn't, what can we do to address the problem?
Consider these levels of management when framing questions:
- preventive
- corrective
- supportive
- consequential
- repairing and rebuilding (see Figure 2).

There is nearly always a workable outcome when these questions are thoughtfully applied.

There is a useful question framework (the 4Ws) for classroom meetings or for consequences that involve students in writing about behaviour (rather than writing unrelated lines).
- What's the problem, specifically?
- What rule or right is being affected by this problem?
- Why do you think this problem is occurring? (This question can be used as a right of reply question in conflict resolution and when encouraging the student to think about related consequences.)
- What can you do, or, what do you need to do to fix up the problem?

I sometimes add the question: How can I help?

Many schools make up a pro-forma for older students to fill in as an exercise during detention (when detentions are used) or as a step in applying consequences, for example, after formal uses of time-out. Naturally, we would never force students to do this if we knew their writing skills could not match the task. Instead, the questions would be used as a conflict resolution exercise with the teacher recording student feedback. The key role of consequences is not to increase intentional suffering but to enable resolution and restitution.

Key questions for use in evalution of programs, strategies, policies and plans

What's working well in our classroom/school and why? (Relevant considerations include plans, activities and strategies. The 'why' is important—the answers are revealing.)

What's not working well and why?

What can we do to change things for the better in line with our aims as well as functional utility?

These questions are also ideal for a classroom meeting format (p 64 ff).

Based on the answers to these questions, we can form an action plan to address:

• concerns we can respond to quickly
• matters which will take more time, especially those related to restructuring and buying equipment
• non-negotiable items such as a responsive bureaucracy supporting schools!

Chapter 2

DEVELOPING PREFERRED PRACTICES OF BEHAVIOUR MANAGEMENT

A framework for common practice

At the heart of a whole-school approach to behaviour management are our behaviour management practices—what we do when students call out, butt in, don't pack up, come late, answer back and argue with us, fight, run in corridors, bully. Rather than leave teachers to decide 'on the run' how to deal with the range of disruptive behaviour, staff make preferential decisions about behaviour management based on shared values and aims. These practices are 'preferred' in the sense that they enable us to better fulfil our aims of 'leading and supporting behaviour that is responsible in a way that acknowledges and protects mutual rights' (see Figure 1). Management and discipline procedures seek to develop in students an acceptance of responsibility for their own behaviour, especially as it impacts on others' rights.

Within a school, some degree of certainty and clarity about what is appropriate management is necessary for staff and students in order to create a stable teaching, learning and social environment. These practices can also provide a framework for collaborative planning when addressing behaviour problems.

It is unhelpful to have one teacher (especially the principal) shouting or screaming at a 'corridor runner': 'Oi—you, yes you! Why are you running in the corridor?' and another ignoring loud swearing and teasing, and yet another, while off duty in the playground, turning a blind eye to rule-breaking behaviour. A united approach makes an impact. Research on bullying for example, has shown that 'low-bullying' schools have a clear commitment to a whole-school approach in fundamental aims, values and practices.

No practices are value free

Merely gaining control over students (or others, whatever our managerial role) is no proof of good management. There are teachers who use sarcasm, put-downs, ridicule and intentional embarrassment—even to other teachers. This is not acceptable, even if it 'works'. Some of the worst excuses for public vilification, humiliation and corporal punishment were based on the value that students were subordinate to teachers and must do whatever the adult says. They certainly must not question or disagree with their superiors. Physical pain, for example, was once sanctioned because students were perceived as subordinates, so fear, guilt, blame and criticism were seen by some teachers as effective methods of punishment. They were effective in the sense of simply gaining social control but, of course, utility is no proof or measure of psychological or ethical probity.

To say that certain practices are acceptable or unacceptable, implies certain values.

When staff discuss their preferred behaviour management practice, they are, in effect, asking:
- How do we gain 'control' over students?
- How do we foster self-discipline?
- How much negotiation is appropriate?
- How should we treat students who are disruptive (especially the 'pains')?
- What do students learn from our discipline?

All these questions imply values which must be addressed, as they balance the utility of management practice with the educational message of why we correct in certain ways or use particular kinds of consequence. As the OECD report, Lowe and Istance (1989) noted, a characteristic feature of an effective school is the pursuit of school-wide values rather than individual values. Developing a needs analysis regarding behaviour management gives staff the opportunity to clarify their values and beliefs. This is a fundamental part of any review process that leads to policy and action planning.

The operation of common and preferred practice

Within a whole-school approach, it is expected that teachers will take active responsibility for behaviour management, using preferred practices both in the classroom and in the wider duty-of-care role (performed in the corridor, on wet-day duty or in the playground).

Preferred practices

1 All teachers will clarify the common rights, rules and responsibilities at the classroom level, and general duty-of-care level

Positive behaviour management is based on a balance of rights and responsibilities. Fundamental rights (p 31) need to be balanced by responsibilities. Teachers need to teach both, and manage within a context that emphasises both. Rights can be protected, in part, by rules and consequences, but rights also need to be taught within the context of a supportive school environment.

The teaching of rights is woven into all curriculums, not just into the making of rules. One of the harder challenges for teachers is to enable an understanding of behaviour that goes beyond, 'Oh, I got caught', or 'I broke the rule', to the ability to see that disruptive behaviour affects someone else's right to feel safe, have their property or person respected, or to learn.

Rules, especially classroom rules, are best developed in the establishment phase of the year. At this stage, students are psychologically and developmentally ready to hear the rules, have them explained, discussed and taught. They are also more ready for the enforcement of rules. It is essential, therefore, that rules are made clear, known—even published— in a positive, workable way (see appendix).

2 The school's rights–responsibilities–rules–routines code forms the basis for all behaviour management and discipline

The 4Rs are the rights, responsibilities, rules and routines we refer to when managing students. Whether we are:

- enforcing rules
- encouraging routines (pp 72–73)
- correcting a student who is calling out, butting in or wandering

or whether we are:

- helping squabbling students with conflict resolution
- applying consequences and sanctions

the emphasis of management and discipline needs to focus on the rights that are affected, not just our personal anger, our status as a teacher, or on mere exercise of control. We need to bring students' thinking and attention back to how their behaviour affects others:

- what they did that affected others' rights
- which rule was broken (in effect, which right was affected)
- what they think they can do to fix things up (reconciliation and restitution).

A right can be seen as a reasonable expectation of what ought to be. One can expect to be treated with respect and dignity. However, a right can only be enjoyed when people are acting responsibly. Because we live in a highly fallible world, we never fully enjoy our rights. Hence the need for rules, order and discipline when rights are infringed.

It is not easy to teach students of any age to think about others' rights. When they affect someone's right, the rule is often a mirror in which that right is perceived. Students have to learn that mutual rights are essential if we are to co-operate with one another at school and enable a positive teaching, learning and social environment to exist.

When teaching about rights, it is important to focus on the essential rights from which all others spring. These rights are non-negotiable. They are not merely culturally based or gender based.

Everyone has the right:
- **to feel safe at school**
Students cannot learn well, or socialise effectively if they feel unsafe in classrooms or playgrounds. Emotional and physical safety, therefore, are high priorities in student management.

- **to learn to the best of their ability**
with the best of assistance

- **to be treated with dignity and respect**
even when they are being disciplined. This is hard, of course, when we are angry with students or when we don't particularly like them.

Even four- and five-year-olds can be taught rights as right things or right ways to behave towards others. Healthy discussion can outline, for example, why it is important for others to feel safe, what this means and how we can go about ensuring this, in and out of class.

3 Minimise unnecessary confrontation when managing students

Students' behaviour can be frustrating—very frustrating—at times, especially when it takes the form of procrastination, playing the clown, answering back and wanting the last word. However (notwithstanding the 'bad-day' syndrome), it is unhelpful, unnecessary and unwise to use sarcasm and put-downs such as, 'You idiot!', 'What's wrong with you? Are you thick or what?', 'How many times have I told you?', 'When will you ever learn, eh?', 'You stupid boy!' and 'You're the worst class I've ever had!'

The sad thing is that some teachers do not seem to be aware of how characteristically, sometimes subtly, they use verbally confrontational and sarcastic practice. Some typical examples:

- I have seen many teachers audibly differentiate to students: 'The worksheets are over here. There are two sets. The first one is for the brighter students, the second one is for . . .'
- The teacher asks the class a question. Silence. The question is repeated. Silence. The teacher says, 'Come on, even Lisa could answer that question.' Such behaviour will hardly gain Lisa's co-operation or enhance her public esteem!
- The student(s) forget, make a mistake, or have an accident with the paint. 'That's typical of you isn't it? You always muck things up!'

Ridicule and sarcasm undermine student confidence and self-esteem. It is also poor modelling by teachers who cavil when they see students doing the very same thing! Teachers clearly convey expectations through their treatment of students, especially in the way they speak to them. Some even use sarcasm proudly, as a way of gaining their Pyrrhic victory—'I'll win, whatever it takes'. Of course, if it takes that kind of behaviour to win, is it worth it? What is of greater concern is that some teachers use undue, even persistent, criticism without apparently considering the effect on the student's self-esteem.

Humiliating young people in front of their friends by, for example, public ridicule, makes good relationships impossible. It breeds deep resentments which can poison the school's atmosphere. Punishments do not need to be humiliating to be effective (*The Elton Report* 1989, p 101).

Teachers need to distinguish assertion from aggression when considering management practice. Assertion is fundamentally the ability to convey one's needs and rights in a way that doesn't trample on others' needs and rights. On some occasions we need to be unambiguously assertive with students, but this doesn't justify screaming, yelling, vilification, poking at students' work, saying, 'Is this the best you can do? You call this neat!', thoughtlessly invading their personal space, or towering over a small student, or . . . It involves a firm, decisive tone focused on addressing the behaviour without attacking the student. This is a fundamental premise of positive behaviour management and conflict resolution.

4 Use positive corrective practice wherever possible

A good deal of corrective discipline and management concerns low-level but annoying behaviour—calling out, lateness, not having equipment, task avoidance, talking out of turn, chair leaning. When dealing with disruptive behaviour, it is often possible to be both positive and corrective (p 48). Several points need to be considered:
- plan the language of corrective discipline
- use a least-to-most-intrusive intervention
- balance corrective discipline with encouragement
- re-establish working relationships as soon as practicable.

Planning corrective language

During the instructional phase of the lesson, one or more students call out. The teacher gives a direction to the group or the individual:

General direction: 'Okay folks, it's hands up without calling out.'

Individual direction: (student's first name should always be used where possible). 'Hands up without calling out, thanks.'

In other words, the direction focuses on the behaviour expected, rather than the disruptive behaviour. For example, 'Don't call out when I'm teaching' becomes, 'Facing this way and listening thanks' or 'Michael, pen down and facing this way. Ta.' 'Four on the floor thanks, Craig' to a student leaning back on his chair.

If a student asks to go to the toilet during instruction time with a grin on his face, the teacher might suspect attention-seeking behaviour. Rather than say, 'No you can't because I'm teaching' or 'Why do you want to go now?' we can use a conditional direction such as, 'After I've finished this part of the lesson, then you can go' or, 'Yes, John, when . . .' or 'When . . ., then.'

A six-year-old asks to do his painting but has left his last activity in a mess. Try, 'Yes, David, you can do your painting when you've cleaned up your playdough' rather than, 'No, you can't because you've left that mess!'

The open interrogative, 'Why?' only elicits unnecessary dialogue such as:

Teacher: 'Why do you want to go to the toilet now?'

Student: 'Well, I didn't go at recess.'

Exasperated teacher: 'Why didn't you go at recess?'

Student: 'Because I didn't have to!'

There are many ways we can focus our language on the expected behaviour when we plan possible words and phrases ahead. (These language skills are discussed more fully in Chapters 3, 4 and 5.)

Least to most intrusive

Effective teachers have a wide, least intrusive repertoire in their language and nonverbal behaviour—tone of voice, gestures etc (see nonverbal behaviour, p 49).

Adam is supposed to be writing in a diary but is surreptitiously playing with a toy troll. The teacher goes over, approaching 'side-on', not 'face-on', bends down to the small student and says, 'Nice troll, Adam. I want you to put it into your "locker" (a plastic tray for student's books etc) or on my desk.' The teacher's tone is pleasant but expectant. Adam has been given a choice rather than a threat. His eyes flicker acknowledgment, and the teacher smiles, moving away to give the student take-up time. Adam puts it away, sighing. Later, as the teacher goes around the class, brief acknowledgment is given to Adam for putting the toy away and getting on with his work. The teacher is balancing correction with encouragement.

A common, more intrusive approach, may occur like this. A teacher with hand outstretched, marches over to a student and says, 'Right! Give it to me. Give it here.' This forces the student to lose face and gives no take-up time. The teacher stands, waiting, forcing the student to act while the audience watches. Incidentally, fast movement unnecessarily stirs up the more kinaesthetic student.

Two students near the window were being silly and testosteronically tapping their rulers in play fighting during on-task time. As I moved around the room I noticed this and quietly asked a student near me for the names of the students who were fighting with their rulers. Rather than go to them and 'over-attend', I called across the room and asked Timmy to come to me. I then gave my attention to the student I was working with. I saw Tim slouch over sulkily, as I gave him take-up time.

I saw all this 'making-statement stuff' from peripheral vision. He came over, 'Yes (sigh and eyes to the ceiling), what do you want?' The words came out as an emphatic whine.

'What are you doing over by the window, Tim?'

'Nothing. Gees!'

'Actually, Tim, you're hitting rulers with Kevin. What are you supposed to be doing?'

'Oh, c'mon, we were only mucking around (last word).'

'Maybe you were, but what are you supposed to be doing?'

'Told you I was just muckin' around an' that.' Tim dropped his head as he whined out this excuse.

'I heard you, Tim, and what are you supposed to be doing?'

'The project' (another sibilant sigh).

'Okay, back to your desk and carry on with the work. I'll come and check it in a moment.'

I turned away, giving him take-up time, as he wandered slug-like back to his desk. Without 'looking' but using peripheral vision, I noticed him have a quiet whinge to Kevin and slowly get on with his work. Several minutes later, I called across the room, making full eye contact, 'Tim.' 'Yes,' came back with a frustrated sigh. Here I gave him the okay sign with curled thumb and forefinger. I think he initially thought I was going to hassle him again. He grinned back sheepishly.

This little fracas was kept 'least intrusive' by:
• calling him quietly aside with a direct, rather than indirect, question
• keeping the focus on the primary issue
• giving take-up time
• re-establishing.

I can address his attitude and silly behaviour one-to-one, away from the audience, after class rather than make a big scene publicly. This approach, which takes no longer, also keeps the relationship workable and intact, and keeps the focus on the current behaviour and the task at hand.

The concept of 'least intrusive' also includes our tone of voice. Even positive language can have its meaning significantly affected by being said in a sarcastic, hostile or demeaning way (close to the student with pointed finger); in a non-assertive, sighing, kind voice with hangdog look and drooped shoulders.

If students argue, we can become more intrusive in the sense of redirecting and clarifying the consequences or even 'exiting' the student from the classroom or playground temporarily. Even this, though, can be done with assertion rather than aggression (pp 32, 50).

5 Keep the focus on the primary behaviour Avoid argument

When we correct students, some come back on task quickly, some slowly, some procrastinate, some want the last word or sulk, pout or argue.

I direct Melissa and Rachel to face the front and listen:

'Rachel and Melissa (a little pause to sustain the attention), facing this way and listening, thanks.'

Here, I resume my instruction to the group. Melissa sighs and rolls her eyes to the ceiling. Rachel leans back in her chair, folds her arms and scowls grudging compliance. The sigh, scowl, eyes to ceiling are secondary behaviour, following on from the primary behaviour of talking out of turn.

'Secondary behaviour is the bane of many teachers' discipline and management engagement, (Rogers 1993).

I ask Melinda (Grade 6) to put her 'chewy' in the bin. 'C'mon,' she says. 'Other teachers don't care if you chew gum.'

This last word is typical secondary behaviour, even if what she says is true! It's the annoying tone and timewasting that advances beyond the rule reminder that frustrates teachers.

I ask Jarrod what he is supposed to be doing. This Grade 1 student is supposed to be putting unifix blocks in groups of two. Instead he is karate chopping a group of ten. When I ask him the question, 'What should you be doing?' he passes the buck. 'Phillip did it too!'

It is tempting to argue with such students and get caught up with their secondary behaviour. This is counterproductive. My colleagues and I have found that it is more effective to:

- **tactically ignore the nonverbal secondary behaviour**—the pouts, sighs, whines, folded arms etc. Obviously verbal abuse and aggressive or persistently disruptive behaviour cannot be tactically ignored (p 111 ff)

- **keep the focus on the primary issue**

    Give a simple direction or a simple rule reminder—

    'Melinda, chewing gum in the bin, thanks' or 'Melinda, we've got a school rule for chewy. In the bin, ta' rather than, 'Why are you chewing gum?' or 'You're not supposed to be chewing gum. Get it in the bin! Now!'

- **avoid argument** (especially in a public forum)

- **refocus the secondary dialogue**

    Student: 'Other teachers let us chew gum.'

    Teacher: 'Maybe they do (partially agree), but the rule is clear in this class. Chewing gum in the bin, thanks.'

Here, give the student some take-up time by emotionally withdrawing and moving away as if she will do it. It gives her a chance to do it in a face-saving way. She 'slopes' off to the bin, spits it in, and sulkily goes back to her seat. This residual secondary behaviour can also be tactically ignored and followed up later, if necessary (p 125).

This skill will be discussed more fully in Chapter 6 which discusses argumentative and challenging students. If students refuse to be redirected, we will need to make the consequences clear (see pp 91–92).

Redirecting secondary behaviour is a skill. It is not easy to do. Our natural temptation is to argue with students: 'I don't care if every teacher in the school lets you chew gum. What did I say?' or 'Don't argue with me!' or 'Who do you think you're talking to?' or 'Which teachers let you chew gum? Come on! Name one, come on!'

6 Invite, model, and expect respect

We can't make every student like us, neither can we like every student, but we can make it very hard for them to hate us. I think it was William Glasser who made that important point for teachers. Respect is an action that does not depend on liking which is affected by preference, taste and looks. Respect can be as basic as 'Please', 'Thanks', 'Excuse me', using first names at all times, and greeting students out of class. I have seen grade teachers walk past their students in the corridor or playground without even a nod or smile, let alone a 'Hi!' Mind you, I've seen even some teachers act this way to each other.

Respect involves:

- **separating the behaviour from the person**
  (This is not easy to do but keeps the respect of the person in focus.)

- **allowing the consequences to do the teaching** rather than an added message of, 'It serves you right, you idiot! You've lost your playtime now!' (Keep the respect intact.)

- **using private, rather than public, reprimands** where possible to consciously enable face-saving by giving take-up-time

- **taking students aside** where possible (in on-task time) **to focus on what they should be doing**

- **avoiding holding grudges** within the day, or from day to day

- **re-establishing the relationship after correction.**

None of this is easy. It is possible, though, because respect is what I can do, not necessarily what I feel or have to feel. This is also true of adult relationships, of course. If we wait to feel the right emotion before we act, we may never initiate positive language, basic manners, resolution, forgiveness or restitution.

7 Utilise related and reasonable consequences

When students do not respond to our positive correction, it is important to clarify consequences and apply them where necessary. For consequences to be effective, staff need to agree on some preferred practices in setting up and applying consequences and punishment. This is particularly necessary for common, disruptive behaviour as well as behaviour which significantly infringes on the safety and fair treatment of others (see also Chapter 7 on playground behaviour and management).

It is unhelpful and unproductive to have a behaviour management policy which consists of a long list of consequences for every possible misdemeanour, piece of silly behaviour, or breaking of rules. It is important to have clear consequences when safety is affected and when treatment of others is unacceptable. If a student:
- throws a major tantrum which affects others' learning
- spits on others' work
- hits out physically to hurt
- hurls a chair across the room
- engages in bullying

clear consequences must result. However, many kinds of behaviour can be dealt with consequentially by using problem-solving techniques that allow students to negotiate how they will fix things up. Most safety-intrusive behaviour will be dealt with by an immediate time-out approach, followed by some form of negotiated (deferred) consequence. Of course, when the pattern of disruptive behaviour persists it is important to set up a conferencing, counselling and contracting process (see Chapter 6).

Consequences can be immediate or deferred

Examples of immediate consequences are:
- sitting away from others (for example, for persistent butting in)
- working away from others (relocation in the room)
- cool-off time in the room
- time-out, away from that classroom or activity (see pp 84–85).

Deferred consequences range from the chat after class, through to students doing work in their own time, or fixing up the mess later (because the student chose not to put the scissors and clag away when directed in class time).

Detention is a common, deferred consequence, but it is important for students to do something constructive related to the behaviour which caused the detention. If they can write, at least have them write about their behaviour (see below).

Emphasise relatedness of the behaviour and the outcome

This is often described in the literature as logical consequences. Some logical connection between the disruptive behaviour and the consequence applied by the teacher is developed or negotiated between teacher and student. For example, rather than writing a hundred lines, students ought to be writing about their behaviour:
- What I did.
- Why I think this happened (their right of reply).
- What rule (or right) I broke or affected.
- What I need to do to fix things up.

This challenges students to (at least) think about and reflect on their behaviour and consider how they might fix it. This consequence is commonly used with upper grades, but should not be forced on a student who has difficulty with writing. It can be used as a teacher–student exchange to resolve a behaviour problem and to initiate appropriate consequences or restitution.

Emphasise certainty rather than severity

Particular students can be kept back to work in their own time because they 'chose' not to do it in class time. Assuming they do not have a learning problem, and the teacher is catering for mixed abilities in the curriculum, this consequence is not unreasonable.

However, if a teacher then gives the student a lecture: 'Yes, Dean, you're inside now. Lost your recess time haven't you! Well it serves you right. You could be out playing now, couldn't you? No, you, *you*, had to be special didn't you?' Some teachers (and parents) believe that it's not enough that a student experiences some related consequence, they must make the student suffer as well and put the verbal boot in or the student won't understand! Not so.

This kind of harangue, especially if delivered with hostile body language, will only mean that the student remembers the severity of the consequence, not the certainty that if you do not do your work in class, or you're particularly rude in class, or you don't pack up with the others or . . . then the teacher will follow up, and follow through with you.

The **certainty principle** is crucial whenever a teacher is clarifying consequences. It ties in with the principle of avoiding unnecessary confrontation (pp 32, 91). It can be extended to correction as well as consequence. If students drop litter in the playground, run in the corridor, are silly during lining-up time or at assembly, they need correction. However, we don't have to add to the correction a litany of mixed messages:

'How many times have I told you? Why is it always you, eh?'

'You never . . . You always . . . I'm sick and tired of telling you.'

If we consider, in our professional judgment, that correction needs to be followed up by some sort of consequence, then we need to **let the consequence teach students:**

- **about the relationship between their behaviour and the outcome applied**

- **that the students, in effect, choose their own behaviour** (the YOYOB principle: You Own Your Own Behaviour). The teacher's job is to help students to make better behavioural choices.

- **to work for reconciliation and restitution** rather than revenge. Reparation between student and student, student and work, student and teacher should be the goal of applying consequences. In other words, we go beyond the actual consequence to ask how we can help this student to repair and rebuild damaged relationships or attitudes. This approach is longer term than just applying punishment.

- **about the need to allow cool-off time** when applying consequences. Some consequences cannot be applied effectively while a student is still angry. Apart from the need for immediate consequences such as relocation or time-out, deferred consequences work more effectively because we've allowed cool-off time.

Two students engage in a verbal fracas in class time (Grade 4). One calls the other a 'dumb idiot!' (I've heard significantly more disturbing epithets!) Because it's loud I say, firmly, to the verbal provocateur, 'Jason (pause for effect), that's a put-down and put-downs hurt.' Dealing with put-downs, or verbal abuse, is one occasion when I'm prepared to show anger in a controlled way. Sometimes I briefly refer to the rule, 'We have a rule for respect and I expect you to use it.' Because the voice is firm and unambiguously decisive, the anger, not 'aggro' is heard. The class goes quiet. When we are angry about issues that count, students 'hear' us and the whole class realises that this issue is serious. (Put-downs are discussed in Chapter 6.)

The deferred consequence may include an apology. It will certainly involve some pained conflict resolution. Any apology, though, can wait until ample cool-off time has taken place. If we try to force an apology (or cleaning up mess, or doing the set work right now, or . . .) in the emotional moment, we'll end up with further accusations and force the student into a face-losing situation. We can't make students apologise and it is highly unlikely that they will do so under these conditions.

8 Actively promote, teach and support positive behaviour

When staff are discussing behaviour management, it is very easy to get bogged down by focusing on disruptive students. We may forget that most of our students behave well and positively most of the time. Even the painful ones behave positively and responsibly from time to time. (Didn't Jason say please, once?)

Students are not born responsible, they learn responsibility. (Some even learn it at home!) We need to build school climates that enhance responsibility and co-operation.

We can do this in a variety of ways.

- **Acknowledge students when they are behaving responsibly, well, positively, thoughtfully**—even if this is how they are supposed to behave! Catch students doing the right thing and give a brief word publicly or privately. 'I appreciate it when . . .' or 'It was great to see that . . .' or 'Well done for . . .' or 'Great manners!' or 'You did that well' or 'Good on you'.

- **Build a positive working environment in the classroom.** Through positive rules, simple and clear routines, maximum use of seating plans, effective monitor systems, a balance of co-operative learning and teacher redirected/individual learning.

- **Gear the curriculum and the teaching and learning environment for maximum success in a wide range of academic and non-academic activities.** While a program cannot, of itself, guarantee success, it can promote it by the way it is planned, structured and delivered. Staff teams can plan for good-practice models by collaborating on successful programs, lesson units, styles of group work, special elective activities, and by rotating key lessons such as science and music with teachers who are specially talented in those areas.

- **Give regular encouragement (verbal and nonverbal) and descriptive feedback.** When considering positive behaviour it is important to consider feedback from students. Ted Glynn (1992) makes the salient point that there is more to a positive management policy than developing explicit, even positive, rules. He asks whether schools provide, 'positive feedback for students who are regular attenders, for students who complete four, six, eight weeks without a single incident of disruptive or aggressive behaviour' or 'for a whole class of students among whom there has been no fighting for a term'. He suggests that schools also publicly display, and comment on, their progress towards achieving positive social behaviour goals (in Wheldall 1992, p 21).

- **Hold special events for 'our class'.** Morning/afternoon teas, special chat times and free activities enhance the feeling that the class is important and distinctive.

- **Arrange classroom meetings once the class has established itself in Term 1.**

  Classroom meetings are widely used to enhance the feeling of group solidarity, and give the opportunity to discuss a range of issues such as curriculum, room organisation, the planned excursion, particular problems with individuals or problems that affect the group (p 64).

Encouragement

Encouragement is often distinguished from praise, in the relevant literature, in that encouragement focuses on the effort rather than the person.

'Dave, you handled that well.'

'It's easy to make mistakes—we all do. What did you learn from it?'

'You're working much harder lately.'

'You have a real skill for . . . Would you like to share it with the rest of the class?'

'You've put a lot of thought into this, Paul.'

'Good point, Melissa.'

'Thanks, I appreciate that . . . it makes my job so much easier.'

'What a great idea! Thanks.'

- Encouragement can also be nonverbal: smile, wink, the okay sign, thumbs-up sign, or the pat on the arm for younger students (p 119).

- If students try to reject encouragement (especially those with low self-esteem), give it anyway. Avoid over-servicing in the form of something like, 'Look, I really meant it. Don't say your work is no good. It is.' Keep the encouragement brief and focused on the effort. Leave it at that.

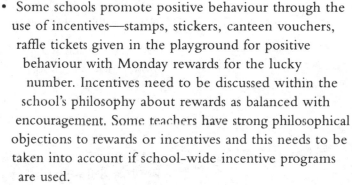

- Some schools promote positive behaviour through the use of incentives—stamps, stickers, canteen vouchers, raffle tickets given in the playground for positive behaviour with Monday rewards for the lucky number. Incentives need to be discussed within the school's philosophy about rewards as balanced with encouragement. Some teachers have strong philosophical objections to rewards or incentives and this needs to be taken into account if school-wide incentive programs are used.

- Ring the parents (or use notes or diaries) for positive as well as disruptive behaviour. One of the successful programs I worked with at an inner-city school involved ringing up parents when the student had improved in work and behaviour. Initially, parents were shocked. They were so used to being contacted only when things were going badly. We can also, of course, give a brief word to the parents when they pick up their child after school.

41

- Involve parents in positive ways in their children's education. Make sure the school has a welcoming atmosphere for parents, with planned ways they can support the school's educational and social culture.

Parents should be contacted and involved early when significant behaviour problems begin to appear (p 67). The school should have a basic, due process that staff are aware of, for communication with parents about their child's disruptive behaviour. The emphasis should be on parent–school support in resolving the problem, rather than on the use of such communication to 'get back' at the student or parent. This is especially important when applying consequences such as detention and suspension. It is also important to have a published policy that outlines the school's aims, practices, plans and consequences for behaviour management (p 18). Indeed, many schools involve parents in this process. This ensures that the policy reflects, or at least makes clear, community values rather than those of any extreme group who might want to bring back the cane, construct gun turrets in the playground or schedule Saturday and Sunday detentions.

9 Have a clear, school-wide, agreement on the reasons for and use of time-out

A clear time-out policy and practice is essential in a community like a school. Some behaviour, because of its persistence and intensity (especially where safety is at issue), needs to be dealt with by a dignified, decisive, even immediate removal of the student from the audience to allow cool-off time and a chance for the student (and the teacher) to regain control.

The practice of time-out is discussed more fully in Chapter 4. The key point here is that a school needs a common practice. There are school principals who, unhelpfully, communicate to their staff by fiat, that, 'no student should ever be sent out of class'. Either they have forgotten, or don't care, how stressful and dangerous some student behaviour can be.

All teachers and students need the protection of an exit/time-out/cool-off policy that has school-wide backing and support.

The key questions we need to ask, school-wide are:
- What sorts of behaviour would occasion exit and removal from class for time-out?
- How will we exit such students from the class with dignity?
- What will we do in the extreme case (not so extreme in some schools) of a student who refuses to leave, or be taken?
- What will be our back-up plan?
- Where will the student go (during time-out)?
- What should occur during time-out?
- On what basis does the grade teacher follow-up with the student?
- At what point are parents notified?

These questions form the basis of a school-wide policy. This policy needs to be published and explained to parents. As time-out is one of the most sensitive and intrusive areas of corrective and consequential discipline, it is essential that thorough planning, and monitoring of its use, be a school-wide issue.

The policy needs to explain:
- the reasons time-out is used, and on what occasions
- that it is a consequence not a punishment
- that it is applied appropriately, with dignity and certainty (not severity expressed this way, 'Right, you idiot. Get out! Get out! You can go to the principal. I'm sick and tired of your stupid behaviour!')
- the significance of adequate follow-up beyond the immediate consequence of the time-out itself.

Students cannot be allowed to persistently disrupt classes or create an environment where other students' learning or safety is affected. To achieve clarity and consistency, it is important that the questions noted above, are seriously discussed with staff. Each grade teacher needs to explain to students what time-out means in the classroom and the playground.

10 Build, promote and utilise a united approach to behaviour management

While this may sound patently obvious, there are still schools who leave teachers structurally or emotionally isolated. The hearty whingeing that goes on in schools, must be accompanied by essential discussion, planning, and action together as a united group, when it comes to managing behaviour. It is necessary to go beyond whingeing to problem solving and action planning.

I've sat in staffrooms at recess and seen colleagues observing students, through the staffroom window, fighting or pulling a branch off a tree and seen them turn a blind eye. I've seen teachers walk down corridors, ignoring loud swearing, running and silly play fighting (the karate kicker!). I've observed teachers who walk across playgrounds and ignore students blatantly dropping litter, or ignore a student who asks for help. Some teachers think that if they are 'not on duty', they don't have a duty of care. The ones who do not take this role seriously make it more difficult for their colleagues who give the role some effort and thought. There is a sense in which we always have a duty of care wherever we are in the school.

The issues and problems associated with behaviour management need to be addressed on a school-wide basis, not an isolated or ad hoc basis, or simply by leaving it to a few. If a teacher is really struggling with a class, or a particular student, there is a sense in which this is a whole-school issue and others can offer emotional, problem-solving and structural support (p 194). It's disconcerting to find teachers in schools feeling, and believing, that if they 'opened up about a problem, then their reputation would be shot', as many teachers have explained to me (Rogers 1992). Teachers feel they will be criticised for exposing a problem or, if they are given any support, it will be in such a grudging fashion that they will feel they shouldn't have asked in the first place.

I've been in many schools where some teachers' tragic way of coping in such an environment is to block themselves off emotionally from their peers, not speaking at team or staff meetings, getting away from school as quickly as possible, even covering over their windows with posters so no-one can see them slowly fall apart.

Creating a united whole-school culture is not easy, but it is essential if we are to have a supportive environment. It can be powerfully modelled by senior staff and team leaders. In fact, if it is not modelled by them, it is unlikely to occur at the grade teacher level. As one school policy states it, 'If you are working alone, you will fail. Throw away the idea that seeking support equates with incompetency. The reverse is true.'

Crucial areas where we need mutual support in problem solving and action planning

Management of behaviourally disordered students

These make up about five per cent of the student population in many schools. Their disruptive and disordered behaviour is frequent, intense and generalised (not confined to the class they are enrolled in) (p 149).

The 'hard–class' syndrome

We need to assist teachers to deal with this syndrome by being supportive colleagues early in the year. This might avoid a bigger problem developing by Term 3 or 4 with the teacher degenerating into the-straw-that-broke-the-camel's-back mode (p 158).

Further, it is grossly unfair, in terms of teacher welfare, if such classes are given to new teachers to the school or, worse, first year teachers—especially where the blend and mix of the hard class is known. Difficult classes should be well planned for and placed with more experienced and effective teachers. If those classes are given to a teacher who is new to the school, adequate backup and support must be given from the outset.

Playground management

If there is one thing that taxes teachers it is yard (playground) duty, with the squabbles, litter, teasing, tale-telling, out-of-bounds play and silly play fighting. If we are going to take duty of care seriously then a common collegial responsibility, and playground management approach, is essential.

Consistency

Aims, rule enforcement, positive reinforcement, correction and consequences have proved to be effective within whole-school approaches. Students take the rules and responsibilities more seriously when there is a common approach by staff to behaviour management.

Summary

These preferred practices describe the way a school prefers to manage its students. More specifically, they describe the way teachers lead, guide and manage students towards self-discipline and respect for others' rights.

It would be expected that individual teachers would reflect on these practices in:
- their classroom management and discipline plan
- the plans made for behaviourally disordered students
- the plans made for duty of care outside the classroom:
  supervision—wet days, corridors, excursions and school camps
  duties—bus, swimming and playground.

Of course, some teachers choose not to work within these preferred practices. Some simply refuse to do so. This creates some difficulty for the school in meeting its aims and objectives. Where these practices are school policy, and a teacher's practice, by default or design, is significantly at variance with preferred practice, particular care must be taken. That teacher will need support, assistance or a decisive reminder that we work consistently as a united group at this school and we don't have private policies for managing behaviour.

While a school's culture has to be patient with a wide range of teacher skill and practice, it does not have to sanction:
- behaviour that tacitly endorses characteristic humiliation
- sarcasm
- unjust or inconsistent consequences
- the 'blind-eye' syndrome that does not take duty of care seriously (p 164).
- action on significant policy issues, independent of colleagues.

I've seen appalling practice defended under the guise of professional independence such as:
- students told to wait in cupboards as a parody of time-out
- students standing outside the classroom for a whole class period without the option of coming back in
- refusal by teachers to negotiate or solve problems with a difficult or behaviourally disordered student
- teachers demanding that principals make students feel guilty, 'head kick and don't send them back until they're grovelling!'
- passing the buck for behaviour problems rather than working in consultation on a whole-school plan.

It is a matter of professional responsibility to support the school's practices and plans. This is essential for realisation of the aims of positive behaviour management.

Professional development

Professional development on behaviour management issues can use preferred practices as entry points into the debate. They are also relevant to action planning. In fact, staff need regular in-service in this area, especially if they have moved to a school whose student population presents as more challenging and more dysfunctional.

These practices can also be used as a reference point for our action planning, so we find ourselves asking value questions such as, 'How does this plan fit in with our preferred practice of . . .? Which skills are relevant to these practices?'

45

Chapter 3

POSITIVE DISCIPLINE

Positive discipline sounds like a contradiction in terms. Discipline is often seen in punitive terms—and correction and consequences in discipline are clearly necessary—but primarily, discipline is to do with guidance and instruction to teach and enhance a social order where rights and responsibilities are balanced.

Corrective discipline

All students need corrective management: they forget, they are annoyingly human and some seek disturbing forms of behaviour in order to belong to their social group (Dreikurs et al 1982). Teachers should, and most do, make every effort to plan for a positive working environment, cater for mixed abilities and have thoughtful routines for the smooth day-to-day running of the class, but still, corrective management will be necessary. In class, in the corridor, in the playground, when students are lining up, on bus duty, at excursions—even if corrective management is merely reminding students, it is still more positive if consideration is given to our language and manner. Compare the effect of these reminders given by a Grade 2 teacher to the class as students line up:

'Okay, everyone. Remember to sit on the mat when we go in to class.'

'All right, don't forget to sit on the mat when you go in. I don't want to see people wandering. Is that clear?'

Positive discipline is about creating the best environment and social climate for teaching and learning, so that correction is given in a way that minimises unnecessary stress, and considers the self-esteem of those being corrected.

Balancing

Like any multi-task role, teaching requires that several elements of behaviour are balanced—all at once! Teachers have to consider:
- content
- lesson flow
- crossover of tasks (transition to set tasks)
- feedback to students
- timing of lesson structure (what amount of time to give to instructions, on-task time, packing up, transition to different tasks)
- management of disruptive behaviour (when to intervene, what to say, how to deal with persistent problems, how much correction to address in the immediate emotional moment and what to defer until later).

Any multi-task skill requires observation of, and relative control over, many factors. However, the more relaxed the control, the less stressed we are. It is a bit like driving. If we had to drive every day at the same level of conscious control and effort we exercised when we initially learnt to drive, then driving would be a very stressful exercise. Fortunately, people normally master driving skills so that much of their driving is appropriately unconscious, leaving energy in reserve for the unexpected. Skilful drivers, like skilful teachers, even consider how they will cope with the unexpected, so that they are not totally overwhelmed when it occurs.

The analogy can be extended to management skills. It is important to have a general discipline plan (p 100 ff) and, occasionally, a targeted discipline plan for particularly difficult students (p 151). When I first began teaching my daughter to drive—indeed, when I first began to drive, myself, there was a degree of stress associated with the learning curve. It's difficult trying to remember all the elements of driving as well as coping with the unexpected happenings on the road! It's like that in the classroom. A teacher can plan a lesson thoroughly, consider necessary board work, plan materials and resources and still have disruptions. The mark of effective, planned discipline is a balance of:
- prevention and correction
- short- and long-term discipline
- correction and encouragement
- repairing and rebuilding strained relationships.

Discipline in the emotional moment

If, whenever we had to correct a student, the situation was calm, and if they responded to our correction straightaway without sulking, pouting or answering back, and if we weren't tired and thinking about the next curriculum meeting or having to rush off to do duty (and make sure we got a cuppa on the way) and if . . . well, discipline would be easy if . . . but that is not reality.

When we are tired, and trying to balance many things, reaction from the gut rather than the head is understandable. I have heard many teachers say, 'I can't help getting angry with him! He whines so much! And when he argues with me (little liar) I just lose the plot!' At least there is some honesty in this description. Managing the emotional side of our role is not easy. Some teachers deny their anger or anxiety, or feel guilty for being angry when they discipline students. This is psychologically unhelpful, even damaging. However, it is socially destructive to just let it go—to open our mouths and say the first thing that our emotional state produces. There are clearly times when, 'a teacher's anger is immediate and justified in response to totally unacceptable behaviour, such as the reckless endangering of life and limb . . . where a teacher's anger is manifest it should also be under control' (Dobson and Gale 1990).

Plan the language of correction

The last thing we may actually think about when we're stressed is what we are saying. It is very easy to use negative language when we correct because of natural emotional arousal. In fact, it is unreasonable to expect that when we are stressed we can always structure our corrective language to suit our management aims most effectively. That is why it is important to plan our language of correction in the light of our management demands.

A common expression of stress in corrective language is the overuse of 'Don't'—'Don't call out when I'm talking!'—'Don't get out of your seat without asking my permission!'—'Don't use bad language.'—'Don't chew gum.'—'Don't run.' Overuse of 'Don't', 'Stop' or 'No, you can't' is often unreflective habit triggered by emotional arousal. Teachers may be unaware of their language and tone or even their 'global behaviour'—all the messages conveyed by tone, gesture, body language, words, spatial proximity. Mixed messages can also occur in the emotional moment when frustration, dislike of a student and the need to manage, all coalesce. We may say much more than we need, or intended, to say.

Jason (Preparatory Grade) has a task with playdough and recording groups of different shapes on paper. He finishes quickly. Up goes his hand. 'Miss, I wanna do the play blocks now. I finished!' The teacher, spying the mess and the poorly executed task, says, 'No, you can't, because you haven't cleared up your mess. How many times have I told you about packing up, eh? (hands go to the hips). If you leave the playdough out, it gets hard, doesn't it, eh? And who has to clean it up? Me! Me! And who has to make the playdough in the first place? Me! Muggins! And look at your work! Is that the best you can do?' This extra information goes well beyond the, 'No, you can't, because . . .'

Many teachers find it helpful to consider and plan what they will say in discipline transactions. Most corrective discipline is concerned with giving directions, reminders, making statements, using appropriate questions and dealing with argumentative students. Leaving the language of correction to the vagaries of mood, chance and circumstance increases the likelihood of negative language when we're under emotional pressure. I believe that it is necessary to plan the language of discipline as carefully as we plan teaching and learning. Positive correction comes from a conviction that corrective, assertive management is not inconsistent with the emphasis on positive teacher–student communications. Basically, it is substituting negative language, where possible, for positive language, while keeping the corrective focus. A framework for corrective language is given in Chapter 5.

Global set: teacher behaviour

We can rephrase many uses of 'Don't' with 'Do' (p 104).

'Walking quietly, thanks' rather than, 'Don't run!'

'Share the pencils on this table' rather than, 'Don't argue and fight over the pencils. Why can't you share?'

'Hands up without calling out, thanks' rather than just, 'Don't call out.'

'If you hold the pen like this (teacher models), it will be easier' rather than, 'Don't hold it like that! Here give it to me! I'll show you! No wonder you can't write neatly if you hold the pen like that. How many times have I told you?'

'Language alone, though, is not enough. Language is affected by the "global set" of our behaviour' (Rogers 1993).

Positive language is also affected by our tone of voice, how hurried or snappy our speech is, by eye contact, proximity to the student and body language. Do we often poke at the air or their work with an extended index finger when making a point? For example, saying the phrase 'walking quietly' in a sarcastic tone of voice, pointing and gesticulating with a leading chin, nullifies any positive words used by the teacher. How our management language is heard by students depends greatly on our characteristic nonverbal behaviour.

The National Education Association of America has noted that 80 per cent of all teacher communications are nonverbal (in Grinder 1993). This makes sense in our teaching experience. Think back to situations where you were managed by others outside your family, for example, school, clubs, work, even being 'line managed' as a teacher. What we tend to remember about management is how we were treated—the way we were spoken to, whether correction was balanced by encouragement, how private correction was, whether the teacher or boss gave us face-saving time and take-up time, how they treated us day-to-day rather than on isolated bad days.

The significance, and presence, of nonverbal behaviour can be demonstrated easily in staff development sessions with communal good humour. Take some basic, positive directions and convey different meaning, intent, expectation and relational tone by changing the nonverbal cues. The direction on paper, 'Denise and Kerry, looking this way and listening, thanks' is a more positive way of directing talkers to stop and refocus than 'Don't talk when I'm teaching'. However, the same words can be said in a sarcastic voice, head rocking from side to side, emphasising key words with a sneer or two, 'and listening, thanks' (as if the thanks is merely a given concession, rather than an expectation).

The same direction can be given with an indecisive or whining tone of voice, the teacher sighing over the words, shoulders bowed, face pained, conveying little conviction. When teachers engage in this kind of composite behaviour, they convey the message that they don't really believe the students will do as directed. Most of the message is conveyed nonverbally. I've been in many classrooms where students appear to be able to determine a teacher's degree of assertion and expectation in the first five minutes by observing all these bits of behaviour. The global set is seen as a characteristic whole by the observer, the listener.

There are teachers whose corrective style is characterised by a snappy tone of voice. They use dominating gestures which invade personal space, coming directly face-on to students instead of side-on, or just reach over to the students' work from behind. They take, rather than ask to see, students' work. They display little 'managerial civility' or relational respect. For some, this is intentional—a form of conscious authoritarian control. Even positive language can be destroyed by walking up to students, pointing in the air near their faces and saying, 'Denise and Kerry, facing this way, thank you!' Here there is a 'wounded silence' as P G Wodehouse describes it. This is the difference between using our leadership power over others rather than for the benefit of others. When we discipline or correct, we do so from within (from and to) the teacher–student relationship. This relationship is tested at times, especially in the establishment phase of the year. Sometimes, it is challenged. It is always present. Each correction, each reminder, each follow-up, enhances or works against that relationship.

The key aspects of global set

Gaining some congruence between nonverbal behaviour and our language requires some reflection on our characteristic management behaviour. After all, the only behaviour we can directly influence, and bring some change to, is our own.

- **Tone of voice**—how expectant, pleading, indecisive, assertive, hostile, anxious, sarcastic, do we normally sound? Is there some lift and energy to the flow of our voice?

- **Bearing and general body posture**—do we normally look confident and expectant? Do we stand and move in a relaxed or rushed and nervous way? If a teacher makes extremely fast jerky movements during instructional time, the more kinaesthetic and motorically restless students focus on the movement rather than on the teacher's words or task direction, or what is being done on the board.

- **Postural/gestural cues**—do we smile when we begin group transactions? Do we show some animation in our faces? Do we smile with reasonable frequency, even to the unlikeable—bad days notwithstanding? Do we point at students when we manage and correct, or use an open hand? Does our characteristic posture convey confidence? expectation? indecision? defeat? appropriate assertion? tension?

Look at me when I'm talking to you.

- **Proximity**—teachers spend a lot of time moving around the room during on-task time to encourage, assist, correct and discipline where necessary. It is important to consider how close we are, whether we come sideways to the student, how fast our movement is to the student's eyes, whether we bend down to younger students to maintain some parity of eye level, or tower over students—all of these actions affect the emotional nature of personal space.

- **Eye contact** is a basic and necessary feature of human communication. As a social cue it can demonstrate attention or interest. It can reflect obedience, compliance or fear. Forcing eye contact—'Look at me when I'm talking to you!'—is unhelpful. It is better to request it and if it isn't given, speak to the ears, using the student's first name. There are sometimes cultural expectations associated with direct eye contact. Extended eye contact with students may provoke unnecessary confrontation, especially with the small percentage of (mostly male) students who selectively attend to social cues (Dodge 1981) and give a biased attribution to the classic teacher stare or extended frown. Such students are likely to say, 'What you looking at me for?' or 'Don't you pick on *me*!' or even throw a tantrum. It is more effective to gain some eye contact and follow with directional language to remove unnecessary ambiguity in the eye contact.

• Take-up time and face-saving time have been referred to already (p 34). They, too, are nonverbal cues that can often enhance expectation. The use of pausing, within our management language, is also a powerful social cue and is discussed in the section on privately understood signals (p 107).

Our behaviour is not accidental

By themselves, these nonverbal elements of behaviour have little effect. Taken 'globally' they can convey a positive, managerial tone. These elements of behaviour affect the working relationship within which we teach, manage, encourage and discipline. By altering our behaviour and use of language we can alter, affect and influence the behaviour of others. This is not manipulation or mere technique—students can see through that. It needs to be a conscious effort of will to convey worth to another, to convey behavioural respect. It needs to be driven by purposeful, managerial aims, not mere expedience or utility. Some teachers say, 'You can't teach an old dog new tricks.' Maybe, but a person is not a dog. If commitment, need and purpose are there, human beings can change.

Some teachers say it doesn't matter what they do or say, 'This is me. Why should I change and become something I'm not?' If being 'me' is equivalent to being:
• snappy, rude, short-tempered
• unaware of how my voice, bearing and manner appear to others
• indecisive and non-assertive
• uncaring about how our words and meaning come across
• unthinking about what we say

then change will be necessary, if effective interpersonal management is to take place. This is as true for adult management as it is for management of students.

If behaviour is chosen, as well as the product of habit, teachers can choose to behave differently. We engage others in human transactions constantly as we go through life. Rather than merely allow circumstances to dictate to that relational dynamic, we can consider behavioural choices in the light of reflective awareness. And there are pay-offs:
• we feel better, more 'in control' when we need to be
• students relate better to us when there is congruence between positive corrective language and the nonverbal messages we convey.

As Hastings (1992) notes, 'In a good relationship, each party feels that they are important to the other and that the other is important to them. They feel that what they say and do matters. This feeling does not arise out of thin air, however. It is generally experienced because a reciprocal contingency actually exists in behaviour' (in Wheldall, p 55).

Common excuses against positive discipline and some replies
• 'I haven't got time for all this positive stuff and reflecting on my language and behaviour!'
  We've all got the same amount of time. The vital point is how important we

51

regard the effect of management style relative to our goals.'

- 'It's too hard, this positive approach.'

  'Too hard or are you unwilling to give it a serious go?'

- 'I tried that approach and it doesn't work!'

  'What exactly did you do? How long did you try the positive approach? How often? Did you follow through? Did you re-establish? What exactly does a positive approach mean to you? The approaches described in this text do not deny the need for appropriate assertion.'

- 'I can't help the way I am. It's just me. I can't help getting angry.'

  'Can't help? Let me show you some ways that <u>can</u> help.'

- 'There are too many obstacles. It's too difficult.'

  'Okay, what are the obstacles? Let's list them and begin to work on them, a bit at a time.'

- 'There's no-one here who will support me.'

  'No-one? Can you not think of one? I will support you, so will . . .'

Ms Davis— a case study

It's the timetable slot after morning play. Ms Davis has a Grade 2/3 composite. It's the third week into first term. The class is lining up but restless. Craig is bouncing the basketball, a couple of the boys are hassling each other playfully outside the portable classroom. She greets them as she goes to the front of the line. 'Nice to see you lining up. All ready to go in, eh?' She comments briefly on the ones not fidgeting, 'Thanks Halid, Dean, Lisa, Michael, Michelle.' The rest basically follow suit. She looks at Craig who is bouncing a basketball on the path. She nonverbally gestures using eye contact, her hands simulating holding the ball. He grins and holds it to his chest. 'Before you go in, what do we need to remember?' Her voice and posture are positive. There is an expectant tone. 'Yep, we sit straight on the mat. Craig, ball in the box, okay?' They file in.

- She could have said to the line, 'Right you lot! I could see you weren't lined up from back there. Can't you line up just once, without me having to tell you, eh?'
- She could have said to Craig, 'Right! Give me the ball!' and 'Don't argue!' when he said, 'But Miss!'
- She could have shuffled in, wearily, noise and all, accepting that nothing can be done about it and deciding to just put up with it!

As Ms Davies walks in, she expects them to sit on the mat. She communicated this expectation in week one, on day one. She has key times—share time and group-instruction—when she expects them to sit on the mat. At other times, she directs them to sit on the mat as the need dictates, for example, for classroom meetings. She gives them some settling time. She has her book ready, the easel to the right of her chair, has the learning tasks set out in several key points which were covered at instruction time. She even has little drawings against each of the key points, for example, a drawing of a pen in hand for dictation, a diary and a thinking face for diary writing.

She scans the faces. All the students are on the mat. There's a bit of noise. Craig is rocking backwards and forwards. She tactically ignores him for the moment. She claps her hands three times. The class copies, grinning. She repeats a more difficult rhythm. Most clap it and a few laugh as they miss the rhythm. Now that all eyes are facing her, she shares the story that will form the basis of the language activity. If Craig is persistently annoying, she will either direct him ('sitting up and facing this way'), or distract him, by asking him to sit near her, or to help by holding a book. I've had students hold a whiteboard marker, paper or even my cold cup of tea as distractions.

If difficult behaviour occurs each time a student comes onto the mat, she may consider a behaviour teaching plan (p 152).

- She could have begun by talking loudly over the noise, 'Right! C'mon, settle down. You—yes, Craig, is it? Sit up properly.'
- She could have focused on every noisy student, or waited for total silence, or she could have used the 'shh! shh!' method, but she has learnt that several 'shhs' tend to set up a counter-reinforcing habit.
- She could have used the ultimatum, 'Right! I'm not starting until every one of you is quiet. Do you understand? Yes, you! You, Lee, isn't it? You're talking aren't you? Why are you talking?'

During the story, she scans the room and the faces of her class, using peripheral vision to assess how it's all going. David is turning around talking to the student behind him. Others, too, are mildly distracted. She stops talking. This sustained pause triggers David's attention and he turns around. She continues the story. On some occasions she has to direct students. When she does, she directs them behaviourally: 'David, facing this way and listening, thanks'. She then resumes the lesson flow, giving David take-up time to respond (p 109). By giving take-up time, she conveys the expectation that he will do what she has directed. She also avoids unnecessary, prolonged confrontation.

- She could have left her seat, walked across to David, and said, 'Don't talk while I'm teaching!'
- She could have said, 'Why are you turning around and talking?' and 'Don't lie to me. I saw you' when he said, 'I wasn't!' She could have questioned and argued.
- She could have sighed her way through an 'I'm-so-fed-up-with-having-to-remind-you' dialogue. 'How many times have I told you, David? David! Are you listening to me? I'm talking to you.' By this time the class is totally distracted.

She asks some questions about the story. Paul and one or two others call out. Some students 'forget' the rules, some are impatient and others want attention. She tactically ignores the calling out, giving no eye contact to those students. 'Yes, Dean. Thanks for putting your hand up.' She beckons to several others as she sees their hands go up. She will come to them in turn. In week one, she reminded the students to, 'Put your hands up without calling out.' This is one of several simple, clear rules she has published on attractive cards around the room. Students have drawn pictures illustrating positive social behaviour reflecting the rules. Later, she will take photos of positive classroom behaviour and display them with the published rules.

It is frustrating when students call out, and she knows that by simply accepting it, group discussion can become a free-for-all with the loudest or most attention-getting students dominating the airwaves. Now and then she gives a general rule reminder, prefacing her questions with, 'Before we begin, remember our class rule for . . .' Sometimes she prefaces group discussion with a general question, 'What's our class rule for . . .?' She knows that rule enforcement doesn't necessarily have to be negative, but it does have to be consistent. Tactical ignoring seems to convey to most students that the teacher will notice you when you've got your hand up.

Sean puts up his hand. 'Yes, Sean.' His question is, 'Can I go to the toilet?' She reads the situation as a non-desperation request and says, 'When I've finished this part of the lesson, then you go, Sean.' This seems to satisfy him. He grins and screws up his face. He suspects she knows. She chooses conditional directions in preference to unconditional, negative directions ('No, you can't . . . because . . .'). She saves unconditional directional language of 'No', 'Don't' and 'Can't' for issues of importance. She also avoids using open interrogatives such as: 'Why?' as in 'Why do you want to go to the toilet now? Why didn't you go to the toilet at recess?' because she knows this invites unnecessary discussion (p 116).

Please Miss, can I go to the toilet?

She reads the situation as a non-desperation request . . .

Lisa and Mia are chatting privately, distracting others, while Ms D is explaining the set tasks. She pauses and directs them to face the front and listen, 'Mia . . ., Lisa . . ., facing this way and listening, thanks.' She has learnt that a simple pause after a student's name helps sustain attention prior to giving the direction (p 107). She often uses 'Thanks', even when correcting, as it communicates an expectation that the behavioural direction will be complied with. Lisa, miffed, says, 'But we was only talking about the work.' Ms D is not interested, at this point, about the veracity of this statement. She redirects, 'Maybe you were, but I want you to face the front and listen, thanks. You'll need to know this.' Ms D gives brief take-up time and resumes the task instructions as Mia sulks quietly.

Ms D has been pleasant, but firm.
• She could have tried to reason, 'Look, girls, can't you see I'm trying to explain something?' 'But Miss . . .' She could have pursued a pointless discussion on whether they were telling the truth.
• She could have argued, called them liars, heated up the conflict unnecessarily—'Don't lie to me. You weren't talking about the work at all.'

Ms D has learnt that it is not relevant whether the students were talking about the work. The issue in the immediate short-term is to refocus attention on the necessary behaviour or task.

Ms D turns her eyes away from the talkers and resumes the lesson flow. She has communicated nonverbally that she expects compliance, but it has all happened without a big drama. Before the girls go to play at recess, she will have a brief chat about their behaviour away from the audience (p 139).

Finishing group instruction, Ms D directs the class back to their tables, reminding the monitors for each table group—materials monitors, noise monitors and group helpers who can assist in task clarification—what they need to do. Watching them go, she sees Dean playfully push Hung in the back. Hung frowns but shrugs it off. Ms D chooses not to ignore this, although it was just playful. She believes that shoving, pushing, elbowing and play fighting is unacceptable, even if 'boys will be boys'. Without making a scene, she calls him over, beckoning with her hand, 'Dean'. She repeats his name, pausing, to gain and sustain his eye contact and attention. 'Over here, thanks.' She turns aside to chat nonchalantly to the group she is working with, giving Dean some face-saving take-up time. The class see him shuffle over with an 'I-know-what-you're-going-to-say-to-me look'. She turns to face him. 'Dean . . ., what's our rule for respect?' 'What?' He sounds surprised. She repeats. She has explained and discussed the meaning of safe and fair treatment in class. She has discussed what respect means—our actions toward others. She also uses stories to explore themes such as respect, consideration, co-operation. 'I saw you push Hung.' 'Gees,' says Dean, 'I was just mucking around.' 'Maybe you were, but we've got a rule for respect, Dean. We don't push or shove here, okay?' 'Yeah,' he says, unconvinced. She has kept her voice quiet, but firm, in this exchange. He goes back to his seat. Before play, she'll have a brief chat with both of them.

As she moves around the room, encouraging, teaching and managing, she has a brief chat with Dean and Hung about the work. This re-establishes the teacher–student relationship. 'How's it going, Dean? Can I have a look?' She is aware that the interpersonal tone is affected by the way she speaks to students. How she enters their personal space, coming side-on rather than face-on is also important. She often bends down to establish eye-level relationship and always *asks* to see a student's work. She is careful not to point at the work, or tap the book or table in a derogatory way, or make disparaging remarks about the work such as:
- 'Give me a look. Is that all you've done? C'mon. I asked for a full page of writing. You've only done a few sentences. What's wrong with you?'
- 'Is that the best you can do?'
- 'Can't you write more neatly than that?'
Even if the work *is* messy, Ms D is careful not to make an issue of that in front of the student's peers.

She notices a couple of students whose conversational working noise is too loud. While still kneeling at Dean's table, she turns her head and, lifting her voice tone a little, says, 'Halid . . ., Simon . . .' They look across the room to Ms D. Holding their eye contact, she lifts up her right hand, bringing her index finger and thumb together in a closing motion. She repeats this little nonverbal signal, completing the action by bringing her hand to her mouth.

This private signal is understood by the class as the teacher's quiet reminder to bring the noise level down. She does something similar with chair leaners. Rather than say, 'Don't lean back on your chair like that'—or worse, tip the chair back and say, 'That'll teach you!' she says, 'Michael . . ., sitting up, four on the floor, thanks.' She extends four fingers downward as an accompanying signal. Sometimes, especially from a distance, she just uses the signal without saying anything.

- She could have marched over to the noisy students and said, 'Look, I can hear you on the other side of the room. Don't speak so loudly or you'll be sitting apart!'
- She could have said to the chair leaner, 'No wonder you can't write well, when you're always leaning back on your chair, Michael' and 'Don't argue, Michael! Just sit up. All right?' when he said, 'But I don't always, Miss!'

Later she goes back when he is sitting up and says, 'Nice to see you sitting up (wink). How's the work going? Can I have a look?' She is aware that encouragement and re-establishing after correction, maintain a positive working relationship.

Adam has a set of footy cards on his desk. Students are not supposed to have toys or play objects on their tables. They know this. She could snatch it off his table, saying, 'Right! Give them to me. Now!' She gives a directed choice instead. 'Nice cards, Adam, but where should they be?'—'I wasn't playing with 'em, Miss.'—'I still want you to put them in your locker (she pauses) or on my desk.' He slowly gets up, sighs, and puts them in his locker.

Halid calls out across the room, 'Miss, Miss, I need you.' She tactically ignores for a while. As a form of negative reinforcement, it often works. Students notice what she does attend to—students who follow the rule and put their hand up and wait—and they often follow suit. If students' behaviour affects other students' right to learn or her right to teach, she will give a simple direction or reminder, 'Halid . . ., hands up without calling out, thanks' or, 'Remember our class rule.' Here, she will signal with a hand up and hands to her mouth as a cue. If several hands are up, she will number them off and deal with each in turn, though this is rare as the routine is, 'Ask three before you ask me.' Students share and conference quietly at their tables unless it is an individual task. If a student hassles her by bringing work to her and pestering, 'Miss, see my work, Miss!' she tactically ignores or turns with a blocking hand and says, 'Waiting quietly, thanks'.

- She could have said to Halid, 'Look, I can't be in two places at once, can I?'
- She could have stopped the whole class to make an issue of his behaviour.
- She could have simply gone over and helped him, or answered him, reinforcing the unhelpful association that when he calls out, she will always attend to him.
- When students whine, 'Can you see my work?' she could say, 'Look, don't whine like that. Do I whine like that? Do I? Now you can just wait till I'm ready to see your work.'

If she says anything about whining voices, she usually says, 'I'll listen to you when you speak in a normal voice.' She then tactically ignores them until they do.

Ms D continues her rounds of the class, thinking of lunch. She notices Melinda and Lisa, distractedly off-task. She has spoken to them twice and they had settled for a while. The time has come to be a little more intrusive. She walks over. 'Melinda . . ., Lisa . . ., I've asked you twice to settle down and work quietly. If you continue to talk loudly, and distract others, you'll need to work separately.' Melinda protests, but Ms D holds up a blocking hand and repeats the choice and targeted consequence. She walks away, giving take-up time. They settle to the task. They know she is serious. She will direct them to work separately, as she has a couple of times already this term.

When students procrastinate or exhibit task avoidance, she gives the directed choice/consequence. 'If you choose not to do the work now, you will need to do it in your time' or, 'during catch-up time' when those who have completed their set work can do special activities such as board games, personal projects or computer activities. She has learnt that the language of choice conveys the impression to students that their behaviour is *their* responsibility and they, directly, have some control over how they behave. Teaching this kind of responsibility is one of the more difficult aspects of her role. Having learnt that responsibility is not a natural given—even some of her colleagues don't wash up their cups, or clean up their mess, or return books to the library—she makes the effort to teach it.

- The rules and routines outline the responsibility side of the rights they enjoy as a class.
- Monitors are taught their role as well as given opportunity to discuss how they can contribute to the welfare of the class.
- She avoids taking responsibility for students when they get into trouble outside her class.
- She makes clear through discussion, stories and the way she treats them that their behaviour is, in effect, chosen. We don't just behave without thought, although it seems that way with some students. By explaining choice, and thinking about consequences, she emphasises that we are responsible and accountable for our behaviour and how it affects others. By treating students this way, she is treating them as if behavioural choice is a reality (pp 117-118).
- She also uses classroom meetings to support group responsibility and accountability when the class is well established.

If any student is persistently disruptive or aggressive, she uses her time-out plan in class (Chapter 4). In an area away from others, partly shielded with a small table and chair and a three- or five-minute eggtimer, disruptive students are given cool-off time and rethink time. More serious behaviour results in withdrawal from the classroom for time-out. This has been planned with the support of senior colleagues.

If students maintain a pattern of frequent, intense disruptive behaviour, she will not merely rely on daily correction, however positive it might be. She will explore any 'causative' pathology (Rogers 1994 b), but will also set aside one-to-one time to teach them how to: put their hand up without calling out; move through the room without disturbing or annoying others;

how to gain the teacher's attention in an appropriate way . . . This process of Behaviour Recovery (Rogers 1994 b) needs whole-school support to enable grade teachers to effectively give this one-to-one teaching time (p 152).

It is almost time to pack up. Ms D prefaces this by getting the group's attention using the clapping signal, a bell, a song—any conditioned reinforcer (pp 108-109). 'Listening everyone . . . pen down, Michael.' This is addressed to a student who is still distractedly playing with a Texta. 'It's not a pen. It's a Texta,' he grins. Michael has a penchant for the last word (mostly sotto voce) and a bit of clowning. Ms D ignores this as she gives her countdown to pack up. 'Okay, it's pack up time. You know the routine. Counting back from 30 . . . 29, 28, 27.' Organised activity is better than just nagging. As they sit up, ready to start lunch, she sends off the lunch monitors and has a chat prior to the lunch bell. Just before they go out to play, she will remind them to put their chairs under their tables. 'Remember to . . .' is a phrase she prefers to, 'Don't forget to . . .'

At this point of the year, Ms D's discipline is more focused, more consciously prepared than later in the year. She knew she had been given a challenging class with some 'reputation' students. Consistent with her views on discipline, she realises the importance of being positive, but is well aware of the difficulty of translating that aim into day-to-day teaching. It is easy to let frustration with student misbehaviour just take its natural course—('I know what I'd like to do when they are being pains!'). She knows it is easier, in a sense, to discipline from her emotions, but she has learnt that having a discipline plan is as crucial as a lesson plan. This plan includes a language framework for correcting students so that she doesn't spend a lot of time and heat on discipline transactions, but keeps the focus on teaching and learning. Such a plan enables her to be as reasonably consistent as one can be in a job like ours. She's had a few bad days when she's been a bit snappy in tone but has let the class know how she felt and why. She has made sure to start and finish each day as positively as possible. Already, she can see the students becoming more co-operative and responsive to her style of management. Later in the term she will build on this establishment (p 71) and use classroom meetings (p 64), co-operative learning strategies and activities. The mentor systems will be extended, and work on peer monitoring will be introduced. For now, she emphasises 'how this classroom should be'—a place of secure social order—not merely teacher-controlled but teacher-led, where students' rights and responsibilities are expected, developed and managed.

Are you all right, Miss Smith?

She's had a few bad days when she's been a bit snappy on tone . . .

Personality or skill

Some teachers will argue that Ms D is effective because of her personality. They might draw attention to her relaxed sense of humour, the way she winks, cajoles, says, 'Hi, guys!' and the way she joins in a footy game while on playground duty. True, they are personality traits to some extent, but the language she uses in corrective management and discipline, her characteristic tone of voice and manner, her body language and gestures are all skills of effective behaviour management. She has learnt them, and especially at this time of the year, she uses them in a purposeful and planned way.

Is it personality to
- say, 'Do' when directing instead of, 'Don't'? I have heard many teachers say that even replacing a negative directional focus with a behavioural focus ('I want you to face this way' rather than, 'Don't talk') has made a difference in their management.
- remind rather than nag? or redirect rather than characteristically argue? or threaten rather than give controlled choices?
- plan one's discipline and opt for least intrusive discipline where possible?

Positive discipline is a learnt behaviour. It can make a difference.

THE IMPORTANCE OF HUMOUR IN BEHAVIOUR MANAGEMENT

Humour can relax, engage, encourage—even defuse tension. As Cornett (1986) notes, '. . . humour disarms. You cannot be angry and laugh at the same time'.

Working with a very difficult senior class, I observed a boy not doing his work but wandering around the room. I called him over.

'I noticed you haven't started work. Any problems?'

'Don't wanna do this *shit*,' he replied, eyes averted.

'This?' I pointed to the work.

'Yeah!' His face looked angry.

'You sure?' I asked, then started to seriously sniff the work. He laughed, almost involuntarily.

'C'mon. Let's have a look.' He came over expecting to see something. The tension now defused, I was able to discover that he couldn't read the set work. Reading it with him, I was able to redirect him by modifying the task.

In another class I heard an older student, clearly frustrated by something or other, say, '*Shit!*' as I walked past. He put his hand over his mouth. He knew I had heard. I winked and added, 'No, you don't need a *sheet* for this work, Dean.'

We've all been in meetings where tension has been released by a humorous comment, a turn of phrase or saying something the wrong way which sounded funny. A principal opened a workshop on discipline by saying, 'Many people think it's important to bring back capital punishment.' He did not realise why all the staff were laughing, until it was pointed out to him.

Laughter is healthy. Students enjoy teachers who can 'lighten up', tell a joke now and then, or use their voice and facial expressions to give licence to life's incongruities. I've had students call me 'Mum'. Now that's a joke. When called 'Mum', I change the register of my voice for a laugh. I've made faces to miserable students, pretended to cry when students said they didn't like the work I'd prepared, laughed at myself for misspelling a word by walking back to the board and putting my eye directly on the chalkboard, pretended I couldn't see what they were pointing out.

59

Try walking up to students who look jaded on a hot day and fan them with a book to get a ready smile. Look for opportunities for small jokes:

'Can I have some Blu-tack?'

'No (wink), I've only got Green-tack.'

The class monitor was looking a bit fed up that day as she put up the class work. She smiled at the Green-tack 'joke'.

Using language and mathematics games, when appropriate, can ease the tension of learning and bring some fun and group laughter to problem-solving. When I gave classes daily writing from the board, I often made it funny so that the students could be heard chuckling while writing. Student literature—Roald Dahl's rhymes, joke books, funny pictures, funny turns of phrase, spoonerisms—is replete with the humour of life's incongruence.

Even as adults attending lectures or professional development courses, we appreciate laughter and good humour. It can make learning more enjoyable.

Passing notes

Students sometimes pass notes, little billets-doux in class. Rather than snatch or grab, sometimes I ignore, sometimes I direct them to give the note to me. I then read it out to all, acting as a student looking ultra-pained, 'Mr Rogers is a deeply caring and respectful teacher. He would never embarrass me by reading my private notes in class.' I then hand it back to the student. Folded. With a smile.

During morning talk with Grade 1, I brought in a witchetty grub. We had been writing about caterpillars and insects. The grub was in an ice-cream container—at least, they thought it was a grub. It was marzipan and food dye. I explained how it was an edible grub and could be eaten alive. Under the magic of imagination I made it move as I put it in my hand and showed it to all. Then, in hushed tones, I said,

'I'll eat it right now.'

'No, Mr Rogers, don't eat it', said several concerned front-row observers.

'You'll all have to be quiet', I said.

Hamming it up, I dropped it headfirst, chewed and then collapsed in a minor paroxysm of sickness as a sea of wide-eyed, open-mouthed students watched. We had a terrific laugh when I sat up, with appropriate gravitas, and explained what I'd done. No doubt, they too had a laugh recounting to their parents what had happened.

In her excellent little handbook *Learning Through Laughter*, Claudia Cornett (1986) gives forty-eight practical ideas on how to include humour in teaching. Here's a few to remind us of the place of humour in a well-rounded class:

• read aloud something humorous each day
• have a humorous quotation collection
• collect spoonerisms
• share personal humorous anecdotes now and then

Next time you have a frog in your throat . . . if you can see the funny side, it will help.

- encourage students to do the same
- use tongue twisters (have students practise and record times on a graph)
- parody television programs and advertisements (a great one for a Friday afternoon or to encourage a grade to do a drama triathlon)
- give a project on what makes people laugh
- put different laughs on cards and have students pantomime them (their task is to mimic a: guffaw, giggle, snort, snicker, beam, grimace, half-smile, polite smile).

Of course, humour is idiosyncratic and is not well developed in everyone, nor is the ability to use repartee and the bon mot. Nevertheless, we can all lighten up when appropriate, by using facial gestures and suitable voice. We can use humorous literature and read from a good joke book now and then, to create a bit of fun. Laughing at ourselves, when appropriate, is beneficial to all. As Cornett (1986) has pointed out, we can, '. . . make others laugh, not by becoming a clown but by letting [our] own natural sense of humour emerge' (p 31).

Humour is distinguished, in kind, from sarcasm (p 32). Sarcasm puts heat into an already tense situation. It demeans and unnecessarily shames. It creates resentment and damages self-esteem.

Next time you have a frog in your throat or catch a cold or get so annoyed about something that it drives you up the wall, if you can see the funny side, it will help. Use the humour to educate, ease the tension and make the classroom an enjoyable place to be.

Balancing correction with encouragement

Apparently Vincent Van Gogh appreciated the way a friend gave some critical feedback on his painting. In a letter, he writes, 'If he says this or that is not right, he always adds but how about . . .' (trying this, or doing that).

Encouragement is the balance needed to round out correction. It is one of the too-obvious-to-mention aspects of teacher behaviour. We know that people—even teachers!—generally, like to be acknowledged, affirmed, encouraged, and praised for their efforts. Yet it is easy to forget encouragement in the busy process of running a classroom.

I recently team-taught in a Grade 5 class which was doing a self-esteem activity. Several students on the mat were fiddling with the presented work they were about to share. The teacher, however, calmly thanked the students who were sitting, holding their work patiently. She said it without a patronising tone, within the general flow of the share time. It had an effect on both the acknowledged and the distracting students.

It is easier to scrutinise for weaknesses in others rather than focus on effort, strength, or the small contributions an individual makes to the group's welfare. As Harris (1973) notes, 'A winner seeks for the goodness in a bad man, and works with that part of him. A loser looks only for the badness in a good man, and thereafter finds it hard to work with anyone.' Conveying positive regard even when the student is a 'pain' is not easy. For encouragement to

61

work, we know we have to make an effort to remember, to notice and convey to students, in a non-sycophantic way, that we care about specific things they do:

'You do a good job of . . .'—specific focus on the effort or contribution made; especially when they don't ask for it (Dreikurs 1982).

'I've noticed you've improved in . . .'—notes their progress as well as effort.

'It helps us/We like it when you . . .'—acknowledges their usefulness, their contribution to the group. Students will remember this and often try again in this area.

'It's a pleasure to see such a tidy, organised library corner. Thanks.'—describes what we see, and comments (Faber and Mazlish 1982, p 186).

'You cleared your desk well. I like the way you organised your books like that—good on you.'—focuses on the observable, positive action and behaviour.

'You worked hard on that . . .', 'Good on you for . . .', 'Thanks for . . .', 'I appreciate it when you . . .', 'You really help by . . .', 'I value your help in this way'—simple encouragers are as basic as a smile and a few well-meant words.

When students feel they've failed or are a failure, teachers can acknowledge:

'Okay, you made a mistake. That's all right. What can you learn from it? How can you do it better next time?'

'You think you can't do it. We think you can. Let's try together.'

'Good try. Hang in there.'

'I'm sure you can fix this up/work this out. If you need help from me or a member of the class, let me know.'

'Okay. Let's try looking at this a different way.'

This approach is important in our own failures and mistakes. Rather than call oneself 'stupid for . . .' rephrase—'Okay. I messed that up. How can I fix it up or do it better next time?' (see Rogers 1992 b). If students hear us speak positively about our mistakes and failures, our modelled behaviour may appear more desirable. Even when they've been disciplined—with dignity, it's hoped—no grudge will be held.

The exterior messages of encouragement from teacher to students are, 'You are respected, you are worthwhile and you belong', not just because of relative goodness or badness. If students' basic emotional needs are not met in the one-third of the day they spend in school, it will show up in their behaviour. Many of us have had students whose primary sense of worth and belonging has, in fact, been met through school. They have been treated with respect, acknowledged as worthwhile, have known daily care, have been listened to, been affirmed and had a consistent adult role model.

Points to consider when offering encouragement

Phrasing

This depends on age and situation. While we might say to a student in Infant class, even to one in Grade 2, 'I really appreciated the way you tidied up the unifix blocks so neatly', we would phrase similar encouragement differently to a Grade 6 student. We also need to consider that older students prefer private rather than public praise—except in sporting areas! Said quietly to a Grade 6 boy recently, 'It really helped, Brett, when you reminded Craig to work quietly. Thanks for doing it without a lot of fuss.'

Tone

This will convey how sincere we are. Sometimes genuine, unprompted admiration is appropriate, but over-ebullient praise is unhelpful. Recognition of the effort and application is enough, 'You put a lot of thought into that piece of work.'

Remembering?

It is easy to forget students who are normally co-operative and thoughtful—the shy, less vocal, students who make an effort. I've observed in many classrooms how the louder, more articulate, clever or pretty students are more likely to be noticed or included in activities or called on to help. All students need simple, little encouragers like, 'Well done' or 'Nice to see a tidy desk' or 'Thanks for . . .' as well as the nonverbal messages of encouragement.

One of the valuable outcomes of a rotating monitor system is that everyone has an opportunity to be actively responsible and contribute to the general sense of social worth. I've seen previously shy students stand up with a monitor partner, and with a big smile on their faces, read out the names on the lunch orders they've just picked up from the canteen.

Because it is easy to forget encouragement, except when it is involuntary, it helps to make a note of the little acts of unprompted kindness, generosity, thought and care:
• how Thomas's manners were evident when he said, 'Excuse me' instead of pushing past
• how Melissa helped David, a student who struggles with numeracy, by quietly going over, sitting alongside him and offering help without actually doing it for him
• how Rachel and John tidied up without being reminded
• how Lee put all the lids back on the felt-tip pens and made sure they were all packed away
• how Dean and Hung made sure they left the library corner a little tidier than they found it.

Some teachers use classroom meetings as a forum for compliment giving. A notebook records the teacher's weekly observations. Teachers initiate the meeting by noting aspects of positive behaviour. Members of the group are encouraged to do the same if they wish. As with encouragement, the key to giving compliments is to focus on the specific where possible. Young students often say, initially, 'I like Craig because he is my friend.' Jane Nelsen (1981, p 118) suggests teaching students to begin their compliment by saying, 'I would like to compliment (the student's name) for (the specific thing that class member did—accomplishments, helpfulness, sharing)' (see also Rogers 1994 b, p 65). Nelsen adds '. . . most of the encouraging experiences involve very little time on the part of the adult to offer a few words of recognition and appreciation'.

It is important to be aware of how we use qualifiers. Encouragement can be devalued if we add, 'And if you put your hand up like that all the time, we wouldn't have a problem, would we?' Consider, also the principle of unobtrusive marking and comments on a student's work. I've seen some teachers scribble, explain and circle in red to the point where the student's original work is actually devalued.

It's the balance. Someone once told me that teachers should give three encouragers for every correction. I don't know if that has statistical validity, but it's sound commonsense to me.

Classroom meetings

Many schools use classroom meetings to enhance whole-school commitment to problem solving, clarification of values, sharing concerns, and even developing school-wide policies and plans.

A classroom meeting is sometimes called a 'magic circle' (at Lower Primary), 'group time' or 'group think'. It operates on these assumptions and attitudes:
- students can contribute to decisions that affect them
- students can learn responsibility through the exercise of planning, sharing and decision making that can occur in such groups
- it is important to allow students some involvement in decisions that affect them
- students learn that they have rights and can use their appropriate right to participate in this way
- through effective use of classroom meetings, students can develop listening, lateral thinking, oral and co-operative skills as well as values clarification.

Effective classroom meetings
Points for teachers to consider

Purpose: a planning session (say before an excursion), an educational session (to focus on a new learning topic or activity) or a meeting to address a concern or problem that affects an individual, several members of the class, or the whole school.

Time: 15–20 minutes is normally ample, though a whole-group meeting can be balanced by mini-groupings, meeting for 5–10 minutes on an issue or topic, then regrouping to a full-class group. Also consider the best time in the day for a meeting—generally in the last 15–20 minutes of a set timetable slot. Some teachers have a standard weekly meeting (a general meeting) and call ad hoc meetings as issues arise.

Seating: is more effective in a circle or semicircle. Plan with the group how this can be done quietly and quickly. Practise the best option. If students sit on the floor, it is helpful for the teacher to sit at that level as well, so that people can hear and see one another comfortably.

Agenda/Rules: some simple rules can help. These can be published as rules for group time, covering communication, respect and length of time for contributions. It is important for students to realise that we are here to help one another. This means we will respect and listen to one another (unlike some parliamentarians!) and work together on solutions for concerns or problems.

The rules overlap with general classroom rules:
• one person speaking at a time
• listen when others are speaking
• hands up to make a point
• positive contributions—no put-downs
• all remarks made through the chairperson.

Facilitation: it is important that teachers avoid moralising or preaching. Use a balance of open and direct questions.
• Give feedback:
   'Are you saying . . .?'
   'Do you mean . . .?'
   'Could you explain that a little more?'
• Manage the more vocal in the group
• Keep to the fair rules of the meeting
• Keep the meeting on track
• Encourage the hesitant without forcing a contribution:
   'Does anyone else want to contribute? share?'
• Students can learn, in time, to take the chairperson's role
• It is the teacher's genuine tone that will encourage participation. If the meeting is flagging, draw it to a close:
   'It seems that most of you are saying . . . Is that right?'
   'Does anyone want to say any more?'

Recording decisions: it helps to write up points, suggestions, or outcomes on a whiteboard or large piece of paper (especially for the visual learners). This role can be shared among the students. In time, and with practice, students can assume the role of chairperson.

Practice: students and teachers need to practise the skills of group/class meetings. In the first several meetings, it may help to begin with some simple warm-up games (Rogers 1990) that can be done sitting on the mat or on a chair (see also McGrath and Francey 1993).

In problem-solving sessions the range of options—plus, minus, and interesting—can be tabled. Minus options are those that clearly do not fit the test of our classroom rights and rules. Initially, students tend to go for draconian measures, especially when discussing consequences for behaviour.

If teachers have key skills in running classroom meetings, they can invite colleagues to join in and observe. This is the easiest and most effective way to learn how to do it.

When exploring issues such as lying, stealing, aggressive behaviour, teasing and bullying, it is important to discuss with students what we mean by these terms.

It is quite surprising to find a range of opinions about basic values as well as this kind of behaviour, especially teasing and put-downs (p 104 ff).

Values clarification

It is hard for many teachers to resist the temptation to jump in and make up students' minds. Encourage discussion of these questions: How do you think a person feels when . . .? Has anybody felt . . .? How does that (the suggestion, the answer, the stated belief) fit in with our classroom rights and rules that emphasise fair treatment, safety and respect?

It is important that these matters be thoroughly discussed, before asking subsequent questions: What do you think we should, and can, do when people tease? when our property is stolen? when we find out who has stolen something?

Solutions should focus on helping students:
• own their behaviour
• plan as a group
• make restitution
• solve problems with a focus on related outcomes rather than just punishment.

As Lemin et al (1994) note, students can be given information about what their community believes, and what its values are, in ways that do not put them under personal duress. This is not easy, however, and requires some skill in both teaching and management. 'They can also be given practice in values negotiation, to acquire the patience and tolerance needed to achieve values agreement in a group or a community.' This is important, because skill development in this area can help students to '. . . make intelligent choices based on a generous awareness of other people's interests as well as their own' (Brian Hill foreword to Lemin et al 1984).

Classroom meetings can provide a group-based focus for students to clarify what their values are—what they mean in given situations; how one justifies one's values in terms of real living; and how they, as emerging adults, can balance some consistency of values with life's inevitable suffering.

> Where they are listened to, treated as people with ideas and opinions, involved in making decisions about their programs and progress, and generally given the responsibility for their own actions, students are less alienated than they are in custodial schools where they are regimented and subjected to directions for the majority of the school day (Oates 1991, p 199). When students participate in the regulation of their own behaviour they are obliged to examine personal motives, social consequences, educational and moral values, and every other aspect of what makes a community worth belonging to. Under these conditions, students are more likely to accept and internalise the values underpinning an agreed code of conduct, rather than just passively submit (or actively resist) an imposed solution (Dobson and Gale, 1990, note 16).

I was working with a group of Grade 5 students on concerns they had about their classroom and playground. They were not used to having their views listened to and it took them a while to become attuned to the fact that we were taking their concerns seriously.

First we split them into pairs for ten minutes or so, to share common concerns (see the questions, p 27). Each pair then had to join another pair to form a group of four whose task it was to share their views and then come up with other views. The last grouping required the group of four to add another two (where numbers permitted) to make a final group of six or seven. When this group had spent five minutes or so sharing and listing their common concerns, a spokesperson for each group reported back to the class and the teacher.

I directed a student to list all the suggestions on the board. They included concerns as widely spread as provisions for play options for senior students and better seating in the playground through to unfair allegations made about senior students by some staff. They were keen to take their list straight to the principal.

I asked them how the principal might feel if they just barged in, en masse, with a list. 'Can you go away and come up with a plan that gives you the chance to share your concerns in a fair way?' I asked. To their credit, they suggested a delegation be formed who could plan a dignified presentation. They spent some time planning this. The result was that they made an appointment, prioritised their list of concerns, appointed a spokesperson for the delegation and some follow-on questions as to how the concerns could best be addressed. (Of course, I gave them a hand!)

To her credit, the principal also planned to receive them, and even had an afternoon tea prepared for them. It was a mutually profitable meeting, key outcomes being that the students learnt a great deal about how to present themselves, and their views, and also discovered that they were taken seriously.

Parent support

It is important to notify parents whenever a student develops a pattern of disruptive behaviour. Most students, especially senior students, appreciate the opportunity to work on behaviour concerns with their teacher without their parents' involvement. Quite often, after-class chats and class-based restitution give the teacher and student time to focus on behavioural and attitudinal change (p 124 ff).

Parents, however, need to know—indeed have a right to know—when things are clearly not working out. Involving parents in behaviour concerns at school requires some sensitivity. Few parents like to think their student is a 'behaviour problem', a troublemaker, or has a bad reputation. Some parents are unsupportive, some blame the school or even inflame the issue. Most want to help, if they can.

It is important that the school has a due process for initiating parent communication on behaviour concerns.

- Grade teachers initiate parent dialogue (even formal dialogue) with senior teacher support.
- It is good policy for parents to make an appointment if they want to raise any behaviour concerns with a grade teacher. Obviously, the principal needs to know of problems with particular students, and the grade teacher needs appropriate protection from hostile parents.
- While making an appointment may seem unnecessarily official, grade teachers need time to prepare for parent dialogue or conference. Records kept by the grade teachers and the administration will be descriptive, focusing on behaviour, the context and date. This can be helpful in discussions with parents, especially if there are problems at home that interfere with the student's life at school. It is important that the conference be planned to focus on the behaviour of the student without attacking the person or parentage. It is also helpful to start with concerns about the student's learning at school, as this is the affected outcome of disruptive or dysfunctional behaviour patterns. Parents often feel threatened when asked to come to the school to talk about their child's behaviour. It is important that the tone and process of the meeting is one of problem-solving. The school, through the grade teacher, will emphasise how the school values and needs parental understanding and support.

The environment and timing need to be considered (Rogers 1990, pp 139–141) and whether the student will be present. Certainly at the first meeting it is more productive if the parent(s) or guardian, grade teacher and senior teacher meet without the student. Some students become quite embarrassed, moody or cantankerous when adults speak about their behaviour in their presence. This is not to say that we shouldn't do it, just that initially the parent may feel more comfortable and more open about discussing concerns and problems without the student listening. There may be sensitive issues relative to home life that the students, especially young students, do not need to know about. For example, most teachers are very supportive and understanding when they realise how a particular student is affected by difficult weekend access visits or other emotional problems at home.

The student's presence is helpful at the end of a meeting—or at a second meeting—when a behaviour agreement is being discussed. This is where parent support is essential. Any behaviour contract or agreement works best if the parent is clearly aware of why it is being used and how it works (p 151). The grade teacher can take the student through the agreement, focusing on specific, positive behavioural outcomes in the light of class and school rules, rights and responsibilities.

For students who come from at-risk home environments, it is necessary for the school to liaise with community welfare, social workers and, where appropriate, with ethnic liaison officers. Home background can help to explain why some students behave as they do. However, it cannot excuse behaviour that significantly affects learning and safety at school. Parents need to be aware of the school's behaviour management policy, especially on aggression, bullying, use of time-out, detention, use of consequences, suspension and contracts (or behaviour agreements). Above all, the tone of a conference with parents should communicate that we are committed to helping their child in every possible way without excusing, tolerating or accepting disruptive behaviour.

Modelling by staff

When addressing behaviour management in schools, it is easy to focus on the discipline of students, on *their* behaviour. Whole-school behaviour management is more than that. It involves everybody's behaviour to everybody.

Consider this kind of event: a senior teacher enters a first year teacher's classroom without knocking and simply wanders around the room picking up students' work, making cavalier comments which, in effect, put down the class teacher's effort. This behaviour affects self-esteem, general staff morale and cohesiveness, and is patent bad manners.

Examples of poor modelling by staff:
- pushing into canteen or tuckshop queues without any reasonable deference to students, not even an 'Excuse me, everyone, I apologise for coming to the front of the line but I'm in a desperate hurry.'
- yelling at students who run in corridors instead of calling them aside to remind them of the rule
- not using common, interpersonal courtesies such as, 'Please', 'Thanks', 'May I borrow?'
- taking a student's pen to use without asking permission, or simply picking up work without the basic courtesies of, 'Do you mind if I check your work? Where are you up to? Do you mind if I write the correct spelling for . . . in the margin? I'd like to read/share/show your work to the class. Is that okay?'
- not letting students pass them in doorways just because the teachers are adults
- entering a colleague's class without knocking or not waiting for them to extend the normative okay, unless the school has an open-door policy. I've seen many senior teachers over the years rudely knock on the window of a class, gesture to the student they want out, then speak loudly in an embarrassing way, sometimes with a thinly veiled reference to the host teacher. This behaviour is an abuse of relational power
- making a colleague who is late to work feel worse by interrogating rather than allowing cool-off time, and problem solving later
- putting staff down in front of students
  Imagine a colleague who is seen by the deputy coming down the corridor at 9:30. The deputy (within earshot of the classrooms in the corridor) takes the colleague to task, 'Listen . . . I've had to cover your class! You could have rung me, couldn't you? What's wrong with you?'

Who knows why the teacher is late or didn't ring? There could be sickness at home, relational problems or perhaps the car broke down. A more effective approach balances short- and long-term considerations—the quiet, private word, 'I can see you're late. Paul is covering your class. Grab a cuppa, get yourself settled. I can see you've rushed. We'll make a time to chat later, okay? Paul can cover your class till 10:45. I'll see him now. Catch you later.' Even if your colleague has been late several times, humiliation won't win co-operation or solve the precipitating problems.

- putting staff down in front of other staff
- not taking meetings seriously

Some staff chat loudly while others are speaking up-front or chairing the meeting, some do their marking or work programs in an attention-seeking fashion to suggest that this meeting is a waste of time anyway, some butt in rudely, put down, snipe or make derogatory remarks. If their students were to come late regularly, read comics in class or talk loudly out of turn, how would they deal with such behaviour?

If senior teachers shout at students, put them down, label students rather than their behaviour, do not use cool-off time, use unrelated consequences, speak to staff in a condescending or arrogant way—their actions will have a more powerful impact than any behaviour management policy. Building a supportive school environment needs leadership modelling.

70

Chapter 4

THE ESTABLISH-MENT PHASE OF THE YEAR

The first four weeks are crucial in developing the smooth running of a class. Taking twenty-five or more students of mixed ability, background and temperament, and building a co-operative, rights-respecting group is no mean feat.

There are several areas that need crucial, whole-school attention during this phase.

Rules

The primary function of rules is to establish 'the way we do things here'. The more co-operative the group is, or becomes, the less we need to be rule managers. We apply rules, like the brakes on a car, when necessary. If it is found that rules or routines are not achieving their purpose, consideration may need to be given to change. They are the framework for desirable social behaviour, not an end in themselves. Dialogue, negotiation and classroom meetings all enable the class to address behaviour, not just in terms of rules but of people's fundamental rights and the supporting values—co-operation, sharing, and care for others and the environment. In terms of developmental, moral reasoning, teachers need to extend the concrete expression of the rules to why we should behave like this (Kohlberg 1976, Piaget 1932). Depending on the comfort level of teachers, the discussion process can range from teacher-directed discussion through to role-playing the behaviour related to the rule. It is also essential that these classroom rules fit in with the school-wide rules.

At this time of the year, students are psychologically and developmentally ready to have rules made clear and to participate in appropriate discussion about them. If teachers do not establish productively in the first few weeks, they lose that developmental advantage. Doyle (1986) has shown that all teachers introduce some rules and procedures in the first few days. Effective teachers integrate such rules into a workable system, anticipating the need for rules, expectations and appropriate cues such as 'hands up'. They responded 'consistently to appropriate and inappropriate behaviour', significantly reducing the number of 'call-outs' and inappropriate movement around the room (pp 410-411).

Consequences

It is also important to discuss consequences for breaking rules and explain to students how behaviour is a choice. It is especially important to explain what time-out is and why it is used in school (p 82).

Manners

It may seem old-fashioned to talk about manners; what may be basic to a teacher is not so obvious to all our students. 'Please', 'Thanks', 'Excuse me' when moving through personal space, 'May I borrow?', waiting one's turn—

these basic good manners are not always experienced as normative in their backgrounds. We may, therefore, have to teach and encourage manners as part of the rights/responsibilities framework of a classroom—not merely expect, demand or assume them. Manners are not the be-all and end-all in human relationships but they are, at least, the social oil that tempers incivility.

Class routines enable the smooth running of the class. Students need to know clearly how to behave: when entering and leaving the room, during mat time in younger grades, at toilet breaks (preferably not during instruction time), after 'big' play, when hanging coats, at lunchtime and during quiet reading. They need key signals about how to gain the teacher's attention and what are appropriate noise levels (p 79 ff).

It is important that routines are explained, modelled, rehearsed and encouraged. Clear reasons for routines should be given. Positive practice can also help a routine to become *routine*. Before teachers direct students in or out of a classroom (especially at Preparatory level and Grade 1) they can give a reminder: 'Before we go in, what do we need to remember?' or 'Before we go to art what do we need to remember? Let's discuss it together.' Encourage students who remember routines without being reminded. 'Thanks for remembering to put the chair away.' 'I appreciate the way Michael and Lisa packed up without being reminded.' 'You remembered to put the Clag bottle away with the brush in. Thanks.' 'The monitors did a good job when . . .'

I would much prefer that my students were in a class whose smooth running (at times running by itself) resulted from planning, than in a class whose routines were ad hoc and dependent on the vagaries of mood, necessity or crisis.

Checklist for routines

It can be helpful in the first team meeting at Infant, Middle or Upper school to reflect on the routines necessary for the respective age groups. Characteristic patterns of teacher behaviour are best set in this establishment phase so that students are clear about how their teacher manages the class.

Questions to ask include:
- How do we cater for mixed ability ranges?
- How do we set up the rules?
- What's the best seating plan to begin the year with?
- What do we do on Friday after lunch or during stressful times?
- Do we have a wet-day plan?
- Have we established how the exit/time-out will work in this area of the school?
- Have I communicated clearly how I want students' attention at critical points in the lesson?
- Do I talk over noise to establish group attention?
- How do I settle the group down to begin instruction or discussion sessions?

- How do I send or direct the class to a learning task from an up-front setting? (for example, transition to seat work)
- How do I reclaim their attention in the middle of on-task time?
- How do I manage changeover of activities?
- How do I manage different groups doing different activities?
- Are there any preferred forms of room organisation we can all consider?
- What is the preferred toilet routine for use during class time? (This is especially important with Infant classes.)

It helps to have a common checklist for routines updated each year.

Monitor systems

Monitors can be allocated for a wide range of tasks to enhance co-operation and responsibility: table monitors, lunch monitors, noise monitors and monitors to distribute materials, are all basic to most classroom settings. Many schools now give badges for these duties. Certainly there should be a rotating system to give all students the opportunity to display responsibility and co-operation, to enhance the 'collective care of our classroom' and to care for one another.

- Label cupboards well with laminated signs or pictures at infant height. Consider seating arrangements and appropriate movement around the room, especially movement to and from lockers. I've been in classes where students cannot avoid bumping into the table behind them when they push back their seat to move away from their table. This creates unnecessary noise and stress.
- Have an attractive photo display of class members with names and interests (see Borba and Borba 1980). Later, add baby photos for students to identify.
- Have a name-learning activity. Include name tags or name cards for the first week or two.
- Display clearly a large timetable, a canteen price list (perhaps a monitor could update the prices), a list of monitor jobs and changeover dates.

Communication and organisation

- Have a weekly journal or news-sheet for parents to stay in touch and share information, such as new letters or words being learnt this week, special activities, monitor lists and duties. The first journal shares class rules, what we hope to achieve, as well as basic facts about our class, and invites parents' co-operation and support. Keep the tone positive and user-friendly, enhanced with student artwork.
- Have a simple routine for what to do with completed work and how to get teacher attention during on-task time. Provide a tray labelled 'To Be Marked'. Clarify which work goes in folders or lockers. Some teachers are happy to have a line of students at their desk. Others prefer, 'Hands up. I'll come!' or 'Ask three before you check with me.' Some teachers ask students in older grades to write their names on a 'teacher help board'. Each student is then visited in turn by the teacher.
- Teach students that bell times and the bell signal are not signals to prove survival of the fittest! Reinforce quiet movement from the classroom to the corridor exit. If necessary practise it.

- Teach 'freeze' and attention signals early (p 108 ff) and reinforce them.
- Plan for early finishers, and when the ability range is recognised, cater for mixed abilities.

Many of the elements of establishing a positive class are almost too obvious to mention, but are essential in building a positive tone and a workable, enjoyable teacher-student relationship.

- Be prepared for classes and lessons by being on time (human fallibility notwithstanding). I've been in many schools where those who are frequently late back from morning tea or lunch have a 'ratty' line of students to contend with, and they're off to a bad start. It's especially important to be early in the morning for chats as you establish the day, greet and remind monitors, direct returned notices and collect swimming and lunch monies. Most important of all is to be there to greet students—most of them look forward to seeing their teacher each day.
- Begin and end the day positively. A positive farewell is more helpful than just letting them go—even if it's been a bad day. Basic as it sounds, it is also important to have time to end the day—to pack up materials and equipment; put work away or in the TBM box (To Be Marked); chairs up or under; to sit on the mat for debriefing, notices and anything to remember for tomorrow. These pack-up routines need to be taught as well as explained.
- Balance correction with encouragement.
- Learn and use the first name of students, in and out of class. This is particularly important.
- Remember special things about students and comment when appropriate. This is not mere technique, it is relationship building. Recognise birthdays and special events (make lists), acknowledge a range of student talents—not just sporting achievements, know what clubs they go to, whether they are having first communion or an important cultural event.

Once the class is established in the first few weeks, consolidation and cohesion is enhanced by:

- classroom meetings
- peer support and cross-aged tutoring
- promotion and use of the Student Representative Council
- programs like *Friendly Kids, Friendly Classrooms* (McGrath and Francey, 1993), *100 Ways to Improve Self-concept in the Classroom* (Cranfield and Wells, 1976)
- balancing the individual focus of the curriculum with appropriate opportunities for co-operation. Enhance the curriculum around access/success by focusing on the individual and the group, utilising students' interests as well as (and within) the set curriculum. Encourage students to use their special talents. Build confidence and risk-taking by legitimising mistakes and failure.

Co-operative activities and learning need to be:
- built on positive establishment of classroom routines and expectations

- taught slowly, over time
- set in structured activities rather than by simply putting students into groups to be co-operative.

My colleagues and I have often found that the best way to teach parents the value of the co-operative classroom is to set up a learning experience where, for example, we:

- seat the parents facing the board in traditional seating mode
- explain that we will be doing decomposition, subtraction, spelling, process writing or . . .
- direct them not to talk while they do, say, five algorithms using the decomposition method (fractions without using concrete materials is another good example)
- ask, after a set time, 'Hands up how many got less than three right?' Before taking that horrible expose-your-ability stance, quickly add, 'After I've counted to five, I'm going to ask how many got more than three, less than three or half the correct words on the spelling list.' Give a spelling list that has the difficult blends and prefixes. After all, isn't it a fact that people in their generation are better spellers?
- stop and say, before the count of five, 'Do you really think I'd embarrass you in front of your peers by asking you what you got right or wrong and make you feel lousy about it? Maybe that happened to you as a student, eh? It happened to me.' Direct them to do a co-operative mathematics or language activity, and the working noise rises and smiles appear on the faces. This is especially powerful when using concrete materials in mathematics, such as bundles of iceblock sticks to represent groups of ten, and decomposing them to the units column so we can subtract rather than just take away. Parents thoroughly enjoy these activities and can readily see the power of focused co-operative activity in the classroom.

I do the same thing with discipline techniques. Model a few strategies (positive, ineffective and confrontational) and ask them what they'd prefer, as a student, even if they were in the wrong.

I've had parents who, on the one hand, argue for the reintroduction of corporal punishment, yet agree that they don't like being put down in front of others or made to feel stupid. They say this especially when I role-play a sarcastic teacher snatching up work, 'Is that all you've done, eh?' or use labels like 'stupid' and 'idiot' or make implications by asking, 'How many times have I told you, eh?' These same people who want the cane reintroduced, say they don't like verbal punishment. After being shown a number of alternatives, almost all agree that there are better ways to discipline people without being punitive, that one can be authoritative without being authoritarian.

Changeover of teachers

It is important for teachers to remember how students feel at the outset of a new year, with a new teacher. This is especially so, when one is new to a school and there has not been the opportunity to meet the new class and familiarise yourself with them at the close of the preceding year.

Most students grow quite attached to their grade teacher and are naturally apprehensive about a new one. What kind of person will the teacher be?—someone who is kind? who growls? who is like my old teacher? How does this person teach? Where will we be asked to sit? (Of course, sometimes, they may be looking for a change!)

This is especially important for younger classes (Kindergarten to Grade 3), especially when they have never had a male teacher before. It helps to check with last year's teacher on special routines or idiosyncrasies that may give insight into how to begin with this class. Leave out a rundown on 'bad' students. That insight may turn out to be incorrect this year, with this teacher (the 'new-start' syndrome). The exception to this may be a student who requires special medication linked to behaviour.

Developing rules

Whenever rules are developed in a school for use in a classroom or at general duty-of-care level (corridor, playground), there are a number of points to consider.

Clarify the purpose for the rules. Rules should have a reason which should be explained to the students. Rules are to protect students' rights to be and feel safe at school, to be treated with respect and to learn (p 31).

Make sure that classroom rules are congruent with school-wide rules regarding uniform or dress code, chewing gum, movement patterns around the school, use of toilets during class-time. Some rules will clearly be school-wide. These hinge on safety and fair treatment (see Playground management, Chapter 7).

It's mildly annoying as a specialist teacher to reinforce a school rule on chewing gum only to be told, and it may be true, that, 'Our grade teacher lets us chew gum!' We need to practise consistent enforcement and encouragement of school rules. Enforcement can occur in the least intrusive way—even with humour at times.

Our grade teacher lets us chew gum!

Clarify and enforce the rules acutely in the establishment phase. As noted (p 71) students tend to be psychologically and developmentally ready to hear their teachers speak about rules and enforce them at the beginning of the year, and to re-establish them at the beginning of each term. When teachers do this positively and with reasonable certainty, then a habit, or pattern of expectation, is established.

Make the rules few in number. Make sure they address the essentials. In an ideal world, we wouldn't need rules. We would live with expectations of rights to be enjoyed, but we do not live in an ideal world.

Make the rules positive in expression where possible, or at least balance the positive and negative elements of the rule. If rules are expressed only in negative terms, they will direct students to what they are not supposed to do but leave the positive behaviour to memory, unstated rather than stated: for example, 'Don't hurt others', 'Don't hit, push, punch, or kick', 'Don't run inside', 'Don't kick the ball over the fence', 'Don't leave chairs or equipment out', 'Don't call out'. When rules are expressed this way, it is more likely the enforcement will be negative:

- 'Hey! Don't run in the corridor' rather than, 'Hey . . . Adam and Lee . . . walking, thanks.'
- 'Hands up without calling out' rather than, 'Don't call out.'
- 'Speak one at a time. Listen when others speak' rather than, 'Don't butt in' or, 'Don't interrupt while the teacher is talking.'
- 'Keep hands and feet to yourself' rather than, 'Don't push, shove, fight, or hit in class.'

We can discuss the negative caveats when we're discussing rules with the class. Many students immediately opt for the negative expression, just as when discussing consequences, they herald the most draconian. Our job is to direct their thinking, attention and expression to the positive features of the rule. Instead of, 'Don't swear and don't use bad language,' we can focus them onto, 'Let's use language that helps us to feel good about ourselves and good about others.' Then discuss what this means. This helps to balance the positive intention of a rule with the negative behaviour it is addressing.

While discussing rules with a Grade 6 class, I asked for suggestions about a rule for class communication. Craig called out, 'Don't call out in class!' In the face of the incongruency, I asked him if he could make the rule more positive. He said, 'Please, don't call out in class!' I gently pushed him for the opposite of calling out—in fact, the opposite of what he'd done a few minutes earlier. 'What do we do instead of calling out?' We finally got there.

Some rules are situation and place specific. In art when we use sharp knives or the kiln, when we go swimming, away on an excursion or school camp or play football away from home, there are specific rules.

Rules overlap routines. Generally speaking, rules connect to social and personal rights and key aspects of social behaviour. Routines—the way we line up, use, distribute and pack up equipment, sharpen pencils, and have our lunch—enhance rights protection and promote the smooth running of the class.

Rules are best expressed simply and clearly. Focus on the key points such as safety, solving problems co-operatively, positive language, good manners and fair treatment. It helps to use plural pronouns such as 'we' and 'our' to preface the rules both in the classroom and school-wide.

Here are a couple of examples from a composite Grade 5/6 class:

'In our classroom, we use language and actions that are appropriate.' The meaning of 'appropriate' would not be clear to students in this class unless they had discussed it and shared many examples of appropriate language and actions.

'We take care of our own, our classmates' and the school's property.' 'Care' was thoroughly discussed. These rules were published on a large sheet and an A4 copy was sent home in the class magazine. Each student appended their signature to the sheet.

Rules must be enforceable. Rules must be enforced with certainty and fairness, not with mere severity.

All rules occur within relationships. Behaviour management is relational. It is the way we make and enforce fair rules and how we follow up when they are broken that counts. Rules are not merely separate entities from the person (teacher or parent) who is responsible for enabling and facilitating a positive and safe learning environment.

Rules are a means to an end. They are not the end itself. While rules can provide acceptable limits to unacceptable behaviour, as well as focusing on the behaviour, they cannot create the behaviour. Rules can give some protection for rights, but they cannot guarantee rights.

Human fallibility, human ignorance and wilful wrongdoing will always compete with what the school community states is right. At the very least, rules give a yardstick within which 'the right' can be explained and enforced, but responsibility will always need to be taught, supported and encouraged.

Common classroom rules

A number of schools I've worked with have encouraged grade and specialist teachers to have a common set of classroom rules based on fundamental rights of safety, fair treatment and learning. Safety extends to health and concerns litter, chewing gum, even spitting, as well as environmental matters such as graffiti. These class rules would overlap the school rules.

Figure 3   Here are some examples of rules at Spring Gully Primary School.

Rules in class		Rules out of class
We speak kindly and respectfully to each other.	TALKING	We speak kindly and respectfully to each other.
We work quietly and helpfully together. We take turns.	LEARNING	We co-operate with others. We share the playground.
We walk quietly in our room and put things away carefully.	MOVEMENT	We take care when we are moving about or playing outside. We look after equipment.
We are kind to each other and use good manners.	TREATMENT	We are kind to each other. We play friendly games.
We try to solve problems in a fair manner. If that is hard, we ask a teacher for help.	PROBLEM SOLVING	We talk to each other and try to work problems out. If we need help, we ask a teacher.
We try not to hurt people. We use equipment safely.	SAFETY	We play safe games. We play in safe areas of the playground.

Establishing workable noise levels

Teachers have differing tolerances to noise levels in their classrooms, partly due to their own tolerance levels to life's stresses and also to the variation in noise according to activity and time of day. It is important, however, to clarify with students when/how noise levels work in their room and what is meant by working noise. My colleagues and I have found it helpful to teach noise levels through the use of a noise meter.

Noise meter

The noise meter is a large (30 cm) laminated circle of cardboard with four coloured quadrants.

- White symbolises the noise level where hands up, without calling out, is appropriate while students do individual work or quiet reading (I used to call mine SQUIRT—sustained, quiet, uninterrupted, interesting, reading time).
- Green symbolises conversational talking time—quiet talking so that others can get on with their work and teachers don't have to raise their voices to gain students' attention during on-task time. I model this so students understand what I mean. With art, physical education or drama activities, louder working noise is expected, but this needs to be discussed with students. Generally speaking, a teacher shouldn't have to shout to be heard. I've been in classes as part of peer observation and stood directly behind students who do not hear even when the voice is raised, so loud is the residual noise.
- Amber signifies a warning that the noise level is too high and too loud. It is a privately understood signal, (p 106) a bit like a traffic light.
- Red signifies 'Stop' when the teacher needs to stop and redirect the class.

The meter has an arrow with a split pin that can be rotated to direct students' attention to the colour on the meter and what it symbolises—hands up, quiet working noise, warning and stop. The meter is positioned so that it can be seen easily by everyone in the class. It is introduced through discussion, teaching the levels, and making a bit of a game out of it. The noise meter can be enhanced by having noise monitors in each group or in key places in the room. The monitors are elected to keep an eye on the meter so they can nudge or signal fellow students if the meter shows amber. The four coloured quadrants can be enhanced by a cartoon symbolising the behaviour identified by the colour.

The whole emphasis of the meter activity is to enhance understanding and co-operation so that workable noise levels can be quickly learnt and established. The meter activity can be withdrawn once the class is clearly operating within reasonable guidelines for classroom co-operation.

For more difficult classes, the teacher can introduce a group-reinforcement activity. A chart for each day can indicate points earned (noted) when the class has responded to white and green zones or the private signal of amber, and dropped their noise level. When twenty points have been reached, the class is allowed a five-minute chat session just before a nominated recess, as long as no student is sitting alone. I've used this approach with very noisy classes to bring down the group noise level. The points program can also be linked to general rule-keeping as part of a group reinforcement process for managing difficult classes (p 161 ff).

Classroom tone and teacher leadership

When teachers exercise their leadership well, they exercise their authority so that rights are protected and enhanced. An authoritative, as distinct from an authoritarian, stance exercises power in a thoughtful way to ensure social order, not mere control. It is seen as the characteristic tone set by the teacher. We've all seen the phenomenon of a difficult class exhibiting different outcomes, depending on the classroom leader. Indeed, I've seen a palpable change in classroom feel and tone when another teacher has taken over a previously co-operative class. The tone of a class does depend on a teacher's characteristic behaviour, rather than what happens on a bad day.

Questions: As a student, would I want to go to this class every day?
Would I want to be a student of the kind of teacher I am?

1 Relationship building
   - know students as individuals
   - find out about their interests, personalities and friends

2 Planning and organisation of classroom and lessons to keep students interested
   Consider
   - ways to minimise opportunities for disruption
   - furniture layout
   - grouping of students
   - mixed abilities (matching)
   - pacing the lesson
   - conveying interest with enthusiasm
   - humour
   - positive atmosphere

3 Scanning (up-front, on-task)

4 Personal behaviour awareness (stance, tone of voice)

5 Modelling expected courtesies

6 Emphasis on rights-enhancing behaviour, with regular encouragement

7 Reprimands
   - use them sparingly
   - be firm, not aggressive
   - target specific behaviour
   - address behaviour, not the person
   - make them private rather than public
   - avoid sarcasm and idle threats

8 The importance of follow-up

Figure 4 (Adapted from *The Elton Report* 1989, Chapter 3.)

EXCLUSION FROM THE CLASSROOM GROUP

The purpose of time-out

The most intrusive consequence we can impose, in or out of the classroom, is exclusion from the group. It is serious because of the behaviour that occasions its use and because it excludes students from their learning and social environment.

Exclusion of students from their peers is commonly known as time-out. It is time away from, and out of, the situation where the student is being disruptive. Time-out is not a first option. Like all corrective and consequential management, it is normally preceded by least intrusive approaches (p 103).

During a language lesson I was conducting with a composite Grade 1/2 class, I saw two wrigglers annoying each other. I directed them, briefly, to face the front and listen. On some occasions, I use distraction, diversion or relocation. In this case, I'd hoped the direction would be enough. It wasn't. In a flash, I took in the quick punch and hair-pulling by one and the explosive tears of the other. In this room, we had a small table and chair near the library corner. Without negotiation, I directed him to the cool-off time area until that part of the lesson was finished. He sulkily stamped off to sit moodily away from the others as I reclaimed the group's attention. Later he rejoined the lesson. At the close of the lesson, I directed both students to stay after class for some conflict resolution and restitution (p 126 ff).

Time-out is an appropriate consequence:
- when students lash out, hit, kick, spit, push furniture over
- for any aggressive behaviour to others, including verbal abuse
- for persistent calling out or interfering with other students' right to learn or the teacher's right to teach.

Students need to learn that their feelings and desires are not bad, per se. All of us have a wide range of feelings and, at times, experience great frustration and anger. When students have 'bad' feelings and desires, '. . . even those at odds with the limits . . .' teachers need to acknowledge that, like us, students have these conflicting feelings and not imply that they are 'bad' for having such feelings (Deci 1985). At the same time, students need to learn that there are consequences when they exercise those feelings in socially destructive ways. Time-out can be used as an appropriate consequence for badly handled frustration, anger and aggression.

Time-out is normally distinguished from relocation in the classroom, a consequence that includes working away from others. While cool-off time and take-up time are important in general behaviour management, in time-out usage, cool-off time can be formalised within a known procedure and process. Time-out can range from three to five minutes sitting at a spare desk away from others in class, to five minutes outside the room 'cooling down', to time-out in a colleague's room nearby or in the office area, or (in larger schools) withdrawal from peers in a designated time-out room. In this sense, there is a least-to-most-intrusive approach in its use throughout the school. These options are discussed later in this section.

In the establishment phase of the year, teachers explain time-out or cool-off time and why it may be necessary. It is also important that the meaning, and application of time-out be explained as clearly as possible in the school's policy document, especially for parents.

Time-out is normally distinguished from mere punishment. It is the logical extension of continuing to disrupt others or acting towards others in an unsafe way. This consequential step is serious and its usage entails special difficulties. Therefore staff need to thoroughly discuss the key components of a whole-school policy (pp 42-43).

A whole-school policy for time-out

Focus of discussion

1 The philosophy of time-out (why it is used). It is important for parents and teachers to know that:
- its primary purpose is to protect students' and teachers' rights which have been threatened in the situation preceding time-out
- time-out gives the disruptive student appropriate time to cool down, to regain control and relative composure
- it also gives the class and teacher necessary cool-off time
- it is not an end in itself, but part of a consequence chain that will later involve appropriate restitution.

2 When time-out will be used at classroom and duty-of-care level.

3 Most importantly, how time-out can be appropriated, especially when the students are resistant, aggressive or violent. How can we get them out of, and away from, the room if they refuse to leave?

4 On what basis does the student come back to the room and when?—after cool-off time? at the beginning of the next class period? after a statutory 10–15 minutes?

5 At what point are parents notified?

6 If time-out is not achieving any change in behaviour, what additional support can the school offer to the key stakeholders?

While time-out is not an easy option for a teacher, and certainly never a first step except in a crisis, it is a necessary option. Teachers are often faced with a situation which can be controlled or managed only by temporary exclusion of a student from the classroom. Nothing is more debilitating to teachers than their sense of powerlessness when the option of temporary exclusion is denied by an unresponsive administration. I have been in schools where principals declare by fiat that, 'No student shall be sent out of class, or to me, as a disciplinary measure'. Do they forget? Have they never had a class with a repeatedly disruptive or aggressive student?

Without a common whole-school agreement on time-out philosophy and a supportive context for its application, teachers—especially in difficult schools—are placed under significant, unnecessary stress.

Connecting behaviour to outcome

What the student learns from time-out is that there is a connection between behaviour and outcome. Whenever they are persistently disruptive, hostile or aggressive, they face time-out. When reminders, redirection and clarification of consequence (p 103) have not resulted in an effort by the student to act responsibly or safely, then they are directed to time-out.

Guidelines for the application of this consequence

- Use the principle of certainty rather than severity (pp 38-39).
- After the warning (clarifying the consequence) the teacher firmly directs the student to time-out in the classroom: 'David, you've chosen not to work by our class rules or what I asked, so it's five minutes time-out for you.'
- 'Stay calm and keep it brief' (one school policy's wording).
- Avoid discussion or bargaining.
- Avoid arguments. If students refuse to go to time-out in the room, the teacher needs to consider whether to clarify a deferred consequence or use procedures for supported exit from the room (p 87).

Time-out in class

It is essential that time-out is explained to the class during the establishment phase of the year. Students need to know what behaviour will result in temporary exclusion from the group and cool-off time. They need to understand that exit/time-out is a very serious matter. The central emphasis is on students' right to feel safe and to learn without undue or persistent interruption.

Time-out in the classroom is normally in an area set aside with a table and chair, without toys, books or games. During time-out students are cooling off and, ideally, thinking about their behaviour. Students are directed there for a set time: 'When you've settled down and done your time-out, you can come back to continue your work.' Time-out is normally distinguished from relocation in the room where the student works away from others.

In Lower and Middle Primary, teachers often have eggtimers labelled three-minute, and five-minute, on a small table. Students are directed to have three or five minutes time-out. In this sense, students monitor their own time-out. One school calls it 'Take five'. Avoid terms like 'naughty corner', 'bad corner' or 'sin-bin'.

In Upper Primary classes, effective and positive use can be made of an area which is cordoned off or screened, where students can cool off. This makes an impact in the establishment phase of the group's life when students learn quickly that significant intrusive and disruptive behaviour means that one has chosen temporary social exclusion.

In one composite Grade 5/6 class, the teachers set aside an L-shaped alcove at the back of the room, screened to shoulder height with a chair behind it. A poster on the wall displayed four focus questions (p 27) accompanied by cartoons of sad/annoying faces progressively growing happier as key, reflective questions about behaviour are focused on.

It is essential that the teacher's direction to time-out be done with dignity, without vilification or public shaming. Going to time-out is embarrassing enough in itself. In fact, if some students are too upset, angry or aggressive, it is better to use exit time-out.

When students have had time-out (in or out of class) they are accepted back into the group without recrimination. They don't need the threat, 'Right, if you're stupid like you were before, you'll be back in that corner or out on your ear—do you understand?' Repairing and building will be necessary at some stage during the day following time-out. Sometimes, all that is necessary is a word of assurance, the reminder that, 'Tomorrow is another day.'

If a student has had time-out on several occasions, a behaviour plan or contract will be necessary to consider:
• situations that may precipitate disruptive behaviour
• alternative seating
• clarification of behaviour that needs to stop and behaviour that needs to be worked on and why (see Chapter 6).

Temporary exclusion from the classroom group: exit time-out

The most intrusive form of time-out requires students to leave their class group completely for a set time. In some schools, this may be as basic as five minutes cool-off time outside the room. Five minutes is ample. I've seen students standing outside for twenty minutes or more as a result of a dispute with the teacher, culminating in a statement like, 'You can stay out there until I say you can come in!' Worse, some teachers, when passing a recalcitrant in the corridor, feel obliged to demand why the student has been sent out—even though the main reason is obvious. The student then faces an interrogation by a senior teacher, and possibly a detention as well!

Unless the student in the corridor is being very disruptive, staff who pass by should be encouraged to ignore the student, leaving the discipline process to their colleague. The use of a five-minute cool-off time outside the room needs whole-school acceptance, especially when some students are likely to be as disruptive outside as they are inside!

Time-out in assembly time

I've seen senior teachers in assemblies yell through the microphone and ask a student who is misbehaving to come and stand up in front for public embarrassment. Time-out in this setting is more appropriately instituted by a teacher quietly calling the student aside from the assembly to an area at the back of the hall or assembly point. The behaviour precipitating such time-out needs to be followed up at another time.

Exit from the room

Exit from the room needs significant collegial support and a well-planned due process. The exit/time-out plan should be published with a clear explanation of what is meant by time-out and the situations occasioning its use. Before students are directed from the room to time-out, they should be warned of what will happen if their present behaviour continues.

The school's policy will outline the options for teachers:
• five minutes outside the room
• fifteen or more minutes in a colleague's room nearby
• fifteen or more minutes in a time-out room or time-out area
• supported time-out procedures.

It is very important that staff consider how a student will leave a room to go to a time-out place. The preferred, successful ways of directing students from their rooms to time-out can be discussed by staff. A student's exit is potentially emotionally charged. It is vital that the teacher remains calm, and directs the student away from the group in order to initiate time-out. Older students can be directed aside by the teacher who might say something like, 'Since you won't calm down I'll have to ask you to leave. I hope we can get together later and work this out. If you're not willing to settle down, it's better you leave now' (Glasser 1991).

• Teachers need to clarify how they want senior staff to support them in the use of time-out. Is it acceptable to direct a student, unsupervised, to another classroom or to the deputy principal for time-out? Should the deputy principal be the first option for support and the sole provider of time-out? In some cases, this may be the only option available. Unfortunately, some teachers believe the principal's role is to punish students during time-out. This creates unnecessary anxiety in students. Going to the principal's office should normally be a positive experience.

• For younger students who are likely to do a 'runner', or students who refuse to come in after recess or refuse to leave the room, it is necessary to have a collegially supported process. Many schools use an exit-card system (Rogers 1992). Each teacher has a postcard-sized, coloured, laminated card with the room number on it. It may be coloured green for go, pink for calm time, or red for danger. Staff decide on a standard colour card which acts as a universal cue across the school. Whoever receives it knows there is a significant concern or problem in the room, hall, library or computer room. The card stays in that room and, if necessary, will be sent via a trusted student to one of several nominated staff, ranging from a colleague teaching nearby through to the principal, according to the problem.

The use of exit cards removes the need to send ambiguous notes. It also saves the emotional win/lose battles some teachers find themselves caught up in while trying to send a student out of the room—'I hate this stupid class and you're a . . . You can't make me leave. I hate you.' The student conveying the card can be from the host class or from a classroom nearby. If supported time-out procedures are used, excesses of temper which cause teacher or student to 'lose the plot' will be avoided.

While waiting for the colleague to come, it is helpful to tactically ignore the disruptive student, unless the safety of others is threatened. Once the disruptive student has gone, it is important for the grade teacher to redirect the class to their work, not give a five-minute lecture about the little 'rat' who has just gone!

- Staff need to agree on what happens during time-out. It is unhelpful if being directed away from the room is associated with a counselling session in the student's mind. A good strategy would be used at the wrong time. Students need counselling, but not when they are emotionally uptight. They have been sent out to regain emotional control—this is the educational and psychological message. It is unhelpful if teachers who are supervising time-out, give the student special duties or activities. This, too, may act as an unhelpful and unwanted reinforcer. The student should basically experience isolation, withdrawal, and the opportunity to cool down and maybe, reflect. The experience should be as non-reinforcing as possible. Older students may be asked to fill in a 4W form if appropriate (p 95). They may also be required to catch up on work not completed due to time-out.

- Co-operation with colleagues on time-out is a widely used option. The initiating teacher sends the exit card to a support colleague nearby or in the same building. Support colleagues need to be able to leave their classes unattended (hence the requirement of 'nearby') while they walk to direct the student to their room for fifteen minutes cool-off time without work. If necessary the disruptive student could stay in the support colleague's classroom until the end of that class session.

- If students try to run off during supervised time-out, they are reminded that they either stay in time-out, sitting quietly, or their parents are asked to take them home. They are given a few minutes to think and choose. It is necessary to have the agreement of parents of behaviourally disordered students that they will pick up their student or arrange for someone else to do so, if extreme antisocial behaviour persists during time-out.

- There are situations where students refuse to leave a classroom even for a teacher. They scream, run around, even hide. In these cases, the exit policy needs to consider the appropriateness of taking the rest of the class out and leaving the student in the room supervised by another teacher. If the student refuses to leave the audience, we can take the audience from the student. Most disruptive students settle down quickly once they realise their audience has gone. Staff need to consider the practicalities of using this approach in a crisis. Like many of my colleagues, I have dragged screaming, abusive students out of classrooms only to see them stand upright and even walk off, once out of their peers' earshot and vision! These days my preference is to direct the class away.

'Okay everyone, looking this way (Craig is screaming under the table).
I want you all to line up outside—now. Leave your work.'

Paul calls out, 'But Mr Rogers, Craig is bashing his head on the floor.'

'That's okay, Paul. C'mon outside, everyone. Mrs Smith will stay with Craig.'

My colleague stands nearby, card in hand, waiting for me to take the class out. Craig had resolutely refused to leave for the deputy principal.

This practice is very difficult to exercise in small schools. One teacher may have to supervise two classes while the other colleague stays with the disruptive student. This, of course, is a crisis plan. It may need to be used only a few times to convey the message to students that if they refuse to come, their parents will be contacted immediately.

Most students want to belong to their social group. Time-out conveys the message that you are always welcome in our class but not when you behave this way. Time-out, therefore, needs to be backed up by repairing and rebuilding strategies.

Time-out rooms

Some large primary schools have a time-out room—a spare room that can be supervised by a senior teacher, or aide, when necessary. It should be a room that is unstimulating but safe. An illustrated chart on the wall could explain the purpose of time-out. Staff need to consider for how long students should normally stay in time-out. If their offence is serious, they stay until collected by a parent or guardian.

If staff and parents support the philosophy of non-punitive use and adequate follow-through, time-out may be an important, effective part of a whole-school behaviour management plan. It guarantees that no teacher has to reach screaming point and that supportive due process is not seen as a sign of weakness in teachers who ask for help and support. It shows students where the bottom line is and makes clear that no student, however difficult their background, will be allowed to persistently disrupt learning or compromise safety.

When using a time-out room, adequate records need to be kept by the supervising teacher and the incident needs to be followed up by the initiating teacher in conjunction with executive staff at school.

Time-out in the play-ground

The protocol and key policy questions noted earlier are also relevant to the use of time-out in the playground. Students will know that if they are aggressive, or fighting, they may face five to ten minutes on a time-out bench, one of several, painted a distinct colour. Yellow is a favourite. Students will be directed there by the duty teacher who notes their names in the behaviour-monitoring book. This book will be regularly monitored by the deputy principal to ensure follow-up and follow-through from playground incidents.

The monitoring book can also record co-operative and meritorious behaviour to be announced at public assembly, perhaps with a merit certificate. One school developed the novel approach of giving a red sash to students exhibiting positive behaviour in the playground. This red sash would be given at the duty teacher's discretion. When I first used it, I felt like a bit of an idiot carrying my bucket of red sashes. A sash would not be given to a student who had clearly set up a co-operative or responsible incident: 'Hey, teacher! Look at me putting rubbish in the bin.' It was to be given for naturally occurring behaviour considered to be responsible, helpful, co-operative or thoughtful. The student would wear the sash for the day and it would be recorded and recognised by the grade teacher with a class chat on the reason for the sash being given. Five sashes would be rewarded with a merit certificate and a canteen voucher. Other schools use a raffle system for similar purposes with a Monday morning draw ('C'mon down number 50!') and a school acknowledgment expressed in a certificate or tangible reward.

It is essential that all staff have clarified:
- their role with respect to time-out
- how they will institute it in the immediate emotional moment, especially if the student refuses to go
- how executive staff can be supportive in short- and long-term follow-up with students
- whether there will be a staffed time-out area for serious playground aggression and violence. Who will staff it? It is, after all, one more burden on teachers. It is worthwhile that all staff, including head teachers and principals, be involved in playground supervision and time-out plans
- a suitable place for time-out
- a method for ensuring that students go. Staff need to discuss how they will deal with students who refuse to go to a withdrawal room/area, perhaps by using a red-card system (p 167)
- the length of time students will stay in time-out
- how parents will be notified
- follow-on consequences: apology, civic duty for damaged school property and restitution where feasible
- use of records/recording and the role of grade teacher and duty teacher in follow-up.

Staff need to consider whether they need such a room in the first place. Some schools have used time-out rooms (withdrawal from the playground for aggressive behaviour, verbal and physical abuse of student and/or teacher, rock or missile throwing and serious fighting). Over-exuberant male play of the testosteronic variety can be dealt with by a warning (short-term) and a healthy whole-school discussion on the issue in the establishment phase of the year.

Use of a withdrawal facility has to be seen in the context of a whole-school plan. It is, therefore, not to be used lightly and each incident is recorded. Notification in the time-out book will be followed up promptly with parent notification and support in the repairing and rebuilding process. Repeated offenders will need to face more intrusive sanctions' such as partial withdrawal from the playground (even going home at lunchtime) with re-entry conditional on a contractual basis. Senior staff will supervise a withdrawal room along with grade teachers as part of playground duty. Most staffed time-out in withdrawal rooms occurs at lunchtime. Some schools use a time-out room as a deferred consequence. If students have had several warnings for unacceptable behaviour, they miss a playtime and spend it in the withdrawal room. To make any time-out system work, as with any whole-school plan, clear guidelines and regular communication are essential, as well as commitment to positive consistency.

Behavioural consequences

Establishing and applying consequences is at the hard edge of a school's discipline and behaviour management plan. When a teacher has to apply a consequence to a student, both parties are often emotionally affected by the behaviour at issue. Sometimes emotions are very strained, for example, when time-out is used. We've all been disciplined as students. We can remember what it feels like to face punishment for wrong behaviour.

High ideals such as:
• consistency of enforcement
• justice
• valid assessment of degree of seriousness
• relatedness to behaviour
• certainty rather than severity
are difficult to appropriate.

Context

Behavioural consequences are the link between rights and rules, and the corrective discipline when students have affected others' rights.

Students learn quickly that they live in a consequential world. They learn about naturally occurring consequences—if you stay out in the sun without adequate protection, then . . ., if you overeat, then . . ., if you keep lying to avoid trouble, then . . . They also learn that adults can affect their lives by setting up consequential outcomes that are linked to their behaviour. Students discover that they are not totally free agents as their parents, siblings, teachers and lawgivers confirm. This is reality.

School is a social institution which helps to prepare students for life in general society. It needs to provide understanding and experience of consequences which are a reality in a society which has laws, rules, procedures, consequences and punishments.

Consequences and punishments

Traditionally, schools have used punishment and rewards (more of the former) to deal with rule breaking and disruptive behaviour. I was caned for breaking a pencil in class, going to the shops without permission during lunch play, answering back and even for disagreeing with a teacher. Oh, major crime!

Punishment was the norm then, consistent with parental and social values. Since the mid-80s most democratic countries have abolished corporal punishment as a way of teaching students that their behaviour is wrong. Many adults of my generation would say such discipline didn't hurt them or impair their futures. That's true. It didn't affect me very badly, but when discussing how teachers can connect punishment to behaviour, the issue is bigger than mere utility. On several occasions in 1954 I was made to stand in a corner as a punishment for talking to someone behind me. I don't think many of my teachers asked, 'What does this really teach the student about his behaviour?' They would have said, 'It'll teach him not to do it again!' Having one's face slapped for rudeness hardly teaches that.

In the 1950s, we hardly had a language of rights in schools. As schools became more democratic and less authoritarian, the language of punishment was replaced by the language of consequence. Many writers on this subject (Glasser 1986; Dreikurs 1968, 1986; Balson 1982) have emphasised:

- the notion of logical connection between behaviour and outcome, when applying consequences
- that students have some role in negotiating consequences
- that the application of consequences is as important as the kind of consequences applied.

Frequently, I've become really frustrated with students when applying consequences. On some occasions, as a young teacher, I know I blew it! I do not agree with corporal punishment in schools, but I have felt the urge at times to leap a desk or two and punch an extremely arrogant or aggressive student. Most teachers in their reflective (saner?) moments would not accept corporal punishment or verbal vilification, but would admit (I do) to being tempted at times to want to use it.

Certainty

The principle of certainty in application of consequences is one of the harder aspects of applying behavioural consequences. It is very easy to want to use consequences to get back at students, to 'teach' them, by our anger and lectures, what rotters they are. We need to keep a balance between:

- addressing behaviour rather than attacking the person (This, in itself, is important modelling.)
- communicating anger on issues that count, and keeping respect intact through repairing and rebuilding by remembering Seneca's dictum, 'The greatest revenge is not to be like them.'

If we can keep this balance, through the certainty principle of applied consequences, then students are more likely to learn something about their behaviour and accountability for it.

Certainty and group establishment

In the establishment phase of the year, it is important that students know that certain behaviour, in and out of class, will result in particular consequences.

Disruptive behaviour is measured by its effect on mutual rights, safety, fair treatment of others and on learning.

When a teacher is discussing class rules, routines and expected behaviour, it is important to discuss consequences relative to rights. Sometimes, students tend to be more focused on punishment than teachers. In discussing consequences, our job is to make sure that consequences:
• relate to the behaviour concerned
• are reasonable
• respect the dignity of the individual
• have degrees of seriousness built in (Rogers 1990).

Legislation—rules and codes—doesn't always change people's minds. Nevertheless, schools can make certain kinds of behaviour unpopular and unlawful by the combination of rules and consequences. This is necessary for natural justice.

What is important to establish in policy and practice is the centrality of rights and responsibilities. Students need to know, within such a framework what will happen if they choose to continue to:
• come late
• call out and butt in
• wander from chair to chair
• interfere with others' learning or teaching
• be abusive, intolerant or aggressive.

Most teachers can tolerate a student having a bad day. It's the frequency and intensity of disruptive behaviour that is emotionally wearing and gives rise to the reactive anger redolent in our profession. To minimise, even forestall this, teachers need to set out a basic framework of consequences so students know what will happen if they affect others' rights.

The most basic framework would follow the injunction that: 'We have fair rules in our class. If people continue to make it difficult for others to work, learn or feel safe, and to be treated with respect, then they will be directed to work away from others. They may be asked to take some cool-off time in the room. They will have to stay back and work on their behaviour with the grade or specialist teacher. If their behaviour is repeatedly disruptive or dangerous, they will face time-out from the class group (p 84).

This process should be thoroughly discussed with the class to invest appropriate clarity and seriousness in the issue and emphasise, again, those central rights. It is also helpful for a school to have clear consequences for serious behaviour out of class, especially in the playground. This, too, needs discussion in the establishment phase by grade teachers with their class.

While it is not possible, even practicable, to have a known and written consequence for every kind of disruptive behaviour, there needs to be whole-school agreement on what the unambiguous consequences will be for totally unacceptable behaviour. It is also highly desirable, for relative consistency, that staff discuss what consequences they would normally apply for common, frequent disruptive behaviour in and out of class. Teachers don't want to have to keep thinking up what consequences to use each time a student refuses to pack up, is late, calls out, doesn't do set work or puts others down. For example, most teachers during the establishment phase of the year develop routines for pack up, tidy up, and leave the room in an orderly fashion. If they don't do these things the positive enforcement needs to include a consequence. Although it may feel like it to the student, this is clearly not a punishment but a way of reinforcing accountability and responsibility.

I've worked with many students who haven't picked up their litter around their tables or desks, or put their chairs away. I direct them to stay back. They often whinge,

'Oh, c'mon. Gees, it's playtime.'

'That's right, it is playtime. I'm sorry you've had to miss your play but . . .'

Here they are directed to do the brief, required, responsible thing. They learn several things out of this exchange:

- I normally follow up issues after class, and when I say, 'I'll have to see you later' it is a promise not a threat.
- The follow-up focuses on their behaviour, and speeds their progress towards good habits.
- That, as a good teacher, I don't have to be popular ('All right. I'll let you go if you promise to do it next time.') but I can be respectful. They'll learn that when reasonable, whole-class rules and routines are in place, they are followed up with reasonable certainty. No grudges are held.
- I've had students sneak off, even run off. I let them go. There are very few occasions when teachers need to chase students. I've seen some fairly overweight teachers running around playgrounds trying to catch students so they can punish them. Certainty, not immediacy, is the key. I can follow them up on the next occasion, and I'll wait at the door next time before I direct them to stay back for whatever deferred consequences may be necessary. This is especially important when students run off in the playground in response to a duty teacher's direction.

There are very few occasions when teachers need to chase students.

93

Telegraphing consequences

Whenever possible, it is helpful to telegraph to students what the consequence will be if they continue to behave in a disruptive way. If a least intrusive approach, such as a direction and a repeated direction, has drawn little or no response in modifying behaviour in the short-term, then an immediate consequence or reminder of deferred consequences is called for. For example:

'If you play in an unsafe way you will be reminded of our safe behaviour rule—you may be directed to time-out.'

'If you bring skateboards or rollerblades to school, they will be kept in the office until collected by your parents.'

'If you push in at the canteen queue, you will be directed to the back of the line.'

A teacher moves across the room to two students who are continuing to talk inappropriately loudly during on-task time: 'I've asked you twice to settle down and work quietly. If you choose not to work quietly, I'll ask you to work separately.' If the students argue or procrastinate, the teacher will redirect (p 134 ff). If the teacher then walks away giving some take-up time, her approach has an element of choice/reminder about it. She has not used a threatening tone, though her voice sounds decisive. If they choose not to settle, the teacher will go back and direct them to work separately.

If either, or both, refuse this immediate consequence, the teacher can remind them that if they choose not to work separately for a time, then she will see them both after class. There is no point forcing the issue in this public domain and, at this point, it hardly requires time-out. A deferred consequence can discuss rights and responsibilities and a possible change of seating, depending on how often such behaviour has occurred.

Throughout this episode the teacher's aim has been to keep the focus as much as possible on students owning their behaviour.

Negotiating consequences

There is a place for negotiating with students the particular consequences of behaviour. This is often the case with deferred consequences. By negotiation I mean giving students the dignity of owning their response. The key question, 'What do you think should happen as a result of . . .?' may see students suggesting illogical, unrelated, even quite punitive outcomes. We can then direct them back to a more educational focus, 'Okay, if I did that, what would you learn from it?' Even if students come up with a consequential outcome we agree with as teachers, we've still given them the dignity of some self-reflection. Not all students appreciate this. I've had students say, 'Look. Why don't you just punish me and leave it at that! I'll write heaps of lines! Why do I have to think about all this?' It takes time for some students to believe that we're serious about behaviour ownership.

Obviously, there would not be any negotiation about the consequences of serious behaviour. In this case the consequence—time-out, exclusion from social play, suspension—is applied without negotiation but not without explanation.

The 4Ws approach

Teachers often use writing as a consequence. Traditionally, this has been the writing of lines. This is empty punishment, unrelated to the problem behaviour. It is more effective in terms of the goal of consequences to direct students to write about their behaviour.

There are several key questions (p 27).
- What did you do? This question focuses on the behaviour relative to the consequence. (Students are required to be specific about what they did.)
- What rule did you break? What right did you affect? (for older students)
- What is your explanation? (this is a right of reply question)
- What do you think you need to do to fix things up?—the consequence or restitution. (This is probably the most important question of the four. It puts the responsibility for the consequence back onto the student.)
We can add this supplementary question:
- How can I help with your plan to fix things up?

It is important to write questions appropriate to the student's understanding. It is essential that we do not force a written consequential step like this on students who have great difficulty with writing. In that case, we can ask the questions and record the answers for them.

Many schools have a standard form, or pro-forma, that can be used by teachers for a written consequence exercise. The 4Ws form is also a record for the teacher (and parent, if necessary). Comments can be made on the back by the teacher, but the student should be shown what the teacher has noted. If students cannot think of what to do to fix things up, the teacher can offer a few suggestions to choose from.

The student may need some clarification and guidance in responding to such questions, but the central effort of thinking about the behaviour at hand and an appropriate consequence should be left with the student. Use of a standard pro-forma for the 4Ws may also be used during class-based detention. It is incredible that there are still schools who have senior students in detention doing nothing! At the very least (if they are able to express themselves in writing) they can fill in a 4W form as part of the consequential process.

Deferred consequences and follow-up

A teacher recently said to me that he made a conscious effort during first term to follow up all rude and arrogant behaviour, all refusals to own behaviour in class time, all sloppy packing up and mess. By 'all' he meant significantly disruptive behaviour. He was especially assiduous in the establishment phase during the first few weeks. His follow-up was not nasty or vindictive—just certain.

He also made sure that he kept the working relationship intact. He explained that he was nearly flattened by the effort in the first half of Term 1 during the establishment phase, but that second term was a breeze. There was no smugness in what he said. He is a fine teacher, ably balancing individual and group work with challenging units of work. He had made the effort to put certainty into his follow-up. If we want students to take our consequential discipline seriously, then we need to follow up and follow through. Even the few chats and simple reminders about seemingly trifling issues such as tidy desks, litter in class, packing away materials, and paying attention to manners will pay off (pp 63, 74).

I was on playground duty recently and, from a distance, I observed a young boy jump onto a stainless-steel drinking fountain. He then jumped off and ran away. I quickly asked his name from some of the students nearby. I called him over a little later, told him what I'd seen and reminded him that people drink from fountains. He said (I've heard this reply countless times), 'I was just mucking around.' I asked him what he was going to do to fix things up. He looked nonplussed. I had another go about hygiene and why we don't walk on drinking fountains. I directed him to clean it up with some paper towelling I provided. Had he refused and run off, I would have followed it up at another time, just as I would follow up any student who refused a reasonable request from a teacher on playground duty. The intention is to call students to account for their behaviour. Some consequences cannot be applied or simply forced on students during the heat of the moment; allowing cool-off time (pp 39, 84) and deferring the consequence still carries the certainty principle. Students are usually very surprised when I follow up incidents related to their playground behaviour. Sometimes I knock on their classroom door the next day or send a note to a colleague's room to ask for a particular student to come to my class at recess so I can follow up.

• Collegial support in follow-up

While it is advisable for grade teachers and specialist teachers to carry through with class-based consequences, there will be occasions when we have to involve colleagues. This is an issue that deserves serious discussion and collaborative planning.

Teachers commonly need support from colleagues on:
- any use of time-out, beyond brief use of cool-off time, when students have to leave a teacher's direct supervision
- serious conflicts where the resolution and consequences need a third party
- situations when the grade or specialist teacher feels overwhelmed or threatened by carrying out consequences
- follow-up by playground teachers or specialist teachers.

In these cases it is important that teachers don't impute blame onto a grade teacher for a student's behaviour outside that teacher's class. ('You know what *your* Jason did at lunchtime, during art or in the corridor or while I was on wet-day duty?') It is both unfair and unreasonable to simply pass the responsibility for follow-through onto another teacher. Reasonable consistency in behaviour management requires shared approaches and support, not blame.

• Senior teacher support

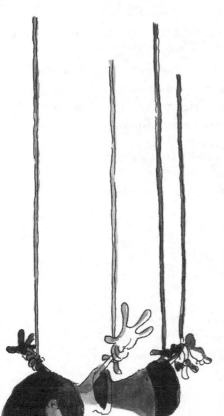

Consideration should be given to what should be expected to happen when teachers refer students to a senior teacher (normally the deputy) for certain consequences. Some teachers want the principal to bawl students out and send them back trembling. Sadly, some principals relish the head-kicking role. It sometimes goes the other way, when senior teachers spend excessive time counselling students who should be faced with the consequences of their behaviour, within the framework of class or school rules. Avoiding abuses associated with referral requires a whole-school understanding of how that support should work for the classroom teacher. For example, some teachers overuse referral by sending students for behaviour concerns that can be dealt with in the classroom. Yet they often expect the principal or the deputy to somehow 'fix' students and send them back with a guarantee that this behaviour will never occur again.

Sending students to the principal to be scared into changing their behaviour confuses students' perception of the role of the principal, who becomes the supreme ogre. It is the principal's job to support grade teachers with time-out provision where necessary and with the problem-solving process that follows time-out usage. This process usually involves the initiating teacher and the student concerned, if that is the context in which the problem behaviour is occurring. When discussing referral and support in the consequence chain, all teachers need to be clear about how support will work, especially when using time-out provisions.

Suspension

Suspension is a serious step (sanction) for any school to take. Most teachers acknowledge that it does not always change behaviour. It can be argued that suspension places some students back into an already dysfunctional family setting which places more pressure on the student in their already vicious life cycle. Nevertheless, some behaviour is so intrusive on others' rights that suspension is the appropriate sanction.

If suspension is considered, it should be appropriately public, an acknowledgment by the school that this behaviour is so bad that the student is persona non grata for the next day or so. The decision to suspend should be made by a team, not just by the grade teacher on the spur of the emotional moment.

Although suspension should be made public by notifying parents and through a brief word to the host class, the school needs to be careful not to give gratuitous attention to the suspension. It's difficult to prevent some students from endowing the suspended student with hero status.

Suspension provides:
- a sense of appropriate justice in the school community
- an appropriate public disapproval of serious behaviour
- a serious cooling-off time for all.

To disavow the charge of deprivation of educational opportunities, the school can send work home for the student, especially if the suspension is more than a day. Before the student returns to school, the student and parents, with school support, will need to meet contractual conditions related to the school's code of behaviour. 'We welcome you at our school, but not with *that* kind of behaviour. Let's work on a mutual plan.'

Re-admission to the school may sometimes involve conditions such as:
- partial enrolment
- withdrawal from certain activities or even from recess, if violent or aggressive behaviour is a problem
- staggered class sessions
- being picked up and taken home (say at lunch times)
- earlier finishing times
- an individual management plan (p 151 ff).

This contractual agreement will be worked out as a team by senior staff, the grade teacher and parent(s) or caregiver. It is essential that the grade teacher be given maximum collegial support without the imputation of fault or blame.

The students we're talking about here can be extremely taxing for everyone, but it is the grade teacher who bears most of the brunt of emotional stress and strain. Difficult as it is, we must avoid an attitude of conditional acceptance or revenge when students return. ('If you put one foot wrong—do you understand?—one foot wrong, you are history! I'll be watching you, all the time!'). It is important to treat them as we would treat any student, and make some effort to acknowledge and encourage positive expressions of behaviour.

In-school suspension

For less extreme behaviour, in-school suspension may be an option. This, too, needs to be decided on by a team.

Students are withdrawn from their host class and specialist subjects, and work separately from other students for the day or as long as the suspension process is in effect. Of course, we can't make students do academic work while experiencing this sanction, but we should make every effort to explain why this consequence or sanction is in force and that it is their behaviour that we are very upset about. They are being asked to co-operate and continue with some special work in a set place, supervised for a set time. In larger schools, where a time-out room is often used, staffing and timetabling need careful consideration.

Almost every student has a powerful social need to belong. Suspension, which is so public, prevents a student from satisfying that need. That is why it needs to be used sparingly within a whole-school approach, observing the normal protocol of consequences, especially the application of certainty (This is what happens when and if . . .) rather than severity (We're going to make you look a fool. We're going to make you suffer and feel horribly embarrassed!).

Questions regarding behavioural consequences
- How 'related' are the consequences you use in the classroom? If you can't think of a related consequence what do you normally do?
- What behavioural consequences have you discussed with your students? How did you decide on them? Do you have any unambiguous consequences?
- How much discussion of typical classroom behaviour and consequences have you had with your colleagues?
- How do you respond to the principle of 'certainty rather than severity'? What does it mean for you? Are you conscious of considering it when applying consequences?
- Have you published any classroom consequences?
- What behavioural consequences relate to playground management? Are these published? Are the students aware of them? How were they made aware?
- What sort of consequences need to occasion collegial support, especially senior administration?
- What support ought we to expect from senior staff on those occasions? Has thorough discussion occurred of senior staff support in the consequence chain? What is the policy?

Restitution

Restitution is, fundamentally, the act of restoring something to its former state, giving back something taken away or lost, making good something which has been damaged. Restitution (from the Latin verb 'to set up') is part of the repairing and rebuilding process (p 25).

As a form of consequence, restitution is about fixing problems, not fixing blame. The teacher will focus on questions such as:
- Okay, this has happened. Now what's your plan to fix it?
- What can you do to repair the damage? How can I help?
- What can you do to make up for it? How are you going to make things right?

Avoid rhetorical questioning:
- 'You know what to do, don't you?'
- 'It's not helping you, this behaviour, is it?'
- 'You need to do this, don't you?'

We can't make students fix things up. We can't make them face the consequences. If they refuse to listen we can point out:
- what we see in their behaviour
- how it is not helping them to belong to their class group and get their work done
- what they need to do if they want to belong.

The tone needs to be decisive without haranguing. The teacher can offer suggestions for restitution, but can hardly force it:

- What can you think of that will do that? (fix things up . . .)
- When can you do it?
- What will this plan do for the other person?
- What will happen if you don't make a plan to fix . . .?

Two boys in Grade 5, caught smashing classroom windows one weekend, agreed to help the window repairers, and contracted to wash the windows for the next four weeks in their own time. We sometimes call this a time–trade consequence. Students use their time to bring restitution to fellow students, a teacher or the school. It involves giving time, effort and thought. Some schools use the 'two for' principle: what two things can you do to make amends? to fix things up for the person you have wronged? It may be helpful if a facilitator brings the victim and offender together to do this. In this sense, there is a social purpose in the consequence—it is constructive for the offender and offended.

- Individuals who have made a mistake, offended or wronged another (or the class) are encouraged and challenged to consider how their behaviour has affected others. Here the teacher needs to encourage the student(s) towards restitution, not aim for punishment. The tone is, therefore, important in how the questions are framed. Students are encouraged to consider not just the school rules but the rights behind the rules.
- The individual is encouraged to make a plan that will work towards social reconciliation, including compensation for the one who has been wronged and ways to make amends.

Di Gossen (1992) suggests restitution requires thought, time and effort. The offended party needs to be satisfied with the result, the restitution act should be related to the offence; it also needs to be genuine without being easy and it should work at making the relationship stronger (pp 52–3).

This is not easy. Our natural inclination is to want to seek retribution rather than restitution. An emphasis on restitution does not deny the need for consequences like time-out, or even suspension. That is why cool-off time is important. It gives offended, affected parties time to consider what has happened and how best to work for reconciliation.

Key questions in developing a classroom discipline plan

1 What classroom rules have you established?

2 How were they communicated to the students? Did students have any part or role in forming the rules? Are they published? In what form? Do they focus on the key rights? Have you discussed rights and responsibilities as well as consequences for significant infringement of rights and rules? How does your definition of discipline compare with that used on page 18?

3 A number of behaviour management practices are outlined in Chapter 2. How does your personal disciplinary style relate to these practices?

4 How conscious are you of having a discipline plan in the sense described in this chapter?

5 How aware are you of having a language of discipline? (see Chapter 5).
- When students engage you in secondary dialogue and exhibit

secondary behaviour? (see Chapter 6, p 129 ff).

- How decisive, or assertive, do you consider your leadership style to be?
- How do you deal with the common range of disruptive behaviour, such as talking out of turn, butting in, calling out, wandering, chair leaning, through to more disruptive behaviour such as swearing, argumentative behaviour, tantrums, hostility, defiance and aggression? Do you have a characteristic least-to-most-intrusive approach? (p 103 ff).
- In terms of behavioural consequences, do you aim for relatedness between behaviour and outcome? Do you opt for certainty rather than severity? How do your class consequences fit in with school-wide consequences?

6 Do you consciously note and affirm positive on-task behaviour in your students? Do you have a characteristic language of encouragement? Do you take time to repair and rebuild with students? (p 25, see also Chapter 6).

Chapter **5**

THE LANGUAGE OF DISCIPLINE

A good deal of our corrective management and discipline involves the use of language. Therefore, it makes good sense to reflect on how we use language to correct and discipline students. Language usage cannot be divorced from context, tone, timing and postural cues (p 48 ff). It is important to consider how the nonverbal aspects of our behaviour are congruent with what we say. There are times, for example, when it is important to have a firm, commanding tone when we need to convey controlled unambiguous assertion. Sometimes it is important to convey anger about certain behaviour and actions in students. Most of the time, however, we will be acting within the principle of 'least intrusive to most intrusive (p 34).

Corrective discipline: Least to most intrusive

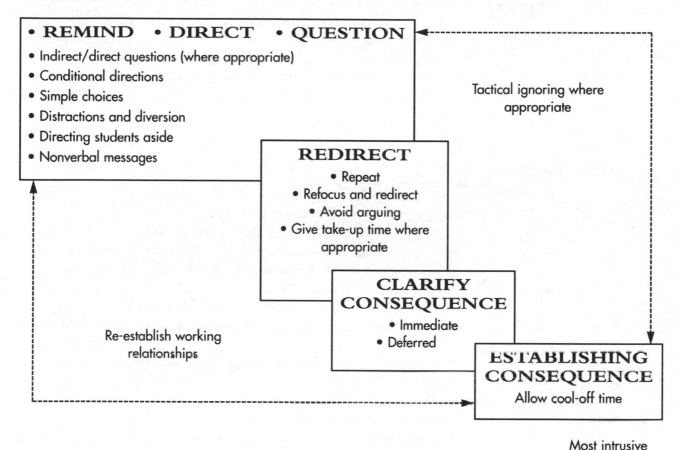

Least intrusive

• REMIND • DIRECT • QUESTION
- Indirect/direct questions (where appropriate)
- Conditional directions
- Simple choices
- Distractions and diversion
- Directing students aside
- Nonverbal messages

REDIRECT
- Repeat
- Refocus and redirect
- Avoid arguing
- Give take-up time where appropriate

CLARIFY CONSEQUENCE
- Immediate
- Deferred

ESTABLISHING CONSEQUENCE
Allow cool-off time

Tactical ignoring where appropriate

Re-establish working relationships

Most intrusive

- Consider the context (up-front, public, on-task time, playground setting).
- Concentrate, focus on primary behaviour; avoid arguing or feeding secondary behaviour.
- Demonstrate expectation, allow take-up time.

Figure 5 © Bill Rogers 1995.

Developing language skills in corrective management

When considering our language in correction and management, we also need to consider the following principles if positive discipline is to operate within our management style:

- focus on the behaviour rather than attacking the person
- be angry about issues that really count rather than a host of minor issues
- be brief when addressing behaviour, even when using commands
- calm yourself before trying to calm the student
- balance correction with encouragement and the re-establishment of working relationships (p 110)
- give take-up time whenever possible (p 109)
- concentrate and focus on primary behaviour, primary issues, rules and rights rather than on secondary behaviour (p 129 ff).

Direct to behaviour

A good deal of teacher management and discipline involves giving direction to students to sit up, go back to seats, line up, put hands up and look this way.

When using directional language it is important to:

- focus on the desired behaviour rather than the behaviour we don't want or the rule-breaking behaviour, for example, 'Wash your brush before you put it away' rather than 'Don't leave your brush like that!' 'One at a time, thanks' rather than 'Don't butt in!'
- always use the student's first name, or ask for their name when giving individual direction. (On one occasion I had a student respond with, 'Guess' when I asked for their name in the playground. I replied, 'I could guess for a while—when *you've* remembered, let me know. In the meantime, let me remind you of the rule . . .')
- rephrase negatives where possible (Rogers 1994). 'Don't walk away from the mess!' as a general direction can become 'Okay, everyone (pause) let's beat the clock to pack-up time. I'm counting: 30, 29, 28' and 'Why is this table so noisy? I'm sick of you lot talking loudly' can become 'Keep the talking noise down at this table, thanks.'
- keep the directions brief. Avoid over-dwelling, mixed messages and labelling. 'Dean (. . .) Sean (. . .) facing this way and listening, thanks' rather than 'Don't talk while I'm talking'. 'Face this way' (the actual direction) rather than 'I'm sick and tired of you two talking. You never listen, do you? Why can't you just shut it!' 'You naughty, naughty boy. You stupid idiot' (the over-dwelling and mixed message component).

When students procrastinate or argue, teachers can redirect. Redirecting is a way of keeping the focus on the rule, the right, or the direction at hand rather than being drawn into secondary issues (p 135 ff).

Conditional directions

'When . . . then' 'After . . . then' 'Yes . . . when'.

A conditional direction simply makes one thing dependent on another: 'When you've washed your brush, you can hang your painting up to dry.' 'After you've packed up your mess, you can go on to the play blocks.'

'Yes, you can go and have a drink when you've finished those four questions (wink).' 'We can all go out for a game when we've done . . .' Contrast this with, 'No, you can't go out because . . .'

Reminding

While it sounds basic, reminding (a staple feature of management) can have a positive, correctional function. Students are forgetful. During the establishment phase of the year, students need numerous reminders about rules and routines. 'We've got a rule for asking questions. Use it, thanks' said positively, with expectation and take-up time, can refocus students quickly to school and classroom rules and routines. When two students are talking quite loudly during on-task time, the teacher walks over and reminds, 'Remember our rule for working noise, thanks.'

Reminders can normally be given in a positive tone. Now and then, as with silly play fighting, or acting aggressively, we need to use the firm 'Stop!' raising the voice to gain attention, then dropping it and referring to the rule: 'We have a rule for safety—Hands and feet to yourself.' For more serious exchanges we will need to direct students to 'Move away'. At this point we would normally have them sitting separately, or each would spend cool-off time in the time-out area (p 84 ff).

Often a few words are enough: 'Sharing, thanks . . .' or 'Remember our rule for manners' or 'Walking quietly'. The reminder is directional. Reminders are often related to routines and are given prior to expected behaviour: 'Okay, everyone (teacher scans the students lining up outside the class), remember to hang up your coats before we go in, or remember to put your toy in your bag, or remember to get your lunch money.' A teacher in the corridor sees a group of boys jostling for the exit door, 'Okay . . ., stop!' He smiles, 'Slow down at doorways and walk through. Thanks' rather than 'Oi! What do you think you're doing, idiots? You can't all fit through the door can you!' Even a brief, 'Fellas, one at a time, thanks' is better than just yelling at them.

We can remind with privately understood (nonverbal) signals. Two fingers extended down as if walking—avoid putting two fingers up, even if tempted!

Special situations require group reminders: 'Before we go on our excursion, what are some of the things we need to remember? Before we go out to play today, what do we need to remember? Yes. Sunhats, sunscreen, lunch boxes back in your bags.'

Teachers often use checklists near the door as reminders, with headings such as: 'Have you remembered to . . .?' Rules can be portrayed on large cards in the room as visible reminders, along with signs on cupboards, monitor charts etc. Our reminder can often be as simple as: 'Check the list.'
• Sometimes we can remind students by getting them to think about the rule or routine through a question. We would normally use this approach one-to-one as we move around the classroom or in duty-of-care role in corridors or playground.

'Sean, what's our rule for manners?'

'What?'

'I saw you push past Dean. What's our rule for manners?'

'Dunno.'

'It's on the wall there, Sean.'

- Redirecting to the rule sometimes elicits the response from the student; if they say it, they are more likely to remember it.
- One way to remind with a positive tone, is to preface with the verb, 'Remember to . . .' 'Remember to hang your coats up before we go into class.' 'Remember to wash your brushes before you put them away.' 'Remember to sit on the mat when we go in.' 'Remember to' is nicer on the ear than 'Don't forget' which sets up two negatives—it says what we don't want, and also says 'forget' which we don't want them to do. We want them to remember.

Privately Understood Signals

One way to keep corrective management least-intrusive is to use nonverbal signals. These signals can be explained to the whole class or to the individuals who need them. In this sense they are privately understood. They can be a positive form of communication reducing the amount of corrective language required, without intrusive fuss.

Jason has leaned back on his chair several times. The teacher could use verbal correction: 'Jason. Sitting up, thanks,' or 'Jason. Four on the floor' (four chair legs on the floor), or the teacher could gain eye contact and give a privately understood signal: extend the thumb and the first three fingers in a downward motion as if signalling 'four on the floor'. This is in preference to 'Don't lean back on your chair like that' or 'Don't lean back like that. You'll break your neck.' The teacher could, of course, combine both the verbal and nonverbal initially and then replace with the nonverbal form as students become used to it.

The teacher is teaching in one part of the room and as she scans the room, she notices Jason leaning back again. Rather than call out and disrupt the group, she gains his eye contact and simply gives the four on the floor signal with her hand. If she can't catch his eye, she will simply call his name and then give a privately understood signal.

Other signals teachers can use are:
- Extending a hand upwards to remind those who call out to put their hands up. The teacher doesn't even have to look in the direction of those calling out.
  - Extending the hands upwards and the four fingers to the mouth communicating 'hands up without calling out'.
    - Using the forefinger and thumb in a closing motion and pointing to one's mouth to remind a student to speak more quietly. This is especially useful when signalled across the room. Contrast this with a teacher speaking loudly, 'Don't be so loud. Can't you speak in a normal voice?' A variation of this can be used while the teacher is moving around the room giving encouragement, reminders and clarification.

If he notices a particularly loud student, he walks up behind and 'turns the volume knob' with his thumb and first two fingers simulating this action while engaged in eye contact with the student.

- As the teacher moves around the room, she notices Craig out of his seat. As a reminder to return and resume his work she cups her left hand as if it is a seat and directs the four fingers on her right hand down into it as if a person is sitting in a seat. No words—just the student's name and the signal.

The pause

When teachers want to initiate and sustain attention, thoughtful use of the pause can help. When initiating attention, especially with a group, it may be necessary to lift the voice a little. Following this with a pause, before giving the necessary direction, conveys the expectation that the student(s) look towards the teacher, listen and subsequently respond. It is an underrated and underused nonverbal cue.

At the beginning of the lesson the pause can be used as a brief wait time or settling time by the teacher when the teacher directs the group to, 'Face this way and listen, thanks' or some group direction which the teacher finds comfortable. The pause acts as a signal, for example, 'Okay folks'. This is said a little louder followed by a pause, then the direction, 'Facing this way, thanks'. If the teacher's tone and general body language is confident and pleasant, the pause indicates, 'I expect you to listen to what follows now that I have your initial attention.'

If teachers rush their directional language, speaking quickly without pausing, they might initiate student attention but not sustain it. They will probably also establish that this teacher talks over, or through, residual noise. A teacher calls across the room to two students loudly talking, 'David and Jarrod, what are you doing?' Because of their engagement in their petty fracas, they may only hear their names mentioned, not the question that follows. When they vaguely turn, the teacher still hasn't actually communicated her question. 'Aren't you listening?' he says. 'What?' they answer. It is as if they haven't heard.

This is very common when teachers give directions from the front of the room. If a student is turning around talking to a student behind him, the direction to 'Face this way and listen, thanks,' will be heard properly if it is preceded by the student's name (a little firmer in tone) followed by a pause for attentive effect, then the direction.

'David (pause), facing this way and listening, thanks.'

'Michael (pause), pen down thanks and looking this way.'

As I was kneeling at a table working on paper puppets with a group of Grade 1 students, I noticed Michael wandering from his seat. Staying with the group, I called across the room, 'Michael (. . .) Michael (. . .).' He looked over and frowned. I gave him a signal indicating 'back to seat'. I saw him sigh, 'tsk tsk' and he muttered on his way back to his seat. Some students need their name to be repeated a couple of times in a firmer tone before they register. After visual registration, assisted by the pause, the teacher can add the necessary signal, direction or reminder. The use of pause may sound unimportant, but along with all our global behaviour (p 50) it sends a powerful message.

I was a guest at a public function where a few hundred people were sitting at large round tables. The master of ceremonies stood up to announce the program for the evening. With microphone in hand, he didn't call for attention but spoke over the noise. It was several minutes before we could actually tune in to what he was saying. Had he tapped a glass with a teaspoon (the noise carries surprisingly well even in a large hall), even stood and waited, it may have signalled some requirement on the part of the audience to face his way and listen.

A group of mostly male young people on my left, continued to talk blithely on, ignoring the MC, so he talked louder. No direction was given to the young lads. If he had directed them to sit down, I'm sure they would have, if it had been done in a positive way. 'Fellas', here the voice is raised to initiate attention and eye contact, and followed by a pause to sustain attention. If they look his way he can then direct them. If not, he might have to add, 'Fellas—the guys standing up, on my right.' Now they look. He's smiling at them, 'Fellas, I'm about to announce our program. Do me the courtesy of taking your seats. Thanks.' These words, said positively without sarcasm or hostility but with expectation, I'm sure would have caused them to sit down. I think he ignored them and continued talking over their noise because he hoped they would get the message from his ignoring them. They didn't.

Well, surreptitiously I walked across and tapped one of the heavy lads gently on the shoulder, and whispered, 'Excuse me, mate, that guy is trying to make an announcement. I'd appreciate it if you'd take a seat and listen. Ta.' To their credit they did. Maybe they thought I worked for the management. Sometimes people need direction.

Establishment phase— gaining group attention

There are crucial times in a lesson when group attention is necessary—the beginning of a lesson or morning talk, or group meeting or instructions, at a crossover activity or during an activity and at pack-up time. It is important to have a simple routine for gaining attention that doesn't require that we resort to shouting or talking over their noise.

Some teachers use a simple nonverbal signal like walking to the centre and front of the room to indicate the expectation of location, then ring a bell or strum a chord on a guitar, or use a clapping rhythm, or even sing an attention-getting song. Students need to know that when the teacher does this they are expected to 'face this way and listen'.

. . . a simple routine

If they are working, then, 'Pens down and look this way, and listen'. Although it sounds basic, when teachers stand or sit at the front of the room and use verbal directions to gain and sustain group attention, it is important to consider the congruence of the directional language with the nonverbal signals such as pausing, take-up time and conveying a positive tone. These include how we stand—a confident body posture with little movement is important—as well as appropriate wait time, and acknowledgment of the students settling on the mat. It can also be helpful to associate the giving of general and group directions with front-of-room location. It is unhelpful to give general, group directions from anywhere in the room, or to give such directions while walking around. The movement, rather than the words, may become the focus for some students.

For example, 'Okay, everyone (pause) facing this way, thanks' or signal with a bell (pause) 'Stop what you're doing (pause) and looking this way (pause). Pens down, thanks' or 'Eyes this way, thanks' or 'Looking this way (pause) and listening, thanks.' The teacher can raise a hand and wait for all to see it and copy. Even this old signal still has currency.

It is also important that a signal like a bell or clapping to initiate and signal group attention is associated with the verbal direction, 'Class (pause) looking this way, thanks.' After a while we can drop the verbal direction and rely on the signal.

Take-up time

Take-up time refers to the time a teacher gives a student to respond to corrective discipline. It also includes the idea of face saving.

A few students are talking out of turn during instruction time. The teacher remains in the teaching space at the centre front of the room and gives direct eye contact as she asks the students by name to 'Face this way and listen, thanks.' The teacher then makes a relaxed eye-sweep of the group, reclaiming the flow of the lesson. If the students actively argue she will redirect with focused eye contact, and reclaim the flow of the lesson (p 135 ff).

It is easy to miss the significance of the nonverbal behaviour in this exchange. By lifting her eyes and smoothly reclaiming the lesson she is:
• communicating an expectation that the students will face the front and listen
• withdrawing tactically from the emotional climate of the interaction
• allowing the student face-saving time to respond to the correction
• drawing the eyes of the audience back to her teaching, as it were, and away from the talkers. In effect, she directs the audience away from the talkers, making it easier for them to comply, and reducing attention time. In this, the teacher nonverbally enlists the goodwill of the group. If she were to walk towards the girls and engage in 'behaviour overdwelling' (Kounin 1971) she would give the disruptive students unwanted audience support (p 132 ff).

By the time the student sighs and faces the front, the teacher has resumed the lesson as if the student will respond to the correction.

Take-up time and tactical ignoring are often combined to convey teacher expectations.

109

Directing across the room or from a distance

If a teacher beckons or calls a student in the classroom, corridor or playground, take-up time can communicate the expectation of the teacher. The teacher tactically ignores the student's sigh and averted eyes as the correction is registered. The teacher turns away, after the beckoning to convey expectation. Several seconds later, the student walks across to the teacher.

Two students are talking off-task in class time. From a table at the other end of the room, the teacher turns her head and, raising her voice, directs one of the students across to her. 'Dean (here she pauses to initiate and sustain the attention), I want to see you over here for a moment.' The eye contact is maintained for a few seconds. She then resumes her assistance to the student she is working with. If she had called the student and remained looking at him until he came, she would be creating unnecessary conflict, especially if she assumed a posture with hands on hips and a snappy get-over-here-this-instant tone!

A note on eye contact

Most students give teachers a normal 60/40 split on eye contact. They look away forty per cent of the time interspersed with direct focus to the teacher. Some students give almost no eye contact for cultural reasons or for passive power seeking. In this case, it is pointless to demand or force it. It is worth asking them to look, but once is enough. After that, speak to their ears. They'll still hear. I have seen teachers force students to, 'Look at me when I'm talking to you!' and then force the student's head up only to have it wrested from the teacher's hold. Who is controlling whom?

Re-establishing working relationships

I've asked Lisa to sit up from some heavy chair leaning. She has a bit of a habit in this department and it detracts from her on-task work. 'Four on the floor thanks, Lisa, and carry on with your work. I'll come and check it later.' It is important to go back later in the lesson and re-establish. 'How's the work going, Lisa?' A positive whisper is added, 'Nice to see you sitting up.' Even a smile or the okay sign is enough. It is the reassurance that beyond the correction the relationship is still okay. They are still accepted. We re-establish a working relationship.

Even if students have grumbled their way to compliance, muttering under their breath, it helps to re-establish the relationship later in the lesson or just before they go to recess. During a science activity, I asked Michael to pick up a small cardboard box. He'd been abstractedly kicking it gently across the room. I called him over quietly:

'Michael, I'd appreciate it if you'd pick that up, thanks. Put it with the other boxes.'

'It's not mine (sigh, tsk).'

'I'd still appreciate it if you'd . . .'

Here he sighed, 'All right, all right.' (sigh)

Later in the lesson when he'd settled, I simply went back and briefly acknowledged, 'I appreciate it when . . . How's your work going?'

He improved—at least in my class.

Brief thanks or acknowledgment say, 'I noticed your effort' and convey that no grudges are held.

Tactical ignoring

I was part way through a story about a baby wombat. One of the pictures in this Big Book portrayed the wombat relieving itself into a bucket. One of the Grade 1 boys said as he pointed, 'He's going for a *piss*!' Several students laughed. A couple chorused the word *'piss'* (sotto voce). Tactically ignoring this, I diverted their attention by saying to the whole class, 'Yes, you can see he's finished his toilet and look at this . . .', quietly turning to the next page. The class quickly settled.

Tactical ignoring is the teacher's conscious decision to ignore certain behaviour and keep the focus on the flow of the lesson, or on acknowledging and reinforcing positive behaviour. This emphasis is appropriate when a teacher ignores several students calling out. A general rule reminder is given to the whole class: 'Remember our rule for hands up, everyone?' The teacher then focuses on the students with hands up, who are not calling out. The student who whines when asked to pack up is ignored, though the teacher may feel like saying, 'Look. Why can't you do something just once, just once, without whining?'

Tactical ignoring is a difficult skill because of the frustration inherent in student behaviour such as whining, calling out, sulking and pouting, the 'tsk tsks' when you ask a student to pack up and the sighs. Yet it is for this behaviour that tactical ignoring is so appropriate.

Tactical ignoring should be distinguished from blind ignorance or hopeful ignoring ('If I do nothing, it might go away!'). One should not ignore safety issues, aggressive behaviour, bullying tactics, blatant put-downs. These need to be addressed assertively, immediately.

Tactical ignoring is also inappropriate:
- when other students are clearly reinforcing disruptive students by giving them overt or covert attention. In such cases it is possible to enlist the support of the co-operative students in a class in group tactical ignoring (see Rogers 1994 b). Because this involves a specialised classroom meeting structure, it needs thoughtful planning with colleagues. The group can be taught how, and what, to tactically ignore
- when students are so behaviourally engaged that they are either unaware or don't care how they are behaving. In these cases, a distraction, diversion or firm rule-reminder or controlled use of time-out is appropriate.

Tactical ignoring is part of a teacher's nonverbal repertoire. Used well, it is quickly picked up by students as a form of reinforcement. They notice when, and for what, the teacher gives attention. It should not be used selectively in the sense that what we ignore in one student, we punish in another.
- It needs to be used within one's comfort zone—one's degree of frustration tolerance! I called a student across the room during on-task time. Matthew had been tapping a girl annoyingly (playfully in his mind!) on the head. 'Matthew . . . see you over here, thanks.' I called, gave him take-up time, turned away to convey expectation (p 109). He replied, 'Not until you tell me what for!' (and folded his arms with a humph). Years ago I'd have raced across to his table and . . .! I repeated the direction, tactically ignoring his little power struggle. (It wasn't easy.) 'You didn't tell me what for,' was his reply. At this, Kylie, a student at his table, said, 'He asked you nicely, Matthew!' Ten seconds or so later, he came, sauntering, arms folded, 'Yes!' Had he not come, I would have walked over to his table and clarified the deferred consequences.
- Know when to use tactical ignoring, and what to move to if it does not achieve its purpose.
- Use it in concert with other management skills as when tactically ignoring secondary behaviour while verbally addressing primary behaviour (p 35 ff). If a student's loud calling out is not affected by tactical ignoring, we need to direct or remind, 'Karen . . . we've got a rule for asking questions. Use it, thanks.' As the teacher refocuses to students with hands up (and not calling out) she tactically ignores her 'humph', crossed arms and sliding down in her chair—her gestural last word.

During an art activity in class, I was moving around the room chatting to students (Preparatory Grade) about the playdough shapes they'd made. At one table while conversing with a student, another opposite me started to pull my clothes, 'Hey, look at this, look at this—mine!' I could have looked. I could have ticked him off. I chose to tactically ignore. Eventually, he gave up. Had he not, I would have shown a blocking hand with 'waiting' and immediately given my attention back to the first student. When I'd finished and he was quieter, still waiting, I went over.

I often say to whiners, 'When you speak in a normal voice, I'll listen' and walk away, giving them the tactical ignoring stance. Tactical ignoring is appropriately used for non-serious tantrums, for example, students who hold on to your leg (Preparatory Grade) while you circumnavigate the room, gently pushing them away and giving attention when they are back in their seat.

It can be helpful to discuss with colleagues how they use this skill and in professional development role-plays, it can be demonstrated how powerful a nonverbal behaviour it can be (Rogers 1990 a). It is another way in which we can manage 'least intrusively'.

Distracting students aside

During the on-task phase of the lesson, it can be helpful to correct some students more privately, as it were, by distracting them away from their immediate audience. As the teacher moves around the room, she notices a disruptive incident, triggered by an attention-seeking student. Rather than walk across to correct him in front of a familiar audience, she beckons him over. She briefly diverts her immediate attention from the group she is working with to direct him across the room to where she is. She gives him some take-up time and when he comes over she directs, reminds, asks a question or gives a choice as the situation determines. By directing him away from his immediate audience she minimises the student's temptation to play to the gallery, as it were. She then disciplines him privately.

A casual question or statement can also direct a student back on task without making a big fuss:

- When a student comes in late, the teacher simply directs him to take his seat, 'Morning, David. Take a seat over there (teacher points), thanks' then refocuses to the lesson. She can speak to the student about his lateness when she is ready, later during on-task time.
- With low-level disruption such as quiet chattering that distracts from a task, students staring out of a window (something I was hit for as a student), or vacant timewasting, a teacher can distract or divert by using a casual intervention such as: 'How's it going then?', 'Can I have a look?', 'Where are you up to?', 'Need a hand?' or 'Lisa, Michelle—having problems?' To two students discussing a television show, 'I'm sure it was a nice program (teacher winks), but how's your reading going?' Casual questions work best when teachers have a positive workable relationship with their students.
- A teacher introduces a new topic to his new class. A class wag calls out, 'We done that last year wiv Mrs Snaggs!' Rather than engage this student, the teacher tactically ignores the outburst and gives a general question to the class, 'Would anyone like to share what you did as a class on this topic last year?' Then the teacher scans for hands up, using the students' answers to initiate the topic from their perspective. This is in preference to the teacher engaging that student in discussion or starting a petty fracas by arguing, 'Listen, smart boy, I don't care what you did last year. I don't care if you've been doing decimal fractions since you were in Grade 4!'

113

- We can ask inattentive students to hold up a book or chart for us or help with an up-front activity. I've had students holding a felt-tip pen, my lesson plan, even my cup of tea. (Of course, if a dribbling Grade 1 has held my now cold cuppa for five minutes while I finish my up-front teaching I don't drink from it again—at least until it's been sterilised!)
- Invite a student to work with a fellow student who has attention-deficit problems (peer mentoring). Work out beforehand which students will best be able to give and receive such assistance.
- A signal to individuals or to the class can distract or divert when necessary— clapping signals, teacher singing a song (in tune we hope) to her Grade 1 when she wants group attention or to change activities or signal pack-up time, even the old-fashioned bell—all have their place as conditioned distracters and attention-getters.

Group directions, group reminders

When directing, or reminding a group, it is important to keep in mind the brevity and clarity of what is being said, and to remember the attention-getting and attention-sustaining cues mentioned earlier (pp 107-108).
- Avoid talking over noise, especially during crossovers when we need to redirect groups in the middle of conversational working noise.
- Have an attention-getting signal.
- Use pausing and scanning the room with eye contact to students.

The teacher wants to remind the students of the hands-up rule, 'Before we begin, let's remember our rule. Hands up without calling out.' If students then call out, the direction or reminder is brief, even nonverbal, 'Hands up without calling out, thanks.' This is said as the teacher scans the room, not to the several students in turn. She will not point to the students either, just give the direction or reminder, 'Remember our communication rule. Thanks.' She'll then be scanning for hands up without calling out. 'Yes . . . Ben, you've got your hand up. What's your question?'

'I' statements

'I' statements: these can be used to convey the teacher's needs and concerns or to tune in to the student's needs and concerns:
- 'David, I can see you're upset because the work is hard (whatever) . . .'
  This tunes in to what the student may be feeling and can be followed by a direction, distraction or question as appropriate, for example, 'I think it might help if you . . .'
- 'Kate and Christine, I feel annoyed (concerned or upset) because you two are trying to fix up your problems by arguing. (The teacher specifically targets the behaviour.) Remember our class rule is . . .' If students argue, protest or procrastinate we can redirect them to the necessary behaviour (p 35 ff).
- 'When . . ., then . . . because . . .' 'When you call out (this, specifically to an individual or group), I feel annoyed (or concerned) because I am trying to teach (give the reason) or others are trying to listen or because we have a rule for everyone.'
- Directional 'I' statements do not refer to one's feelings but assume a personal dimension between teacher and student: 'I want you to put your hand up

without calling out' or 'I want you to sit up, go back to your seat and work, talk quietly at your table, etc.'

- The personal pronoun prefaces the specific, positive behaviour the teacher is directing the student to, 'I want you to . . .' is preferable to the question format: 'Would you face this way and listen?'

Talking out of turn

During the establishment phase of the lesson, students sometimes call out impulsively from habit or for attention. Talking out of turn is a common classroom disruption (Wheldhall 1992). It is important to have a basic rule for question time whether during the more formal lesson, or during group discussions. Teachers at Lower or Middle Primary can also utilise the noise meter game in the establishment of positive behaviour during group discussion (p 79).

The teacher begins the formal discussion of the topic. She directs a question to a particular student, 'Adrian'. However, when other students call out, she snaps back, pointing, 'Is your name Adrian? Is it?' At other times, she says, 'Don't call out. How many times have I told you?' Sometimes, she accepts calling out from students she likes.

Apart from the negative tone created by the teacher's language, her corrective approach is creating uncertainty and confusion in the students. They are not sure what she accepts as appropriate questioning or group-discussion behaviour.

Because the establishment phase is crucial in behaviour management, it is important to deal positively with talking out of turn by enforcing fairly the appropriate rules or routines for asking questions or for discussion. Of course, these rules need to be age appropriate.

When a student calls out or butts in the teacher can choose to:
- tactically ignore each student who calls out while responding to those using the hands up rule
- use a rule reminder, name the student and refer to the rule. 'David, we've got a rule for asking questions. Use it, thanks.'
- give a direction. Name the student and direct them to the required behaviour. 'Hands up, without calling out or clicking fingers or . . .' I find it useful to finish with thanks (rather than please) to emphasise expectation.
- give consideration to whether seating is affecting how students communicate in public forums.

Before beginning each session in the first few days, the teacher can preface the question or discussion time by saying:
- 'Who can remember our rule for question time?' The teacher then reinforces those who respond appropriately.
- 'Okay, folks, before we begin our discussion I want to remind you to . . .' (this for older students).
- 'Before we start it's worth remembering that some of you may be so eager to ask a question you may blurt it out. (Here we can wink and smile.) Remember, others want to ask questions and comment too, so remember our rule, okay? Let's go for it.'

It is important to keep the tone positive, enforce the rule fairly, and be sure to positively target those who remember.

'Michael, thanks for putting up your hand. What's your question?'

'Yes, Lisa, you've got your hand up. Ta. What's your question?'

If several students have their hands up, it helps to acknowledge them briefly by name, 'Thanks, Dean, Lisa, Paul. I see your hands up. I'll be back to you in a sec' or simply number them off and then return in order.

If there are students who persist in calling out or butting in, they need to be warned through the use of class consequences and then followed up later (p 124 ff). A behaviour contract can be used to retrain disordered behaviour patterns.

Using questions in correction

It was noted earlier that the open interrogative, 'Why?' is counterproductive in behaviour management, and discipline in particular. Students don't often know why they behave the way they do, and if they do, the likelihood of coming up with an honest explanation in the immediate moment is rare. What is more likely is avoidance, shifting of blame or denial.

'Why are you out of your seat?' 'Why haven't you started work?' 'Why are you two talking so loudly?' 'Oi! Why are you running in the corridor!' Such questions are counterproductive because they easily draw the teacher and student into secondary behaviour or issues, especially if the teacher's tone is snappy, sarcastic, or hostile. It is more effective to use direct questions, for example, 'What are you doing? What's happening here?' To the question, 'What are you doing?' most students will say, 'Nothing' (some with heightened annoyance that you should even ask). Keep the focus directly on what you saw and give brief feedback. 'You're talking quite loudly here. What are you supposed to be doing?' This question redirects students to own their behaviour by refocusing on the present situation. If they say they don't know, or even say nothing at all, redirect them to the task with assistance if necessary. 'You're supposed to be doing . . .'

Direct questions

A student has dropped litter in the playground. The teacher has seen the student drop it. She calls the student over to her:

Teacher: 'It's Sean, isn't it?'

Sean: 'Yeah.' He looks a little suspicious.

Teacher: 'What's our rule about litter and playgrounds?' or 'I saw you drop it. What are we supposed to do with litter?'

Sean: 'Supposed to put it in the bin.'

Teacher: 'Off you go then.'

Using direct questions challenges the student to take some ownership of what he is supposed to be doing. If he argues, 'I didn't!' the teacher will redirect. 'I saw you drop it. What are you supposed to be doing with litter?' The student wearily replies with the appropriate response. As the teacher walks away, giving him some take-up time she 'sees' him drop it in the bin.

She turns, calls his name, and gives the okay sign. He smiles and wanders off. We don't need to call him a liar, nor do we need to invite a discussion—'Do you think I'm lying?', nor do we need to give mixed messages, 'You always argue. You never listen. What's wrong with you?' If they refuse to pick up the litter and put it in the bin the teacher can note this and follow up later. It is the certainty of deferred consequences that will eventually send the message through. The longer term, related consequence means he will be picking up litter in his own time for five minutes.

Individual rule reminder

'What's our rule for?' If students play dumb or look away, repeat the question. If there is no answer, simply remind them of the rule. Avoid pushing the issue or using threatening language. 'Our rule for learning time is . . .' If the student says he 'doesn't care', remind again and add, 'Can you do it anyway?' (Gossen 1992). If possible, give take-up time. At this point if there is still no willingness to respond, clarify the immediate or deferred consequences (pp 94-95).

Directed consequences

When we direct noisy or distracting students to work away from others in the room (relocation), we need to consider how we direct them from A to B. Grabbing their books and ordering them to follow you is an option but is likely to create unnecessary tension. It is helpful to have a place where distracting students can be directed to work on bad days. If they choose not to work over there in the next few minutes, we can come back and add, 'If you choose not to work over there'—'You can't make me!'—'No, I can't make you, but if you choose not to work over there, you are choosing to stay back at recess.'

Leave them with a deferred consequence. This puts ownership back on students, gives them take-up time, leaves the teacher and student in face-saving mode and lets other students who hear this exchange know that the teacher will follow up. Of course, if they refuse to move and are even more disruptive, the teacher may need to initiate exit and time-out procedures. If a student has had to be relocated several times over a week or two, the teacher will need to look at longer-term solutions (p 146 ff).

The concept of choice in discipline contexts

If we are going to treat students as if they are able to own their behaviour, then giving choices is a reasonable management and discipline option. Of course, these choices are not totally free. How could any choice be totally free? In the context of behaviour management, choices occur within known rules, rights, responsibilities, consequences and teacher guidance. Edward Deci (1985) in a study on motivation, explored the issue of creating structures in schools that, 'support students, guiding them towards desirable outcomes without controlling them inappropriately'. According to Deci, 'autonomy orientated limits' mean that teacher pressure is minimal so that, 'students have real choices to make about how to behave'. When rules, limits, and consequences are positively and clearly outlined students can 'choose'.

Both the limits and consequences for overstepping them must be stated clearly, and the consequences should be appropriate for the severity of the transgression. Given clear limits and consequences, the students can choose to stay within the limits or can choose to transgress, as we all do at times. In the latter case, they will learn there are costs to be paid for their actions. Of course, the consequences must be consistently applied if the learning is to be effective (p 53).

When students are given appropriate behavioural choices they learn that their behaviour can be self-controlled. 'Choices' also clarify the student's responsibility as seen by the teacher and give the student the sense of 'I can make up my mind.' How much the element of choice rather than threat is heard in the teacher's communication will depend on:
• how it's said
• the body language of the teacher
• how take-up time is given
• whether (and how) the teacher carries through the consequence
• how the teacher re-establishes working relationships with resistant students.

This is particularly relevant especially when students respond sulkily to the choices given. When consequences follow a choice we need to make clear to the student that they chose this outcome. The teacher didn't just punish them by keeping them back to clean up a mess or do work in their own time or engage in some act of restitution.

Directional choices

Rather than take toys or objects of art off students' desks, teachers can give a directional choice: 'Paul . . . that's a nice toy but I want you to put it in your bag or locker or on my desk or you can hand it to me' (smile). With appropriate take-up time most students will put it away. If they don't or if they argue, they can be made aware of the deferred consequences. Most will then put it away. There is no point (except satisfying the desire to win) in just wrestling for the toy! It is appropriate in some corrective contexts to precede a direction, reminder or question with a brief prefacing chat, as in the example of the boy with the toy above. In the playground, several students are sitting with (residual?) litter at their feet. 'G'day, how's it going?' Teacher has a brief chat. She then asks for their help in picking up the litter (p 172 ff).

Relocation in the room

Not all students respond to least intrusive correction:
• maybe they're having a bad day
• maybe they are into expressive nuisance behaviour
• maybe they didn't believe the teacher the first time.

Rather than yell at them, we can clarify the consequences of continuing to disrupt others: 'If you continue to (here, be specific about the off-task or disruptive behaviour) then I'll have to ask you to . . . (here outline the immediate or deferred consequence—working away from others, time out, staying back to discuss or fix up . . .)'.

Teacher: 'David . . . if you choose not to do your work now, you'll need to do it at recess.'

Student: 'It's not fair.'

David folds his arms and sulks. The teacher knows he can do the work. His task avoidance is a form of attention-seeking behaviour: service-me-now! Sometimes (like today) he engages in a little power struggle. The teacher repeats the directional choice and walks away giving take-up time. Sulkily David resumes his work half a minute later when the teacher's 'back is turned' though she can still see him in peripheral vision. She goes back to re-establish. If there's no time to do this during the lesson, she will have a word when the recess bell goes, 'I'm glad you made the right choice, David.' She pats his arm as he goes off to play. If students refuse directional choices, the teacher needs to clarify the immediate or deferred consequences. 'If you choose not to put the scissors away now (as the others are) you'll need to stay back and do it at morning play.' The student is left with the choice and a possible deferred consequence. This is treating students as if they can make decisions about their behaviour. It is also holding them accountable for those choices. Applied positively, it enables self-control.

Directional language and 'continent touch'

With younger Primary-aged students, the appropriate use of tactile affirmation can increase the likelihood of compliance in management situations. The affirming pat on the arm can convey relational trust as well as expectation. Katrina, Grade 1, has a tendency to laziness. At pack-up time she still hasn't cleared away her materials—scissors, papers, Textas. The teacher comes over and says, 'Katrina, I want you to put the scissors away (she beckons to the scissors tub) and the Textas. And paper bits go where?' 'In the bin,' whines Katrina. She then says, 'But Sean didn't pack up his scissors yet!' The teacher keeps eye contact with Katrina but avoids arguing, 'I'll speak to Sean. I want you to . . .' She finishes her redirection to the present task and as she walks away to give her some take-up time she says thanks, and pats her on the upper arm as if to say, 'and I know you'll do it'. A few minutes later she shuffles into action. 'I have seen many examples like this where teachers add to their reminders or direction, a pat on the arm that conveys a combination of expectation and affirmation' (Rogers 1994 a).

Wheldall, Bevan and Shortall (1986) and Wheldall (1992) note, 'The use of touch by teachers is an under-researched area . . .' Noting two classroom observational studies, in *Junior Primary*:

> In both classes when teachers touched students together with praising them, on-task behaviour rose by over 15 per cent from around 75 per cent to 90 per cent and disruptions fell from about ten or eleven per session to only two or three instances (Wheldall 1992, pp 57-59).

Caveat on touching or physical affirmation

In the current social climate, teachers are often advised to consider carefully any form of touching or tactile affirmation due to concerns:

> about both potential litigation (this is rare) and connotations of abuse (also, thankfully, rare). In social terms it is perceived as more 'ambiguous' when a male touches a student than when a female does so. When female teachers use 'touch' to affirm, praise or reassure, it is normally viewed in the context of nurture and care (Rogers 1994 a, p 61).

The issue of tactile affirmation or directional touch needs whole-school discussion, as does the appropriateness of physical restraint (allowed under law) in situations where students display out-of-control behaviour. The whole issue of touch and its social and managerial probity should not, in my opinion, be left only to professional discretion.

Redirecting

When students argue or procrastinate (unreasonably) there is little point in arguing or defending. It is more effective to either repeat the same direction, instruction, reminder or question. This is sometimes referred to as the 'broken record technique' (Smith 1991). An extension of this approach is the use of partial agreement before redirecting attention to the direction, reminder, question or choice (see especially p 135 ff). The purpose of redirecting is to keep the focus on the primary issue or concern. The basic message is: 'I'm not discussing this now. We can work it out later.'

Denial and mistargeting

Some students deny, lying through their teeth, that they swore, called out, talked loudly, were chewing gum. If we see students behaving disruptively and they deny this, we avoid taking their argumentative baits.

During on-task time, a teacher hears a provocative swear word, loud enough for several students to hear. He calls the student over in class.

Teacher: 'Geoff, I heard you call Hung a slant-eyed *shit*. That's a put-down.' (The teacher says this to the student aside from the group.)

Student: 'I didn't! Gees, I was just talking to Paul.'

Teacher: 'I heard you Geoff. You said . . .' (Describe what you heard.) 'We have a rule for respect.' (Here Geoff butts in with another denial. The teacher holds up a blocking hand.) 'I heard you. We have a rule for respect and I expect you to use it. I want you to go back to your seat now.'

Later he will speak to Geoff after class, and work out what (if any) restitution may be necessary between the offender and the offended. If we are sure a student said or did something, we can just acknowledge that, 'I saw . . .' or 'I heard . . .' and then remind them of the rule or deferred consequence.

It is important not to mistarget students. If we're not sure who said or did what in a group it is wiser to eye sweep the group and say, 'I don't know who said it, but' (what was said) is a put-down. We have a rule for respect and I expect you (eye sweep) to use it.' If they argue, the teacher can redirect by just repeating the rule reminder firmly and walking away. This is a form of verbal blocking.

Giving commands

In situations of danger or where immediate attention is required, a command can crisply and firmly stop disruptive behaviour. I was doing playground duty and saw a boy kicking another on the ground. I called out with a sharp 'Oi!', to gain instant attention across the play area. As he turned to look, I gave the command, 'Move away now. There!' I pointed to the wall. He moved. With commands, the sharpness of the initial contact needs to be unambiguous. Raise the voice but avoid shouting, unless this is essential. In classrooms we may need to use the 'Stop!' command to immediately communicate to all: 'Look, listen, focus.' When we have their attention, we can command, 'Put that down now' or 'Move away now' in an unambiguously commanding, assertive tone. It is helpful to drop the voice after attention is gained, otherwise it will unnecessarily increase emotional tension. One can keep assertion in the voice without resorting to aggression.

If students are fighting and they won't stop, we need to consider whether to physically separate them or direct the audience away and send for help. It is not easy to stop serious fights. If students refuse commands and they are a significant danger to self or others, under duty-of-care proviso we may need to physically separate them by standing between and firmly (not shouting) directing them to move away. Direct them to sit apart and give them cool-down time. With a bit of luck, the 'cavalry' will have arrived by then. A collegial back-up plan for crises is essential (p 167).

Summary— positive language

Developing a positive language of discipline does not come naturally to some teachers, certainly not to me. It is easier to say the first thing that comes into our heads. My colleagues and I have found it helpful to write down the sorts of directions, rule reminders, questions (direct and indirect), choices, assertive statements, and redirective dialogue that we can use more effectively. This may sound trite, but it is easier to say 'Don't call out' or 'Don't tap or annoy' or 'Don't rock on your chair' than it is to say 'Hands up. Pens down. Looking this way, thanks' or 'Four on the floor' or 'Sitting up, thanks.' It is certainly easier to argue than redirect and threaten rather than give choices.

Practice (even cognitive rehearsal) can help build a more positive language of discipline and management. Being aware of, and conscious of, global behaviour also helps in developing a positive communication style. The big question is—Is it worth this effort? It depends on what we value about our role and the messages we want to convey to our students.

It also helps in one's planning to consider the context within which we discipline: the up-front, public context and the on-task phase. In the up-front phase we need to be more brief and more directive to the group and the individual. We would not, for example, normally use questions to correct students because it invites unnecessary discussion. In this phase of the lesson, we need maximum attention to the front, the board, the elements of the lesson and on active listening.

During the on-task phase of the lesson we can afford to be more discursive with our correction, as the group is diversified and noise level is more diffuse as students normally talk during on-task activities. In the on-task phase we can afford to be more private (one-to-one) with our management and discipline, drawing students aside and using questioning approaches: 'What are you doing?' or 'What should you be doing?' One of the earliest observations I made about behaviour management was that when I modified my behaviour, I saw a corresponding change in my students' behaviour. Even the simple change from 'Don't' to 'Do' had an effect, as did considering how assertive (rather than hostile) my tone of voice was. Conveying expectation and tone through body language, helped me to relate more positively and effectively to my students. Learning to tactically ignore some behaviour and keep the focus on the central issue at hand cut down the easy arguments that can occur between teacher and student (p 129 ff). I also learnt the importance of follow-up with students:

- giving some cool-off time when appropriate rather than forcing a no-win situation in the heat of the moment
- opting for certainty in the long run rather than severity in the short-term. ('You-will-do-what-I-say now!').

. . . when I modified my behaviour, I saw a corresponding change in my students' behaviour.

Most of all, having a plan for my daily corrective language helped me to keep the focus of correction on the behaviour at hand without unnecessary strain on the working relationship. A discipline plan helped me to structure my language relative to the context and disruption so I knew the sorts of thing I wanted to say. The key was being conscious of what I was doing and saying when students were being disruptive. I knew I was saying certain things rather than just opening my mouth and hoping the right thing would come out. Even now, when I take demonstration lessons, I am conscious of managing problem behaviour—calling out, butting in, chair leaning, talking out of turn—with a range of language scripts that are assertive but positive. I don't have to directly think,

'Now what will I say and do in this situation?' Freed from that need, I am more relaxed in my teaching and can spend more time on the teaching and learning needs. A classroom behaviour management plan enables one to meet one's aims more effectively, to keep the focus of management on teaching and learning and do so in as relaxed a way as possible.

Support plans for continuing behaviour problems

With persistent behaviour problems, grade teachers need to utilise:
- time-out plans with whole-school support (p 83)
- daily reports, contracts, individual behaviour plans (p 152)
- changes to basics like seating arrangements
- modifications to the curriculum—to cater for significant individual differences
- daily work plans
- follow-up with parents (planned, supportive parent interviews with senior teacher involvement)
- formal case conferences
- suspension and partial enrolment (in severe cases).

Key questions

How aware are you of how you normally sound when you are correcting students? What is your characteristic language? (Forgive the bad-day syndrome—we all have those.) On those days, students are normally very forgiving.

How does your language of correction (the words, phrases, and manner of corrective management) fit in with the emphases and skills outlined in this chapter?

Chapter 6

SOME PROBLEM AREAS IN BEHAVIOUR MANAGEMENT

Follow-up of students after class

Case study

Veronica was a popular, 'bright' Grade 5 student. She generally completed her work, but in class was the classic, marginally compliant student. Other teachers had described her as having an attitude problem.

In my first teaching sessions with the class I noticed she would wander from her seat in class time and chat with other students. I tactically ignored for a while, then directed her to go back to her own desk. 'Gees! (here her eyes rolled to the ceiling, following a sibilant sigh) I was only borrowing a "rubba" from Michelle.' Here a punctuated, 'tsk, tsk', and averted eyes, finished her sulky retort—typical secondary behaviour. Almost every time I corrected her, even with simple reminders, this would occur. In class, I redirected and defused most of this behaviour but followed up with several chats after class.

Just before the recess bell, I directed her to stay back after class for a few minutes. 'What for?' was her 'injured party' reply. I ignored this and dismissed the class. If teachers want to follow up students after class for a chat, or to follow through with consequences, it is good policy to telegraph the direction to stay back just before the recess bell. This avoids any prolonged discussions based on, 'What for?', 'Why me?' or 'What have I done?' As the class left, she folded her arms and slouched against the wall near the door, and I had a chat with her about her behaviour.

This kind of brief chat, with the door open for ethical probity, is designed to clarify what is happening in classtime regarding the students' behaviour. It is important to remember that our correction, guidance and repair of strained relationships occurs within a working relationship. I need to keep the tone positive and friendly, and avoid threatening body language such as the extended index finger while I say, 'What do you think you're playing at eh! This is the fourth time I've had to keep you back after class!'

Better to talk *with* rather than talk *at*.

I asked her if there was a problem in class.

    Student: 'Nope' (eyes down, subdued sulkiness).

        Teacher: 'Maybe you're feeling annoyed or upset because I've asked you to stay back?'

      I was trying to communicate that I was aware of how she might be feeling.

        Student: 'Yeah. What did I do anyway?' (More sibilance. She may not actually be aware that her behaviour is problematic.)

Teacher: 'Do you remember when I asked you to go back to your own desk? Do you remember what you did and said?'

Veronica gave me marginal eye contact at this point. I could also have said, 'Is there anything you'd like to share that would help me to understand why you argued with me in class when I asked you to go back to your seat.' The tone is one of trying to invite dialogue or, at the very least, showing you're not 'out for blood'. The fundamental respect is still intact. It's not worth the emotional effort of forcing eye contact (p 50).

Teacher: 'Do you mind if I show you what you said?'

Student: 'What?'

Teacher: 'Do you mind if I show you what you said?'

Mirroring

Many students are unsure at this point, about the meaning of our offered demonstration, or modelling.

Teacher: 'Let me show you.'

Here I 'mirrored' to her the postural, gestural and tonal behaviour I'd seen and heard that morning, complete with the tossed head and the hurt look to suggest gross unfairness on my part. Many students are quite unaware of how their secondary behaviour appears. They certainly don't see it as we do. Teachers often interpret such behaviour as rudeness and as an attack on their status. While it is rude, in our value judgment, it's really poor social skills, bad habits or the students' gambit for attention or power within the class group. When we 'mirror' what we see in their behaviour and then explain our feelings and refer them to the class rule for respect or fair treatment, at the very least we've clarified:

• what *we* mean by rudeness
• our point (often the rule or rights being affected by such behaviour)
• that such behaviour affects working relationships and we've let them know that we know they know we know.

There's nothing Machiavellian about this if it's done in a non-pejorative way. It is akin to a more involved process described by Dreikurs et al 1982, as 'goal disclosure' where questioning of students assists in clarifying 'mistaken goals' of attention, power, withdrawal and revenge (p 147).

As I gave the brief demonstration and came out of role and smiled, Veronica fought back an involuntary grin and said, 'I don't do that all the time.' 'No, that's true,' I replied, 'but you do act like that many times.' Here I directed my hand to the space I'd vacated, where I'd mirrored her behaviour. My tone was friendly and non-threatening. I paused for several seconds, then added: 'I don't speak like that to you, Veronica. When you speak like that, I feel it shows disrespect because of the tone and the way you say it.'

Student: 'Yeah, well I didn't mean it.'

Teacher: 'Liar!' (No, I only thought that, I didn't say it.) 'Okay, maybe you didn't mean it, but that's what you said and that's how it sounded.'

Some students then give a cursory apology. Avoid saying, 'You're not really sorry are you? You didn't really mean it.' Accept the apology with a reminder of the school rule about respect and then a goodbye for now. Remember that this is only a chat designed to clarify the problem and explain what happened. What I've described here doesn't take long. It is good practice to follow up all secondary behaviour that you believe works against basic respect. These follow-up chats are to be distinguished from more formal consequences and counselling. A useful rule of thumb is that if a student's secondary behaviour is still characteristically disrespectful after three or four chats, then a more formal counselling/contracting process needs to be set in place (see Chapter 6).

The few chats I had with Veronica didn't stop all her sulky and argumentative behaviour, but they produced a significant reduction in their frequency and intensity.

Such chats are at their most persuasive in the establishment phase of the year, acting as a 'nip in the bud' approach—the message being that this teacher will always follow up on certain behaviour after class time.

The importance of follow-up

There are a number of issues that should be followed up after class:

1 Students whose public behaviour is clearly disrespectful in terms of the class understanding of mutual respect. When students are rude without provocation, the effort of directing them to stay back is worthwhile. After such a chat, I've overheard students in parley with their mates in the corridor, 'What did he say when he kept you back?' Miscreants often say 'Nothing' with a smirk on their face.

Some teachers then assume that the chat and feedback were a waste of time. Do we really expect students to tell their mates that the teacher, 'focused on my postural and tonal language and made me see it in a whole new light. I didn't realise how sulky, rude and provocative my behaviour really was'? Of course, they often say 'Nothing'. They can't afford to lose face.

2 Students who blatantly refuse to follow rules and routines in class time. Deferred consequences would be appropriate:
   • packing up materials in own time
   • cleaning up in own time
   • completing work after class or in 'catch-up' time
   • a time-trade consequence, for example, students engage in some act of restitution. If they've damaged school equipment, they engage in a negotiated time-trade to do some positive things—cleaning up, gardening, extra duties in their own time to heal the damaged school (pp 94-99).

3 Blatant task avoidance. Sonia refused to do her set work in class time. I knew she could do it. I'd checked her other books. It was refusal not merely avoidance, 'raising the banner' stuff. Rather than buy into her power struggle ('Don't want to, can't make me') I gave her a directed

choice: 'You're right. I can't make you do the work. If you choose not to do it now, though, I'll have to speak to you at recess.' 'Don't care!' was her reply. Perhaps she thought I wasn't serious. Perhaps she really *didn't* care. Either way she's right. I can't make her and I'm not going to start making useless threats and giving her centre stage. She did stay back and whinged and said, 'It isn't fair' when I directed her to complete the work at recess. Even then, there's no guarantee I can make her do the work. Had she refused, I would have followed it up with senior staff and developed a more formal process, but it would still have been her choice (p 39).

- It can be helpful to note down who you will follow up and for what. With older students it is beneficial for them to see the teacher write it down in a class record book, not in a smug way, but as a necessary reminder for the teacher that this is serious enough to be followed up and followed through.
- Go for certainty not severity (p 38 ff). There are teachers who direct the student to stay back after class. I did it myself in the early days. The student stays back waiting, only to hear the teacher say, 'Don't do it again. All right?' and then shoot through to the cuppa.
- If we are going to direct a student back, follow-through is important. Have a chat. A prepared format will help. Use either the example noted earlier or the 4Ws approach (pp 27, 87).
- They don't need a lecture: 'Right! You've lost your playtime. You can answer the questions on this form. What did I say in class? Didn't I say not to be rude to me, didn't I? Well you've lost your playtime and it serves you right—and you've made me lose my morning tea time, so you can suffer, suffer . . .!'

Consider how the student is feeling

We need to consider their emotions at this point. The whole class has seen the student kept back.
- Do we attempt to create guilt?
- Do we criticise or work on repairing and rebuilding?
- Do we focus on the solution or on fixing blame?
- Do we distinguish between mistakes, failure, 'stupidity' and blatant disobedience?
- Do we seek to coerce or to use shared dialogue?
- If we need to use consequences, how can we do so without attacking the person but keeping the focus on behaviour?

Follow-up and follow-through, even just the chat:
- convey the teacher's intent. (They're serious. They mean what they say.)
- ensure that the other students see the teacher direct the student back. This, too, is important. The tribal tom-toms will soon convey what happened.)
- allow students to make a connection (in their minds and experiences) between their behaviour and outcomes (p 84). The connection is restrictive but educational.

Follow-up, follow-through

As we cannot always deal effectively with behaviour in the public setting, we have to defer outcomes until after class time—after cool-off time and without the audience.

We need to consider the ethical probity of all one-to-one situations. The classroom door should be open so that brief chats after class and deferred consequences are visible. It may be appropriate to keep a record of follow-ups to see if there's a pattern. These can be used in discussions or case conferences with senior staff. Most schools have a policy on teacher follow-up anyway, especially with regard to extended time (lunchtime) when used for consequences like detention. In this regard, schools are also bound by Education Department guidelines.

Extended one-to-one conferencing, counselling or follow-through or supervision of consequences may need to be carried out
- in an area near the office
- with another teacher (female) present for moral support and ethical probity. This is especially important if the initiating teacher is a male.

DEALING WITH ARGUMENTATIVE STUDENTS

In every school there is a small percentage of students who challenge teachers, who display dumb insolence, who answer back and want the last word. They have ten reasons or explanations why it wasn't them, why it isn't fair, why the teacher 'always picks on them'. I'm not talking about students whose behaviour is mistargeted by teachers or about students who have justifiable complaints about teachers' behaviour. I'm talking about the ones who make behaviour management a contestable affair, purposely or by habit. They chip away at our joie de vivre, have a tendency to create an irascible environment and upset the emotional tone.

The disconcerting reality is that a lot of the arguments between teacher and student begin on such petty issues:

Teacher: 'Jason, why are you wandering?'

Jason: 'I'm not. I'm only borrowing a ruler from Dimi. Gees!'

It's not just his reply to the teacher that's annoying. It's the way he says it and the accompanying body language.

Teacher: 'Look, don't lie to me. You were not getting a ruler. I saw you. Yes, you can laugh!'

The teacher is quickly becoming angry as he sees the grin surface on Jason's face that says, 'I'm conning you.'

Teacher: 'I'm sick and tired of your behaviour!'

Here, Jason looks bored, looks at his feet and sighs.

Teacher: 'Look at me when I'm talking to you!'

Jason screws up his mouth and gives marginal eye contact with dumb insolence. He butts in. 'How do you know, anyway, whether I was getting a ruler or not? You can ask Dimi.'

Here he folds his arms in mega-huff mode. The whole class is watching now. The teacher butts in on Jason's butting-in.

Teacher: 'You think you're so smart don't you? Well let me tell you!'

This invective begins a mini-lecture that sees Jason slouch back to his chair and continue sulking and silent task avoidance. Still smarting from the above fracas, the teacher interprets Jason's leaning back in his chair, with hooded brows scowling, as blatant task refusal and disrespect. He goes over and challenges him.

Teacher: 'What do you think you're doing now, eh?'

The question is undisguised confrontation in tone and gesture. Jason is 'on stage'. What does the teacher expect him to do? Lose face and acquiesce? Of course, Jason *has* been rude, even flippant, but the teacher's attitude and actions have also had a powerful bearing on how this originally minor issue got out of hand.

How we deal with such students depends on how characteristic the behaviour is and how thoughtfully the teacher has developed a plan for positive correction (see Chapters 3 and 5). It also depends on how the teacher interprets, responds to, and deals with secondary behaviour (Rogers 1992 a and b).

Primary and secondary behaviour

If we ask talkative students to face the front and listen during instructional time, we are addressing primary behaviour, that aspect of behaviour that is primarily affecting our right to teach or others' right to learn. If they then fold their arms, lean back in the chair and let out a huge sigh, this behaviour is secondary to the main issue of talking out of turn.

Two students are talking to each other during instructional time.

Teacher: '. . . so, in this decimal fraction, the number after the zero . . .'

(the teacher is explaining a point on the board prior to group activities) 'Lisa and Emma . . . I'm trying to teach!'

Lisa: 'I wasn't talking. Gees!'

Teacher: 'Lisa! I saw you talking to Emma. Don't talk while I'm teaching. Face the front and pay attention.'

Lisa: 'C'mon. Emma just asked me about the work!'

Teacher: 'Look! I don't care who said what. Both of you could have the good manners not to interrupt this lesson.' The teacher is naturally becoming quite irritated—especially by Lisa's tone and body language.

Lisa: 'But, Emma . . .'

Teacher: 'Lisa!' This loud response is followed by 'Shut up!' or 'One more word and I'll . . .' or a stand-up lecture: 'I'm sick and tired of . . .' Whatever, it is collateral damage.

Nothing is more annoying to teachers and parents than these extensions to already annoying behaviour:

- the pouting, snappy, sulky or even sneering tone of voice following teacher correction
- the singsong voice some students affect when you direct or remind them
- the postural cues, such as the way they walk across the room when you beckon them, their insouciant indifference as they sigh and raise their eyes, 'Here we go again!', the way they stand with arms folded, legs askew, head turned away, refusing to look at you, the displays of dumb insolence
- the 'last word' syndrome—'I wasn't the only one talking (whatever) . . . He was mucking around too, you know!' or 'He didn't pack up. Why should I? What you picking on me for? What about . . .?'—the sotto voce last word as they grudgingly comply, the muttered, 'All right! All right! I'm going.' 'Honest. I'm packing up!' (at snail's pace).

I noticed that the student (Grade 7) hadn't started his work. I walked over and casually asked, 'Bradley, I notice you haven't started. Any problems?' I was pleasant. To his response, 'Yeah, well I haven't got a pen, have I?' I replied, 'That's okay. You can borrow one of mine.' (Whenever I teach an upper grade class, I take pens, pencils, rulers, rubbers and spare paper with me—preventive management. Each implement has a band of blue tape to mark its journey back to my remember box.) He muttered something, then said moodily, dropping his voice and eyes, 'Yeah, well I haven't got a ruler have I?' Here I pointed to the box of materials on the teacher's desk. 'You can borrow one of mine.' His voice took on a frustrated edge as he said, 'Tsk, tsk, yeah, well I haven't got any paper. Gee!' Poor chap! I was disrupting his task avoidance game. I was tempted to be sarcastic but I said, 'There's paper on my table as well.' I pointed. 'I'll come and see how you're going later.' Faced with this last helpful comment he said, '*Shit!*' under his breath and as I moved away I saw him go to the teacher's desk to find what he needed. Later in the lesson, I went back to give some encouragement which he received with controlled grunts. It's hard being civil.

Bradley has been described as 'up himself' by some of the teachers at this school. What they are referring to is the sum total of his secondary behaviour and this behaviour has more emotional weight than the primary behaviour that precedes it. Even a mere 'Yes!' in reply to a teacher's question can be annoying to both ear and eye.

While on playground duty, I directed a student to come to me. 'Rose . . . can I see you for a sec?' I want to call her aside from her group as she is more likely to show off if I speak to her about her behaviour with her peers in tow. After I've beckoned her over, I turn aside and walk away a bit to communicate expectation and avoid unnecessary confrontation. She waits, then discontentedly comes across to me, stands near me and says 'Yes'. But it's the way she says it that's annoying, isn't it?—mouth screwed up, sighing, arms folded, a one-syllable word—the global set of behaviour speaks volumes.

Teachers say to me, 'I'd like to slap his face! How dare he? Who does he think he is?' They read so much into the secondary behaviour even when the student has been compliant—'All right, all right. I'll pick it up. Phew!'

I'd asked a student to pick up and bin the entrails of a paper cup he'd been abstractedly dropping on the ground. He did what I'd asked under sufferance, with what we might call uncompliant compliance. I could wander after him and attack this immediate secondary behaviour and say, 'Look, when I ask you to pick up litter, you don't have to make a big deal of it, do you?' or I can leave it at that point and follow up later, if necessary, even during playground duty with a chat about the secondary context in which he complied.

It is easy, even natural, to overreact, or overfocus on a student's secondary behaviour, especially when we're tired—much more so if we impute inherent malignancy into their tone, manner and words, or if we have insistent beliefs about respect and obedience always being shown by students in deferential body language and manner of speech (Rogers 1992).

Respect

It is dysfunctional and stressful to believe that students must respect their teachers at all times simply because they are teachers. Respect and civility are crucial values in social exchange, but one doesn't promote such values by merely demanding that reality accede and conform to our beliefs about respect.

Our modelling and our management style can do a great deal to moderate and even change the nature and extent of secondary behaviour.

Invited and uninvited secondary behaviour

A teacher walks over to a couple of Grade 5 girls who are secretly scanning a magazine and chatting during process writing time. The teacher, noticing this, walks rapidly toward them, comes face-on and snatches up the magazine. 'Right! What do you think you're doing with that? Give it to me. C'mon. Give it to me now!' The tone and manner invite non-compliance. When these students start to protest their relative innocence this fitful exchange degenerates into a power struggle. If the teacher, wanting to win, then snatches up the magazine and orders the students to 'work or else'—she has 'won' but at great relational cost.

The teacher could manage this off-task behaviour differently. She could refocus the secondary behaviour, still see the students come back on-task, and not unnecessarily strain her working relationship with them.

Teacher: 'How's it going Wendy . . ., Michelle?'

She eyes them both. She comes side-on, not face-on. Her finger does not point at, or on, the magazine.

Student: 'Okay.'

The girls try to cover the magazine.

Teacher: 'Interesting magazine.' The teacher smiles and adds, 'I'd like you to put it away though . . . in your desk or on my table. Ta.'—a directed choice rather than confrontation—(pp 117-118).

They try the protest pathetic:

Students: 'Gees! We weren't really reading it.'

Michelle looks pained as she purses her lips.

The teacher partially agrees, refocuses the issue, and redirects:

Teacher: 'Maybe you weren't, but I want you to put the magazine away in your desk or on my table and carry on with your work. I will come and check it later.'

This reassertion prevents the teacher from getting bogged down in whether they are lying or not, or in unproductive exchanges: 'What did I just say?' or 'Are you deaf?' or, 'I don't care if you were reading it, I said . . .' In other words, the teacher doesn't capitulate to the secondary behaviour by discussion, argument or adversarial tactics. It's hard for a student to still keep being objectionable when the teacher is assertive but still civil. Of course, if they refuse to put the magazine away then the consequences (immediate or deferred) need to be made clear (p 95 ff).

Why students behave in this way

Most secondary behaviour is uninvited by the teacher. No matter how positive a teacher's manner, there are students who will display secondary behaviour such as:

- a 'performance'—a way of focusing attention on themselves in front of their peers or indicating that 'You can't really make me comply, you know!' 'Even if I do face the front as you told me to, my huffing, my eyes to the ceiling, my folded arms, my leaning back in my chair, demonstrate that you really didn't make me.' Of course, this is correct. We can't really make the student comply. The authority we possess depends on the kind of relationship we generate through our management approach
- a habit that goes well beyond the 'bad-day' syndrome which appears whenever the teacher calls behaviour into question.

Some secondary behaviour is low level:

- the whining student who asks, 'Do I have to pack up now?' who complies but with screwed up face muttering and whingeing
- the student who shuffles and sighs and walks with slug-like compliance (the bodily last word)
- the 'clever' last word from students who try to be funny, smart or sarcastic. I directed a girl who was running in the corridor, 'Walk instead of running, thanks.' She (aged 7) replied, 'I wasn't running. I was power walking!' A student who was asked to put away the comic he was reading, replied, 'I wasn't reading. I was looking at the pictures.'
- the procrastinating student who says, 'I don't like this work'. This is especially annoying when said in that whiny 'nyah nyah' kind of tone. Our natural reaction is to reply in kind, or mimic them, or have a clever last word of our own. While humour is a very powerful defuser, sarcasm merely feeds conflict and breeds defensiveness.

Whether the behaviour is low or high in its intrusiveness, our management approach will benefit from reflection and planning. Rather than going straight onto the attack, a least intrusive approach is normally more effective. The exception, of course, is when the primary or secondary behaviour is unsafe, aggressive, or verbally abusive. Even then, some planning for how we can approach crises with assertion rather than aggression, needs to be considered by all staff. This is discussed later in this section.

• *Avoid unnecessary power struggles*

The key to dealing with difficult, argumentative and challenging students is to avoid unnecessary power struggles. While we can't directly control the student, we can control how we deal with the conflict, by considering what we can say in the immediate short term and how we follow through in the long term (p 128). Reactive and defensive correction extends the conflict:

- 'Don't speak to me in that tone of voice!' 'You don't have to sigh like that! For crying out loud, all I asked you to do was pack up. Is that too difficult?'
- 'I don't whine at you like that do I? *Do* I?'

If we react like this, tempting as it is, especially when our body language is hostile, we change the behavioural focus away from the packing up—the direction, question or reminder about the rule etc. Students may play out their power struggle in front of the ever accommodating audience of peers. Some teachers will say, 'Who cares whether they feel threatened? The little beasts deserve it. I'm not having anybody be rude to me!' If we simply react to others' behaviour based on how we feel, we will be working against good practice (see Chapter 2) and against the very aims we set for a whole-school approach to behaviour management.

I need to emphasise again that I'm talking about our characteristic approach to students and to our management approach, not the 'bad-day' syndrome we all experience as teachers. Of course, student behaviour can be annoying, stupid, churlish, rude and flippant, but that doesn't mean that we have to reply in kind. It is important to remember that whenever we discipline, we nearly always do so in the public domain of the students' peers.

Some teachers, acting from whatever reserves of goodwill they have, try the discursive approach. This is nearly always counterproductive, especially when the teacher's tone and manner is non-assertive:

Teacher: 'Lisa and Michelle, why are you reading that comic (sigh) when you're supposed to be reading?' Open interrogatives (Why . . .?) are an invitation to secondary behaviour (p 116).

Students: 'C'mon, Miss. We weren't reading. Anyway we're still getting our work done.'

The teacher, reading too much into the sulky and pouting faces (she doesn't want to be disliked by her students) starts to reason with them.

Teacher: 'But I think you were, Michelle. I saw you.'

Student: 'Are you calling me a liar?' Michelle butts in, rudely.

Teacher: 'No, of course not, Michelle. I just want you to put that comic away and . . .'

I have seen these fitful exchanges played out in many classrooms.

Teacher: 'Why haven't you started work yet, Dean?' It comes out as a whine as 'Why do I always have to come and remind you?'

Student: 'I don't like this work!'

Teacher: 'Well (sigh) what work do you like doing?'

So begins a bargaining exchange in front of a ready audience. These sorts of exchange can go on for a long time—wasted time. It is a one-sided power struggle now. The key managerial point is to focus on the main issue in the short term—the primary behaviour.

• *Reflective awareness*

Reflective awareness of what is happening in these exchanges is a useful starting point. This is more easily said than done, of course. What do these diversionary cues mean in a teacher–student exchange? Under the emotional pressure to manage in a busy classroom, it is easy to be drawn in (some teachers have said 'drawn in unconsciously') to the secondary behaviour, even the low-level behaviour.

• *Tactical ignoring*

Tactical ignoring of tone of voice, postural cues and the nonverbal elements of secondary behaviour can help keep the focus on the issue, which, at that point, is important. We can address their tone and manner at a time when they are likely to hear it, away from their audience at the end of the lesson (p 124). Tactical ignoring is a choice we make not to focus on non-essentials as we perceive them (p 111). We see, we hear, we're fully aware of the grunts, the sibilant sighs, the way they walk, but we choose to ignore. This is what makes it tactical. We don't ignore their last word or challenge unless it's something like quiet muttering as they walk away. We can address their secondary dialogue without focusing on the package it comes in. We do not, and should not, ignore the thinly disguised disrespect shown in their tone of voice, postural indifference, and their attitude. What we are choosing to do through tactical ignoring is to tactically distinguish when to address the behaviour.

• *Keep the focus by redirecting and refocusing*

A new teacher goes up to a difficult Grade 3 student and notices that she hasn't started work. His approach is calm, even relaxed:

Teacher: 'I noticed you haven't started work. Any problems?'

Student: 'You're not as nice as the other teacher!'

She says this testily after a wounded silence, and finishes this exchange by screwing up her face and grunting. Tactically ignoring the grunt, the face and the withdrawn, suspicious hostility, the teacher partially agrees with the student.

Teacher: 'Maybe I'm not (the partial agreement), but I'm your teacher this year. How can I help you with your work, Danielle?' (the redirection).

The teacher refocuses to the issue at hand. Another student challenges the work.

Teacher: 'I notice you haven't started work. Do you know what to do?'

Student: 'I don't like this work!'

Teacher: 'You don't have to like it, Paul (the partial agreement), but it's the work we're doing today. How can I help?' (the refocusing, the redirection).

Student: 'But we didn't have to do it like this last year with Mr Smadge!'

Teacher: 'You mean the poor fellow you gave a nervous breakdown to?' (The teacher probably felt like saying this but thought better of it.) 'Maybe you didn't have to do it (he directs his hand to the work) like that, but that's the work we're doing here today.'

At this point the teacher, having dignified the student's words and now refocusing, moves away, giving the student some take-up time. As he moves away he adds a parting redirection, 'I'll come and see your work a little later. Let me know if you need my help.' This signals a temporary end to the procrastination or last word.

Giving direct eye contact to a couple of chatterers:

Teacher: 'Dinah and Carla (here a pause for attention), facing this way and listening, thanks.'

Student: 'But we're still listening!'

Teacher: 'Maybe you are, but I still want you to face this way and listen without talking, thanks.'

The teacher resumes the flow of the lesson, emotionally withdrawing from this exchange to convey that he expects them to respond to his direction and redirection.

The tone and manner in which this is carried out is essential in terms of how it's heard by the student. Two or three redirectional exchanges are

enough for us to convey to the student that we are not going to argue or debate. We've clarified the issue and we are now looking for and expecting responsibility from them. By giving them take-up time, we give face-saving time to comply.

It is also important to re-establish a working relationship as early as appropriate. We do this best by not conveying personal animosity and by not bearing a grudge (p 110).

Teacher: 'Michael, that's a nice toy but I want you to put it away in your locker or on my table, thanks.'

Student: 'But . . .' he argues on.

Teacher: 'Michael, I want you to put the toy in your locker or on my desk, thanks.'

It is also important to re-establish a working relationship as early as possible.

Here she moves away to give him take-up time. Begrudgingly, as the teacher turns away, Michael lets out a huge sigh, puts his triceratops into his locker, comes back to his table, sighs and starts his diary page. A few minutes later, the teacher comes back and pats him on the arm and says, 'Thanks for putting your dinosaur away, Michael. Let's have a look at your work.'

Student: 'It's a triceratops, not a dinosaur, Miss.'

Teacher: 'Thanks for reminding me, Michael. Let's have a look at your work.'

• *Follow up secondary behaviour*

Whenever a student is displaying significant secondary behaviour, it should be followed up after class as well as redirected in class time. During follow up we can explain (even demonstrate) to them what their secondary behaviour looks and sounds like and how it affects mutual rights (p 125). If such behaviour persists, a balance of consequences and one-to-one contracting can often be effective. This is discussed in Chapter 6.

A good deal of secondary behaviour occurs in the establishment phase of the year, most often in the public domain. In this testing of the relationship between student and teacher, the key seems to be in how we address the behaviour in the immediate, emotional moment and in the consistency and certainty of our follow-through. When we follow through, it is essential we convey to students that secondary behaviour is unacceptable in terms of classroom rights and responsibilities. Dealing with this kind of behaviour is a skill. It is natural to want to argue back, counter challenge and interpret such behaviour as disrespect. It takes effort, planning and practice to feel comfortable in addressing secondary behaviour in a non-confronting way. Not every teacher will feel comfortable with the approaches outlined here.

Having used confrontational approaches myself with difficult students (I made some dumb mistakes) I can vouch for these approaches. I find them to be more functional, less stressful and more productive. It dismays me to see experienced teachers engaged in pointless, fruitless, unnecessarily stressful slanging matches over students who display the sort of behaviour described in this section. We need to ask what practices we prefer as a whole school, when managing this type of behaviour and then seek to accommodate these practices within our management approach.

ARGUMENTS AND SQUABBLES: THE RESIDUE OF PLAYTIME

When students come in from play they sometimes carry with them the emotional entrails of some playground fracas. Some are hurt, some have friendships out of kilter, some have been excluded from the game.

Maria and Cherie are accusing each other as they come in from play. Maria is crying and telling Cherie that she 'hates her!' As 'Miss' arrives at the Grade 3 line, Maria rushes out her story, 'Miss, Miss, Cherie she . . . anyway . . . she said she's not going to be my best friend!' The tears are real. Maria is upset. There is an audience. 'Miss' is in a difficult situation. She must deal with this in a way that acknowledges there is a problem, that feelings and needs are affected, yet make sure it doesn't all get out of hand. If she tries to find the truth while the students are emotionally aroused and only focuses on their immediate feelings and perceptions, they are likely to claim and counterclaim: 'Gees! You're a liar, Maria. I didn't say I wouldn't play with you. I didn't, Miss.' Here she turns to the teacher to protest her innocence. She doesn't want to be blamed for Maria's discomfiture. If the teacher tries to deal with this episode at the door, there will often be a few other students happy to 'rat' on these two, to act as agents provocateurs—'I saw it anyway, Miss. She did so tell Maria that she couldn't play in the group!' It's easy to have a kids' court in full swing.

In a problem like this, or when students argue with each other in class or the playground, they are not often amenable to problem solving, at that point. Because of the emotional arousal, it is important to refocus the situation on their behalf.

• Establish priorities

The teacher's responsibility for Maria and Cherie has to be balanced by her responsibility for the rest of the class. She has to take them in and settle them. Now is not the best time for conflict resolution.

I've seen teachers stand at the door for five minutes or more, trying to arrive at the truth of an issue while the rest of the class become unsettled, barrack for their favourite, or just wander into the room unsupervised. What the two students need is a brief reassurance from their teacher and for the whole class to quickly refocus on normal activities.

• Acknowledge their feelings and refocus

'Maria (teacher pauses for eye contact), Maria . . . I can see you're upset.' As Maria starts to rush through her story, the teacher puts up a gently blocking hand, pats her on the arm and says, 'Yes, I can see you're upset but I want you to take a seat in class and I'll help you sort it out later.' Cherie butts in and the teacher gives a similar 'I' statement to her. It is important to reassure them that there will be follow-up later. 'Later' is a difficult concept for small students so at the earliest opportunity, when the class is settled, they may need a brief reminder that you will speak to them after a certain activity or before 'big play'.

• Allow cool-off time prior to conflict resolution

It is difficult to address conflict, let alone resolve it, when there is significant emotional arousal. This is as true for adults as it is for students. By acknowledging, assuring, and then allowing for cool-off time, the teacher can both teach and model more rational approaches to conflict management. Students need to learn that it is not wrong to have 'bad' feelings, nor are they 'bad' for having those feelings or displaying anger. They do need to learn to acknowledge their emotions and manage them. By directing them to cool-off time we say, in effect, 'I know you're upset (or angry), but I need to give you time to settle down before we can find out what the problem is and see what we can do to fix things up.'

Allow cool-off time.

• Take time for conflict resolution

When we direct squabbling or arguing students to cool-off time, we normally just ask them to sit separately for the rest of the lesson until we can bring them together for conflict resolution. 'Maria, I want you to sit over there. Cherie, I want you . . .' The teacher may need to show by nonverbal signals that she is not going to engage in discussion now. She puts up a gentle blocking hand as if to say, 'Yes, I know you are hurting and we'll sort it out later.' She'll direct Maria to take a tissue or two as she makes her way to the mat. Obviously, if there are any cuts or bruises, the student needs to go to the office or to the first aid teacher.

It is sometimes possible, later in the lesson, to send the two students into the corridor or library corner to do some problem solving. They ask each other:

- What do you see as the problem?
- How does it (the conflict) make you feel?
- What do you think we can do to fix things up?

Some teachers at Lower Primary use the problem-fixing table. The problem solving questions are written on a large card with cartoon pictures depicting the key issues. Students sit at a table facing each other with a three-minute eggtimer between them. They then ask each other (in turn) the three questions. Each waits until the other has had their say (the eggtimer times each 'turn' as the issues are focused on one-by-one).

Students are encouraged to work at a resolution and then share it with the teacher when they have finished. The teacher would preface this approach by asking, 'Do you want to work on this together?' If they look too rattled or protest that they need assistance from the teacher, the resolution process would need to be deferred until later. The teacher would then sit them down and work through similar questions.

I have often kept students back at the end of a lesson to work through an issue. 'Okay, Maria and Cherie, you had a problem before. Let's sit down and talk through what happened.' Often the students respond with a sheepish smile and say, 'Oh, it's all right now. We're friends again.' I followed up a hearty squabble with a couple of senior girls—a squabble that had involved some serious and protracted sulking. After class, one of them blithely said, 'We've broken up and made friends six times this week!'

Arguments and quarrels in class

When they do occur it is often over minor issues:

'She took (or "stole") my pen.' 'He won't let me use the red Texta.' 'She won't share.' 'He pushed in first.'

Sometimes (as in the example of the playground) it is a relationship problem. In the short-term, it is important for teachers to keep their managerial focus on:

- balancing the rights of others with the responsibility of those who are disruptive
- referring to rules or routines that protect rights
- avoiding long discussions about who started it (it is not always clear if there is a direct culprit).

The teacher can face the disputants directly and ask, 'What is the problem?' or 'What are you doing?' If they protest loudly and butt in on each other, the teacher can first block them by holding her hand up in a stopping motion: 'I'll listen when you speak in a normal voice' (sometimes this blocking sentence needs to be repeated). 'Okay, you first, Michael, then you, Sean.' After they've shared: 'Now what do you need to do to fix it?' If they can't think of anything, they can be directed to come up with solutions without any more arguing. 'Okay, I'll come back in a few minutes to see how you've gone.'

Students will know within the first week that if they continue to hassle and argue in this class the teacher will relocate them to work separately and they will have to stay back after class for problem-fixing time. This is the value of consistency in practice. If the problem looks too difficult to address there and then, remind them of the relevant class rule: 'You know our class rule for settling problems' and direct them to share. If they don't, the immediate or deferred consequences are made clear: 'If you continue to argue or . . . you'll have to work separately.' Sometimes it is appropriate to give this direction and then give them time to think about it. Some students respond to this as to a warning and settle down. If they do, we can come back later and acknowledge their on-task behaviour.

Any argument that involves aggressive behaviour will require immediate time-out for the aggressor, and follow-up with both parties later. Students soon grow accustomed to the fact that some teachers will not allow arguments or hostile behaviour in class, but will acknowledge the problem, affirm their feelings, and address their needs at an appropriate time.

To solve recurrent problems, the teacher can use classroom meetings as a way of engaging 'all' the students in conflict resolution (p 64). As with most management issues there needs to be a balance between:
- what we can do in the immediate short-term (when students are squabbling)
- what we can do long-term, after the heat has died down—resolving conflict, working through better ways to deal with the same problem next time, making alternative seat plans if necessary
- working with the whole class on preventive management by emphasising and developing co-operation; teaching social skills; exploring themes such as considering and caring for others; valuing others' contributions; using manners and better ways of solving problems. These themes can be explored through literature, drama, projects, and classroom meetings, and whenever positive social behaviour is observed by teachers it can be encouraged, commented on and reinforced (See McGrath and Francey, 1993).

Put-downs by students

. . . classroom banter and some gentle teasing is healthy.

The issue of put-downs by teaching staff has been noted earlier. When students use put-downs they often assume it's okay because he's my mate.' It is often a bad habit, especially with upper grade students, 'Gees! You're an idiot, *a dickhead, a slag, a moll, a skip.*' Racist terms are often used in this way, too. Sometimes the put-downs have vitriol and are clearly intended as abuse to hurt. In the immediate short-term, when the teacher hears the put-down, it needs to be addressed through the class/school rules and rights. A clear reminder, or very brief chat, is enough.

If it is bad habit or poor social skill, students still need to know it is unacceptable at this school. The reasons it is unacceptable should be explained to the class during the establishment phase of the year. Put-downs really concern the use of language, how people feel and the right to be treated with respect, whatever one's background. Put-downs can, and often do, hurt the recipient and while classroom banter and some gentle teasing is healthy, habitual use of '*fat slob*', '*drop kick*', '*shithead*', '*poofter*' and '*turd*' is totally unacceptable (at least in my value system).

Questions we need to ask ourselves as a staff are: Is it worth emphasising positive language? If so what do we mean by positive language and how do we, as teachers, model it? I've heard teachers call students '*dickhead*', '*drop kick*', 'stupid' and similar abusive terms! Describing a behavioural act as a stupid thing to do is different from calling a student 'stupid'.

1 If the put-down is quiet—sotto voce—and the recipient is apparently unoffended, a gentle reminder is enough. Direct students aside and let them know you heard it. Remind them, 'We have a class rule for respect. Remember to use it, thanks.' This can be done positively without drama—even pleasantly. If students say, 'He didn't mean it', or 'But he doesn't care if I call him a *poofter*', simply redirect to the essential point you are making and ask them to go back to their places. Avoid discussion, unless it is a one-to-one setting after class.

2 If the put-down is loud or aggressive, it helps to use an assertive voice that stops the class and focuses attention. Raise the voice and firmly direct the student. 'Craig! (pause)'. The pause here, after firmly speaking the student's name, registers that wounded silence that says, 'This is serious, folks.' Then give the statement: 'That's a put-down and put-downs hurt.' The assertive tone is controlled but unambiguous. Sometimes I refer to our rule for respect and remind them that offensive language is unacceptable here. 'Craig . . . we've got a rule for respect and I expect you to use it.' If a student protests, 'Yeah! But yer didn't hear what he said first, did yer?' 'No, I didn't hear what he (name the student) said, but what you said is a put-down.' If he then protests loudly, the teacher holds up a blocking hand to convey 'Stop', adding: 'Stop . . . I'll speak to you both later.' Then, eyeballing the whole class, the teacher can redirect the lesson, 'Okay, folks, back to work. The show's over.'

3 If the offending students persist, direct them to work separately or face time-out. It is pointless trying to have a whole-class debate on racism or put-downs or gender-inclusive language while emotions are running high. Save the classroom meeting for another time. The protagonists need cool-off time.

4 It is also unhelpful and unwise to force a public apology even when the student swears at the teacher. Forcing apologies while the student is emotionally aroused may gain an immediate victory, but it's likely to create unnecessary hostility—even revenge. Anyway, we can't make a student apologise. We cannot, in fact, make a student do anything. Strong-willed students will resist a teacher's attempts to make them apologise ('No! I'm not going to apologise to that bitch!'), creating even more conflict. In the 'public' arena of a classroom, acceding to a power struggle in this way only confirms the student's mistaken goal (Dreikurs 1982). If necessary, to save face for all, institute a time-out procedure and defer repairing, rebuilding and restitution. After cool-off time, most students are prepared to apologise when it is explained to them what apologies are, how they work and if the apology is being given to an adult, how they might do it.

SWEARING AND 'BAD' LANGUAGE

Teachers are hearing more bad language, put-downs, and swearing in classrooms these days (Rogers 1992). This may be partly due to the influence of television and the social acceptance of conversational swearing. It is not uncommon for teachers to walk past students in conversation who easily drop the *shit* and the 'f'—word, especially the participle form of 'f'—ing.

Different kinds of swearing?

Children, like some adults, swear differentially—some out of habit, especially when frustrated, some for effect, some to hurt others. If students come from homes where swearwords and poor or 'bad' language is commonplace, it will take some of them a while to accommodate and control their easy habituation to swearing. I've worked with colleagues who appear to have some problem with habituation too! This doesn't excuse students' language, but it helps to put it in perspective. Like many teachers, I've had parent conferences to discuss students' behaviour only to have the mum, dad, or de facto say, 'What the bloody hell's he been doing now?' I had a mum respond to a phone call I'd made about her son's behaviour with, '*Shit*! Don't tell me he's in trouble again!'

It helps to distinguish a dislike for certain swearwords and their association (as with blasphemy), from the social inappropriateness, the effect on others and finally, our response as teachers. Our response will be affected strongly by how we feel about the words, how we perceive them and what we believe about such word associations. Swearwords, of themselves, cannot hurt us unless we attribute special power to them. This is not to deny the managerial necessity of addressing swearing at school. However, we can be more functional if our response is not merely reactive.

I have seen teachers become physiologically aroused (clenched jaw, shoulders set, carotid arteries aquiver) at the overhearing of the 'f' word in the corridor or playground. I've seen teachers ascend to 'boil' on hearing students mutter '*shit*' sotto voce, as they walk away from a teacher. They then grab the student and demand to know, 'What did you say, eh?' (Do they really expect the student to reply?). Clearly this teacher couldn't distinguish face-to-face swearing from inappropriate ventilation of frustration. Such arousal is not merely the byproduct of words per se—more is at stake. Many students do not see such language as bad. Our job, as a school community, can be better served if we emphasise what positive language is and address swearing, bad, poor and inappropriate language in that light. In this sense, unacceptable language is explained within the context of how language works in terms of meaning and social effect. There are students who swear (in adult hearing or to an adult) for shock value (Dreikurs 1982). If we overreact, we will easily reinforce such a goal.

Swearing as personal attack or abuse is a different matter. Whether the swearing is directed between peers, or student to teacher, students need to understand that this is personal abuse. While language cannot really hurt us, we need to make it clear to students that:
• this kind of language is socially unacceptable

- it affects one's right to fair treatment
- there are better ways to communicate one's frustration and anger.

Managing swearing

The preventive focus is essential to all aspects of management. A common policy direction might include this statement: 'In this school we use positive language—language that helps us feel good about ourselves and others. This means no swearing or racist language, put-downs or sexist language.' It can be productive for grade teachers to discuss and teach this principle within the policy framework during the establishment phase of the year. The positive language focus can also be used when following up students after a swearing incident.

Incidental swearing

I've had a number of students at Lower Primary level use the word '*piss*' or '*shit*' with a totally straight face—no chagrin. I recall a Grade 1 boy (in my second year of teaching) squirmingly put up his hand to say, 'I gotta go to the *shits* bad!' (and he did).

It is pointless, unnecessary and damaging to relationships to preach at the student. I've heard the following on many occasions, 'I don't care what language you use at home, but you will not use that language here. Do you understand?'

The hostile index finger and the machine-gun voice are inappropriate. Attacking students' language via the home environment over which they have no real control is equally unacceptable. An attack on self-esteem and an exercise in public shaming achieve nothing worthwhile. It is possible to convey to students that their behaviour is inappropriate, wrong, and even bad, without communicating inherent badness to them. Again the principle of 'least intrusive' is important.

I have used humorous defusion with older students (pp 59-60). On hearing a frustrated 'Ohh, *shit*!' I start sniffing around the desk and winking, say 'Can't smell it, Jason.' A colleague recently shared the example of a bon mot to an older student who had used the *shit* word. 'We're not studying organic matter this week.' Most students apologise, grinning involuntarily. While working with a Grade 3 class, I heard a boy loudly exclaim, 'Holy *shit*!' He was struggling with an art activity. Had he been a Grade 6 student, I might have said, 'What denomination is that?' Instead I said, 'I can see you're frustrated, but we have a rule for good language. Now how can I help?' It is important for other students to hear this rule reminder and see me follow up with this student after class.

When students drop a social clanger, there is enough audience reaction of 'Oohh!' 'Ahh!' 'Did you hear what he said, Mr Rogers?' to convey social ineptness, and the teacher can always follow up later. As the student, described above, left the class, a few students wanted to talk about bad language. I did, briefly, by saying, 'Yes, we don't use that word. I'll speak to Sean later. Maybe he doesn't know.' We then returned to our work. I spoke to the student one-to-one about different words we can use and words we use here and it never happened again, at least in my hearing.

I've worked with a number of canteen volunteers (generally mums and grandmothers) who are annoyed by students dropping swearwords while lining up to purchase goodies at the canteen. Some of the canteen assistants admit to becoming angry and 'doing a banshee' out of the serving window, 'Oi! Don't you swear!' Then if students protest that they are 'only talking to each other and not to the canteen assistant', arguments start as secondary exchanges (p 128 ff).

Developing a whole-school approach to swearing around the school involves having a school-wide philosophy on positive language and mutual respect and then developing some common practices for dealing with them in the short-term. It was important to emphasise their managerial status to the mums who ran the canteen. Rather than simply use the term—the 'ladies in the canteen', they were given badges and renamed as canteen supervisors.

First, we discussed with the canteen supervisors the difference between conversational and frustration swearing ('*Shit,* Craig! Don't push in front of me!') and the personal abuse type of swearing. Most of the mums and grandmums admitted that the swearing they heard was the conversational or frustrational type. We discussed our feelings about that and what their characteristic responses were and whether such responses were productive.

Second, we looked at the issue from a preventive focus and held class meetings across the school on conduct around the school with respect to language use, especially in the canteen area. Grade teachers patiently explained to students why positive language is important and how some language, even just conversational swearing, makes people feel upset or annoyed. A general rule reminder card was made and placed in corridors and on the canteen wall, 'This is a positive language zone.'

Third, the canteen assistants as well as the groundsperson, cleaners and caretaker were invited to a mini-workshop on positive discipline. Emphasis was given to what we could do, and especially say, to students who were swearing (loud enough to hear) and behaviour such as pushing in line and dropping litter. The swearing, if audible, was dealt with by reminders:
'We have a rule for positive language. Let's use it, thanks.'
or
'This is a positive language zone. Let's remember that, thank you.'
The canteen supervisors would say this firmly, even pleasantly, to an individual or, if they were uncertain who it was, as a direction to the whole line of students, eyescanning them all. Then, rather than sustain conflict, they would distract from the group, eyeball the first student in line and take the order (take-up time). 'Okay, now you were first. Paul, isn't it? What do you want to buy?'

The hardest part of the exercise was encouraging an assertive/positive tone to the voice and body language. If students argued, 'We weren't talking to you. Gees! We're just talking to each other!' the canteen supervisors were encouraged to briefly redirect: 'Maybe you were, but this is a positive language zone. Remember that. Thanks.' They would then reclaim their serving role. If the student persisted with inappropriate or bad language, their name would be taken and referred to a senior teacher for an appropriate consequence. The key to the success of this managerial approach is that it is a whole-school emphasis involving all the parties. Within a few weeks, we saw a significant, almost complete, drop in swearing, at least in that setting.

All staff can remind about positive language anywhere in the school. Although none of us is foolish enough to believe that this will stop students swearing outside the school gates, it does enable students to think about how they use language at school.

Abusive swearing

As with any abusive behaviour, there needs to be a clear understanding of the infringement on, or damage to, another's right. In the immediate moment, if sworn at, the teacher can use an assertive statement:
'(Student's name) I don't speak like that to you. I don't want (or like) you to speak to me like that.'
or
'We have a rule for respect and I expect you to use it. That language is offensive and unacceptable.'

The tone needs to be unambiguously assertive without aggression and screaming or finger pointing. It is also unhelpful to follow the assertion with a mini-lecture, or to force apologies. An apology can be saved until after cool-off time. The teacher can then direct the student to continue their task, or if they are very disturbed, direct them to cool-off time. Older students can be directed just outside the door for a brief chat prior to time-out.

If the swearing is particularly offensive, aggressive and recurrent, the teacher should utilise the supported time-out procedure (p 87). Some schools use a suspension process for swearing at teachers. This needs to be considered carefully in the light of circumstances after appropriate cool-off time. If a student has a habit of reactive swearing it will be more effective to work in a longer-term behaviour contract (Rogers 1994 c) for positive language.

Caveat

Some teachers 'invite' aggressive responses from students. If a student is disruptive and a teacher comes over finger waving or extending the finger into the student's shoulder, or grabbing at their clothes, shouting at the student, 'Idiot—what are you? Didn't I tell you to put that packet of chips in the bin. Now give it to me!' a swearword from the student may be technically wrong, but it is understandable.

CONTRACTS: BEHAVIOUR AGREEMENTS

A contract is simply a way of formalising an agreement about responsible and desired behaviour on a one-to-one basis between teacher and student. Many students benefit from a structured approach within which their behaviour (in and out of the classroom) can be addressed.

Give time to the student

It is important that the initiating teacher, normally the grade teacher, makes a special time to focus on the student's problem behaviour. This time will need to be out-of-class time away from the student's peers. It may be possible to arrange for a colleague to supervise the class while the grade teacher engages the student in contract time. The tone and setting of this meeting needs to be pleasant, relaxed and non-judgmental. It can be helpful to give feedback about how the student might be feeling, 'You're probably feeling annoyed (upset, concerned, angry) at having to stay back like this, eh?' It is important to show that we understand without condoning their behaviour. 'After the student feels understood, she will be more willing to hear your point of view and then work on solutions' (Nelsen 1987, p 57). The student needs to sense that this is a supportive process not a punishment.

Focus on the behaviour

Keep the focus on the behaviour, without attacking the person. Use direct questions such as: 'Ask yourself this question, David:—What am I doing in class that's causing me problems?' It is important that the teacher give feedback here: 'Is what you're doing helping you in class?', 'Is it really okay within our class rules and rights?' Feedback should concentrate on the specific behaviour: both the disruptive behaviour and the on-task behaviour that the contract is addressing.
- How many times do you reckon you call out? butt in? seat wander?
- What do you do when we sit down to start activities?
- What do you do when it's time to come and sit on the mat?

Rudolf Dreikurs (1982) has demonstrated that students often behave within what he describes as 'mistaken-goals' (pp 13–26)—attention, power, revenge and withdrawal and that students' disruptive behaviour can often be seen (consciously or unconsciously) as their attempt to belong to their social group through this behaviour. It may be appropriate to use 'mirroring' and picture cues to demonstrate these goals to students as a way of identifying and clarifying what is happening when they call out, butt-in, wander, are lazy, argue . . . (p 125). Teacher modelling, if it's brief and illustrative, can be an effective way to convey the message to the student about what the behaviour 'looks' like (Rogers, 1994 c).

Students who regularly call out, wander around the room, and rock back in their chairs may stop when directed, but later start again. The student who needs constant reassurance often draws forth teacher over-servicing. Dreikurs indicates that, in terms of attention, the student is saying, in effect, 'I have a place only when people pay attention to me.' Teachers' emotional reactions to this kind of behaviour often indicate which of these 'goals' are operating.

For example, students who are stubborn, refuse to work or refuse to come inside when the bell goes, or regularly argue, often attract reactions from teachers such as anger, a clash of wills, counterresistance, even defeat. A student's goal, here, according to Dreikurs may be power—'You can't make me behave' and 'I'm important when I'm in a power struggle with my teacher, especially when my student peers see me do this.' Dreikurs argues that by understanding goal directed behaviour in students, teachers can increase their understanding of disruptive student behaviour and (by not giving too much attention, or feeding power by counter-power) can also help students to understand what is happening in their behaviour. They can then work with the teacher to find productive patterns of belonging.

As part of the behaviour change process, Dreikurs advocates that teachers first seek an awareness of the primary goal of misbehaviour and how the teacher is characteristically reacting or responding to that behaviour. An excellent text on this approach is *Maintaining Sanity in the Classroom: Classroom Management Techniques* (second edition 1982, see also Balson 1990).

This approach needs to be matched to the age and understanding of the student. It is most effective at Upper Primary level.

1 During the contracting session the teacher can ask: 'Do you know why you call out a lot in class? or wander? or rock?' Be specific about the behaviour described or modelled (p 125). Allow some time for response. Students often respond with, 'Dunno' or a shoulder shrug. Some argue a bit and say, 'I don't do that all the time!' The reply might be, 'No, that's true. But you do it a lot.' The teacher can even show a written frequency count of wandering, calling out or time off-task. The question, 'Why?' is normally not a useful question in management, but in this one-to-one setting it is used to provoke thought.

2 The teacher can then suggest in a supportive tone, 'Do you mind if I tell you why I think you don't sit on the mat or (name behaviour)?'

3 The next step involves the teacher hypothesising and identifying the likely goal: 'Could it be that . . .?' or 'I think that . . . Is that right?'

• If the suspected goal is attention, the teacher might say, 'Could it be that you want to keep me busy with you when you wander around the room? or that you want me to notice you a lot? or you want the group to notice you? or you want to get their attention by calling out a lot?'

• If the goal is power, 'Could it be that you want to be the boss? be in charge?' or 'Could it be that you want to show me that I can't stop you doing what you want?' (Give the specific, behavioural example.)

• If the goal is revenge, 'Could it be you want to hurt me? the group? your parents, the school?' or 'You want to show me how it feels. You want to get even.'

• If the goal is assumed inadequacy and social withdrawal, 'Could it be you feel you can't do anything and you're afraid to fail so you don't even want to try?'

After goal disclosure—the teacher's attempt to point out the primary goal of their disruptive behaviour—it is important to allow some waiting time. Some students give a simple, 'Yes', some a sigh, most a nonverbal reflex such as a smile or knowing nod that says, 'I know you know that I know.' If the student says, 'No' the teacher can simply add, 'Well I thought that was the reason you refused to do the work. If it isn't, do you have a reason you know that you can share?' (This is obviously more effective with older students.) If a child displays a 'recognition reflex' the teacher can add, 'I thought that was why you . . .'

4 This goal disclosure then becomes the basis for the teacher's contractual plan with the student. 'We all like (want) attention, Craig. I'd like to work on a plan for you to get attention in a way that doesn't upset others or make it hard for me to give everyone the help they need.'

For students who are into power struggles, it is helpful (and a surprise to the student) to let them know that you (the teacher) cannot actually make them do what is right, or what is appropriate, or do the work, or even, simply obey teachers. Admission of this fact is not a weakness by the teacher but a strength. It can become the basis for teacher–student co-operation in making a plan for behaviour change. It is also important to discuss the consequences of the student choosing not to co-operate with the teacher and the need for a behaviour plan (p 151), with an emphasis on supporting better behavioural choices rather than threatening the student.

Encouragement

It is essential to build encouragement into the plan. To minimise over-servicing of attention-seeking behaviour such as whining and calling out, teachers can reflect on how much of the student's behaviour can be tactically ignored. The teacher can explain to the student why particular behaviour is ignored. On-task behaviour can be affirmed, acknowledged and encouraged by the teacher with a visible feedback mechanism. 'Let's see if we can go from ten callings-out to five this week (wink). I'll keep a check—you can too, on this little card.' The student has the same record card as the teacher. The key, of course, is to give acknowledgment for appropriate behaviour. At the end of each day, then weekly, have a brief feedback session, that focuses on:
• what part of our plan is easiest? hardest?
• what areas can we improve, change, modify? or even
• do we still need to keep this plan going?

It can also be helpful to have a class meeting focusing on behavioural issues and linking the discussion to goals. Why do some people choose to frequently butt in? wander out of their seat? call out in question time? sit away from others? lie? steal others' property? Avoid focusing on the individual student. Instead, focus on exploring why people generally behave in these ways.The grade teacher can use this feedback in the one-to-one behaviour contract.

Di Gossen (1992) suggests involving student collaboration by discussion along these lines—You don't have that behaviour for no reason. You learnt it somewhere, some place. Can you work out another way of behaving that works well and doesn't cause hassles or problems for others? By inviting students to co-operate we increase their sense of ownership of the plan.

The plan

The plan is simply an expression of what the teacher and the student contract (agree) together. This can be a checklist, a written plan, or maybe even a pictorial representation (p 153 ff). It needs to be simple, achievable, and focused again on the 4Rs—rights, rules, responsibilities and routines. Most importantly, it needs to be expressed *behaviourally*: *What* do you agree to do? Is it *achievable*? *How* will you do it? Explain it to me. What help can I give? How will you follow your plan on days when you feel 'ratty', and annoyed and don't feel like working?

The plan can be expressed as: I need to *stop* this specific type of behaviour. I need to *start* this specific type of behaviour. It may be as basic as: I need to stop calling out or butting in during question time and I need to start putting my hand up without calling out, clicking my fingers or grunting. The teacher can then encourage the preferred behaviour in class.

The plan may be more involved, such as: I need to stop going to sharpen my pencil several times, and getting out of my seat to get a pen or ruler. I need to start . . .' For example, it may involve a set activity and include a set time-on-task focus (five, eight, ten minutes) and how this will be achieved. It may be appropriate to rehearse the plan (p 156). Certainly there should be some discursive rehearsal, 'Let's go over it again. Do you know what your plan is and how it will work in class?' It is also important to clarify with students:
• where their copy of the plan will be kept
• how they can self-check their plan during the day.

The teacher can also add some positive self-talk into the plan for older students, the emphasis being that thinking is a special kind of behaviour that can help or hinder our performance.

BEHAVIOUR-ALLY DISORDERED (BD) STUDENTS

In many schools there is a small percentage (one to five per cent) of students whose disruptive and disordered behaviour has a significantly detrimental effect on the school's social fabric (Wragg 1989, Morgan and Jenson 1988, Rogers 1994 c). They create a lot of emotional strain for the grade teacher, but they are just as much of a pain for the specialist teacher because their disruptive behaviour is not normally situation specific.

Behaviour can be defined as disordered if it is:
• frequent
• intense (When Jason 'wanders' or is motorically restless he does so frequently and loudly, annoying others en route. He snatches things, pushes others' work, purposely bumps into them.)

- of significant duration—both the episode and the timespan (Such students are often as disruptive on Friday as they are on Monday.)
- resistant to normal classroom discipline
- general (not affected by where the student is in the school).

A student with this behaviour profile may be said to be *behaviourally* disordered notwithstanding any 'causative pathology' or learning disability (Rogers 1992, 1994 c).

Collegial support

When a clear behavioural profile has emerged, with factors such as those noted earlier from grade and specialist teachers as well as aides, then it behoves the school to actively support the colleague in whose class this student is enrolled. Such support needs to be given without imputation of failure—any teacher who has had such a student knows how draining they can be.

A behaviour management plan for such students needs to be based on a collegial, team approach. Teachers who have BD students on their class roll need a lot of support.

Collegial support is expressed through:
- moral support, problem solving—most of all, by senior staff (administration) ensuring that no imputation of blame is shafted home to grade teachers
- a small team working with the grade teacher to develop a program for behaviour change for the BD student
- support for grade teachers in their relationship with parents or caregivers
- a well structured exit/time-out policy to support grade and specialist teachers
- structured release time from class being given to teachers to do some one-to-one behaviour rehearsal. (Behaviour rehearsal is a process that actively teaches new behaviour to students through modelling, cueing and rehearsal techniques.)

While BD students have a right to education in mainstream schools, that right has to be balanced with the rights of their peers to learn without persistent (sometimes bizarre) interruptions and displays of unsafe and aggressive behaviour. It is also essential to consider the welfare of the grade teacher. If it is known at the student's enrolment that there is a history of disordered and disruptive behaviour, it is essential that a support process be set up as a condition of that student's enrolment. Under Education Department guidelines the enrolment of students with disabilities and/or special needs, normally requires an enrolment support group, composed of parent or caregiver, parent advocate, grade teacher, head teacher and relevant professional support staff. I have seen too many teachers unfairly stressed by the unsupported arrival in their class of a student whose behaviour is clearly way outside the normal range of disruptiveness. Worse, the advent of support comes when the teacher has reached breaking point— the outcome of weeks of unnecessary suffering.

Parent support

Wherever possible, the school will be looking for, encouraging, and building bridges of support with parents or caregivers of BD students. Many parents are supportive of programs like behaviour recovery (Rogers 1994 c) and even introduce at home the contracting and behaviour management plans used at school. Unfortunately, some parents disclaim all involvement with BD students' behaviour at school:

- 'She was all right until she came here!'
- 'How come she was all right at the last twenty schools she's been at, eh?!'
- 'It's all the other students' fault!'
- 'It's the teacher's fault.'

  This accusation is rarely true. This is why colleagues must be united in planning a whole-school approach to behaviour management plans for BD students. Art, music and physical education teachers as well as teacher aides, can all contribute to a behaviour profile to be used as ammunition—no, sorry, evaluative feedback to Jason's mum, dad or . . .
- 'You can hit him if you like—that's what he needs—a good kick up the pants!'
- 'You can do what you like to her as long as she's breathing when you send her home!'

The standard line in response to this is, 'In our school we' and refer positively to what our school policy on behaviour management stands for. If written in user-friendly language, such a policy is a powerful focus for parent-school liaison when discussing student behaviour.

When working with hostile or intransigent parents, we need to assure them that:
- we are partners in their students' education and life at school
- behaviour management programs are designed to enable their students to increase their on-task learning and gain success out of their school experience
- this program is also designed to increase the student's social relationship skills such as co-operation, consideration and care for others.

Developing a collegial plan for behaviour-disordered students

The primary purpose of a plan or program for BD students is to increase their self-control skills and enable their social integration at school.

Because these students seem resistant to normal correction and social observation of appropriate behaviour, they benefit from behaviour plans that specifically teach them how to:
- move through the room without disturbing others
- sit on the mat during group time instead of rolling around or sitting away from others and making silly noises
- put their hands up without calling out or 'constantly' butting in
- speak in a normal voice during on-task time
- put their hand up instead of calling out, yelling out, or . . .
- sit on their chair 'four on the floor' without frequent rocking
- use positive, respectful language such as 'please', 'thank you', 'excuse me' when moving through others' personal space, instead of pushing past others, annoying, touching and interfering, or using inappropriate hostile language (swearing, cursing, put-downs).

Developing an effective behaviour plan

1 It is important that the grade teacher develop a profile of BD behaviour (p 149) as a basis for planning for behaviour change. Teachers should be sympathetic to, and aware of, students' emotional pathology and home environment, but while BD students are at school, the focus emphasises teaching them appropriate social behaviour and academic survival skills (Morgan and Jenson, 1988). What may seem basic and simple to other students may be outside the BD student's experience.

2 Make the plan specific, simple and achievable.
 It should:
 • identify the off-task behaviour
 • explain to students why the behaviour is inappropriate or wrong
 • explain how their behaviour affects the class and school rules
 • fundamentally, show how the BD students' behaviour is affecting their peers.

There is little point in describing off-task behaviour in general terms like laziness, rudeness, argumentativeness and attention-seeking. A behaviour-change plan needs to target *how* students seek attention, or are lazy or rude, how often and when they behave this way. How many times do they call out? Is it worse when they are on the mat or during on-task time? Are they worse on any particular day? Sometimes students are more ratty, off-task, and emotionally out-of-it on Monday after the de facto has shoved a dysfunctional oar into an already strained home life. It can help if the grade teacher keeps an observation profile of a BD student prior to embarking on a special program. A daily journal can give a characteristic profile of a student's disruptive behaviour in terms of frequency, seriousness, time-of-day etc.

3 Include release time for grade teacher and the BD student to effect one-to-one behaviour recovery. The grade teacher will have negotiated release time within the constraints of the timetable and the amount of support available from colleagues. The working ideal is that a colleague takes the class for 15-20 minutes while the BD student and grade teacher withdraw to work through the behaviour plan. In small schools, the principal usually covers for a teacher.

Staff need to consider the normal ethical constraints and considerations of one-to-one work with students, especially if the grade teacher is male and the student is female—though most BD students are male (Rogers 1994 c). A suitable place in an appropriate environment needs to be available. It helps to have a student's table or desk and a few chairs for the rehearsal of appropriate on-task behaviour.

Step 1 Clarify the off-task behaviour for the student. One way to enhance the communication process is through the use of picture cues and mirroring techniques.

The teacher can prepare an A4-sized card, illustrating the student's off-task and required on-task behaviour. These simple line illustrations can depict the student surrounded by peers showing both social disapproval and approval (see *Figure 6a* and *Figure 6b*).

Figure 6a

Figure 6b

The BD student should be able to recognise the off-and on-task behaviour in the pictures.

Teacher: 'Have a look at this picture here, Craig. Who do you think this student is?'

Student: 'Is it me?' (He looks at his name.)

Teacher: 'It is. What are you doing in this picture?' (It is unhelpful to ask *why* at this stage, especially with Lower-Primary-aged students.) 'What is our rule for . . .? (Check if the student knows the rule that relates to this disruptive behaviour. Explain how this specific, pictorially represented behaviour affects the rule.)

Teacher: 'Have a look at the faces of the other students near you. What can you tell me about their faces?' (Briefly discuss social disapproval—other students in the picture look upset because they don't like it when the student behaves in the way shown in the picture.)

It can be helpful if the teacher shows students what their loudness, rocking movement patterns, and calling out look and sound like. The teacher's modelling of the off-task behaviour acts like a mirror (p 125). It is important that the teacher ask the student's permission first. 'Do you mind if I show you what it looks like when . . . ?' or 'how loud you are in class?' This should be done supportively, not sarcastically or in an attempt to embarrass. It is helpful to mirror the behaviour spatially, apart from where the teacher is sitting, as if the teacher is stepping 'out-of' the adult role into the 'student' role. After the mirroring, the teacher can reclaim the sitting adult role. Some students laugh at a teacher's 'mirroring', especially if it involves rolling on the mat making silly noises. This is normal—it may arise from embarrassment, even anxiety at seeing how stupidly funny they look. If a student is particularly loud or has raucous bad language, a teacher can use a tape-recording as a 'mirror' and play it back.

Keep the mirroring brief. Here the teacher can point to the vacant space. 'That's what your behaviour looks and sounds like, Craig.' The teacher then sits down to refocus the student's attention on the illustrated card. 'Have a look at the second picture. What are you doing in this picture, Craig?' Discuss the social approval of the now happy faces in the background of the second picture (see *Figure 6a*).

Step 2 Introduce and model the plan. 'I want to work with you on a plan to help you with your behaviour in class. Look—(the teacher shows the on-task picture)—a plan to help you to . . . (teacher describes the desired behaviour).' Explain why the plan is important, how it will help the student, and how it will elicit peer approval.

'I know you can do this. Let me show you how loud I want you to speak at your table in class.' The teacher then models the target behaviour. 'You can do that can't you?' While modelling, for example, sitting at the desk in on-task time, the teacher can think aloud, 'I'm sitting four on the floor, I'm pushing my chair in, and I have my eggtimer. As soon as the sand has run down in my eggtimer I'll put my hand up, without calling out, and my teacher will come over and check my work.' This modelling is important, as it clarifies the desired behaviour visually. Refer the student, again, to the second picture on the card. 'Just like this, Craig' (see *Figure 6a*).

155

Step 3 Rehearsal. If sitting on the mat during group time is the target behaviour (for Preparatory level or Grade 1), the teacher shows the student how to go to the mat first thing in the morning or from the door when returning from recess or from his table. The next step is to encourage the student to copy. 'Okay, your turn now, Craig. Show me how you can sit on the mat, just as you can see in the picture, and just as I showed you.' The picture becomes his aide-memoire. Rehearsal is crucial to behaviour recovery. In effect, if a plan cannot be rehearsed, it may not be a workable plan. During rehearsal the teacher comments on, and finetunes, the student's approximation to the on-task plan. Rehearsal clarifies the task, aids short-term memory, and builds a bond of assurance—the teacher can see that the student is able to behave in the desired way and understand why it is important. Rehearsal also aids recall when the student is back in the 'natural-setting' of the classroom or playground.

Torgenson and Goldman (1977) have noted that learning-disabled students 'both recalled less and rehearsed less than normal students'. When the learning-disabled students could be induced to rehearse, they recalled as well as normal students (Wragg, 1989 p 54). It is our experience that BD students significantly benefit from behaviour rehearsal in much the same way (Rogers, 1994 c).

DEVELOPING A BEHAVIOUR PLAN

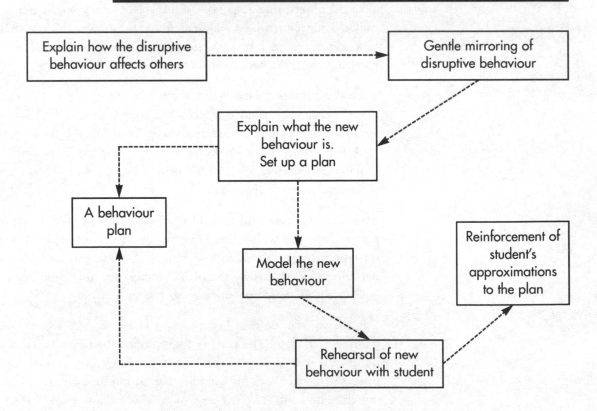

Figure 7 © Bill Rogers 1995

Step 4 Implementing the plan in the natural setting of the classroom or playground. Students are given a copy of the plan, reduced from A4 to half A4 size. They are asked if they would like to keep it in their locker or even on their table/desk, and check it several times during the day.

During class time, the teacher looks for the student's approximations to the plan, and gives encouragement accordingly. This may be as basic and simple as the okay sign, a smile with 'Good on you. I'm pleased to see that' or a pat on the arm with 'Good to see you've remembered four on the floor.'

It may be appropriate to use reward schedules to begin the process. Have places on the contract card where teacher or student can tick boxes. These marked boxes act as a primary reinforcer (see *Figures 6a* and *6b*). They can be exchanged later for stickers, free time activity or even a canteen voucher. Because rewards may be seen as bribery by some teachers—rather than behaviour enhancement outcomes—staff discussion should consider whether this ought to be a feature of the program. The ticks can simply be rewards in themselves. 'This is how many times I caught you sitting on the mat doing your plan. Well done, Craig.'

Once a week, the teacher has a feedback session with the student: 'What part of the plan was easiest?—hardest? How can we make the plan even better? What can we work on next?' All corrective management will focus on the plan. 'What is your plan for? What are you supposed to be doing?' The student can be shown the teacher's copy of the plan during corrective management in the classroom.

Supporting the recovery process

- It is important that all specialist teachers have a copy of the behaviour recovery plan and are aware of its purpose.
- There will be a supported, well-planned exit, time-out plan for hostile and aggressive students. They need to know that time-out doesn't invalidate their plan. Whenever they are in a classroom, the teacher expects students to work by their plan.
- Specialist teachers and teacher aides are also aware of special time-out support for students.
- The grade teacher can enhance the success of a behaviour plan by calling a special classroom meeting to raise key questions with the BD student's peers. For example:

  What is it about Craig's behaviour that upsets, concerns, annoys you?

  Why do you think he does X, Y or Z?

  What do you think we, as a class, can do to help him?

It would be appropriate to have the BD student out of the room working in a colleague's room while the meeting is going on. However, the BD student should be given feedback about the meeting by the teacher.

The grade teacher can also nominate a couple of students to act as peer encouragers or plan helpers. The BD student is asked, 'Which of these two students would you like to help you with your plan?' The chosen student then sits near, or with, the target student to prompt, remind, assist and encourage. The teacher explains this 'job-profile' to the willing peer helper.

- The plan can be enhanced by teaching self-talk skills, especially to older students: 'I can put my hand up without calling out. I can speak in a quiet voice. I can . . .' These 'I can' messages are taught using the same modelling and rehearsal skills noted earlier (see also Downing 1986 and Wragg 1989).

The team supporting the grade teacher can review the plan—weekly at first, then fortnightly, to see if there is any significant approximation by the student to the desired behaviour.

Many students respond to positive behaviour management plans or contracts. When they don't, and a reasonable time for change (with due support) has been allowed, the school needs to consider whether the continued stress and strain of repeatedly disruptive behaviour is unduly affecting the rights and welfare of other students and staff. In this case, with appropriate documentation, senior staff will consider the BD student's future placement in the school and what alternative options are open. It is essential that the local and regional sections of the Department of Education are made fully aware of what is happening and support the school in its formal application regarding the workable options.

Summary

A behaviour management plan is a contractual arrangement designed to support a student's positive behaviour. It should be simple, clear, achievable (a few kinds of behaviour at a time), be planned to increase the likelihood of success, and written in a style appropriate to the student's age and development. All key stakeholders need to be involved in the plan and the grade teacher needs adequate support to set up and administer the plan or program.

'REPUTATION' CLASS

Every teacher has had some experience of a harder than average class. The perception of how hard it is may be relative to one's experience, but it is no less hard for that. Sometimes the class has a reputation of its own. Everybody knows—even if they don't admit it—that this class is difficult.

In some cases, such classes are skewed to new teachers in the school or, worse, to beginning teachers. It's not enough that some first-year teachers have to negotiate a new school, or even the culture of teaching itself, but they then have to cop a hard class—the one with the dreadful reputation that nobody wants.

The nature and personality of the class, as a group, may have come about by poor establishment at the beginning of the year. Having worked with many such classes as a consultant, I've noticed that basics such as clearly published rules and routines, workable noise levels and seating plans have not always been carefully taught and monitored, nor has the teacher catered for mixed abilities.

I've also noticed that individual students have been allowed to become significant problems because early follow-up has not occurred. Lack of support by senior staff in the face of a recognisable, emerging problem, also contributes to the 'downward spiral'. The absence of a supportive culture in the school for problem-solving on issues of behaviour management is a major source of stress (Rogers 1992).

In such a climate, the grade teacher is probably flat out using all available energy to survive. The climate is aggravated still further, by colleagues who make comments behind a teacher's back such as, 'Those kids (or '*Your* kids' to the teacher's face) in Grade 6 are the worst behaved bunch of . . . I've ever seen. If I had them, I know what I'd do. I didn't have any problems with them last year.' Some senior staff 'help' by coming into a noisy, disruptive class to read the riot act for five minutes. 'You pack of animals you . . .! I can hear you from my office! Who the hell do you think you are, eh?' While it is possible to shout a robust Grade 6 into submission, it does nothing for the grade teacher's morale, or the possible re-establishment of the group by that teacher. To add insult to injury, some senior teachers then (once the class is quiet) walk out of the room past the teacher with the parting words, 'That's how you deal with them.' The response must surely be, 'Yeah, great help. Thanks! That's not really the support I wanted.'

The hard-class syndrome may be the result of a poor teacher–student relationship caused by difficulties such as these:
- A teacher who didn't want this particular age group—say one who has taught largely infant grades and has been given a senior class or vice versa. This scenario can be avoided by thoughtful preventive planning and staff negotiation.
- A class which takes out their corporate frustration on a teacher who is not like their old teacher. I've worked with teachers who have had to take over a class midway through the year, only to face the group angst of a class at missing their old teacher.

I've also seen teachers successfully turn such classes around by thoughtful use of classroom meetings, explaining to the class that:
- they (their new teacher) can understand how the students might be feeling at losing their old teacher
- that their new teacher can't be the same as the last one. There has to be a new beginning, however hard it is to let go. The new teacher's job is to make sure that students act in a safe, responsible way; that we work co-operatively together and support the learning programs in this classroom; that we all understand and support the rights and rules, and fulfil our responsibilities.

It helps to know what the previous teacher's management and discipline procedures were, and if appropriate to re-invent them by re-establishing them with the group.
- It is important to explain at this meeting that their current behaviour (be specific without being derogatory) cannot be allowed to continue and that

their co-operation is required in particular ways. Again, be specific.

- It helps to have a senior teacher (who gets on well with the class) present at this meeting for moral support and to lend credibility to the agreed outcomes. These outcomes will be written up as 'our class plan'.

If the class is too disruptive and unwilling to co-operate, the teacher needs to clarify the unambiguous rules and consequences (the bottom line) and proceed towards co-operation from there. Again, a senior teacher needs to be present at such a meeting, not to threaten and diminish the new teacher's authority, but to give genuine support in running the meeting.

The aim of this special classroom meeting is to give the class and the new teacher an opportunity to find out how, why, and where the group is going wrong; to re-establish the rights, rules, responsibilities and consequences, and set some goals for future success. How open or closed such a meeting is, will depend on the group's co-operation and the comfort zone of the teacher. Using the 1, 3, 6 method, individual students write down their concerns and recommendations on their own for ten minutes, then share with a group of three for ten minutes, then the three join with a group of six. After 25–30 minutes, a representative from each group shares their feedback with the whole class. No feedback is allowed to be derogatory or aimed at putting others down. Explain and enforce this. If the feedback is likely to be too personal, the teacher can consider letting the students note it in private correspondence.

Another option is to have a colleague take the class and the grade teacher conducts mini-meetings in another room with three randomly selected students at a time. The outcome of the meeting should be a re-establishment of the class and a workable action plan. It can help to publish the outcome of the meeting. There should be an evaluation meeting with the class four to six weeks down the track, perhaps using the evaluation questions noted earlier (p 27).

Collegial support

The primary aim of any procedures to deal with a hard class is to emphasise staff welfare. While the learning rights of students are essential, those rights cannot be enjoyed if the grade teacher or specialist is not given adequate support. That support should be aimed at developing a common, consistent action plan for the management of the class.

If a teacher recognises the hard-class syndrome, that this is more than just a challenging class, it is essential that the support of colleagues be sought as early as possible. If teachers think it is heroic to struggle on alone, or believe it is weakness to admit there is a struggle, or think that others will think they are weak (if they admit . . .) they will only cause emotional damage to themselves and the class. Even an apparently unresponsive bureaucracy will come to the aid of teachers if an effort is made to explain and describe their experience with this group during the last two or three weeks.

Problem-solving support

1 Are there any ringleaders or powerbrokers in the group? any particular 'sub-terrorist' groupings we can enrol in other classes? One of the benefits of composite classes or vertically grouped classes is the structural freedom to move students who have carved a power niche in a particular class. Moving a student, or even a few students, is a drastic measure but may be necessary occasionally. It helps to offer such students the choice of co-operation or . . .

2 Is seating organisation a problem in the room? Are there any particular routines contributing to disruptive behaviour? It may help to invite a trusted colleague into the class, at key times, to observe the behaviour of the class and use such observations in the ongoing problem solving and action planning. This teamwork needs adequate support by senior administration.

3 It can help to place key powerbrokers or disruptive students on behaviour contracts. It is appropriate to give the grade teacher time-release opportunity to do some behaviour recovery with the most disruptive students. If the teacher does not feel adequate to the task of working with behaviourally disordered students one-to-one, the school can appoint a contract supervisor to set up such a process with targeted students.

4 At a purely preventive level, it may help to use a team-teaching approach to begin the establishment phase with a difficult group. A teacher who knows the bulk of the students, and who has their respect, can help the new teacher to establish credibility by proxy, as it were. The team partner need not stay all day, every day, but it is important to be there in the first critical days or at critical times in the day. The support colleague can leave quietly after the first half hour or so. Such a process is commonplace in a wide range of professional settings outside teaching.

5 It is essential to have a positive, planned, serviceable time-out procedure available if the teacher of the difficult class needs to use it (p 82).

6 It is important to encourage grade teachers to work on positive behaviour management practices (Chapters 2, 3 and 5) and support them in follow-up with difficult students.

7 It is also important to consider issues like curriculum delivery and mixed ability in the group. Some schools, even primary schools, still practise selective streaming, a process that does little to enhance the self-esteem of those who have difficulties in literacy, numeracy and learning generally. While ability nurturing through partial withdrawal is educationally productive, segregated grouping based on ability is likely to increase behaviour problems.

I conducted a problem-solving meeting with a composite Grade 5/6 a few years back and the major complaints from the students were: boards full of writing (all we do is copy work and worksheets), little project work, no small-group or co-operative work, no conferencing of work and few class games. I could see their point.

8 It may be appropriate to use group reinforcement strategies (Rogers, 1990 a). The class is divided into teams, each with a leader. In upper grades, the

161

team leaders are selected through secret ballot by class members. Explain what the basic qualities of a team leader are. Write them on a card. Ask each class member to write on a piece of paper the names of two students in the class who, they think, would make an excellent team leader. After the nomination papers are collected, the teacher sorts out the names which occur most frequently and these become the team leaders for the next week.

The team leaders choose their team with the teacher. This process is carried out privately with the teacher while the rest of the class works on a set activity. The leaders select team members from a class list (one at a time to guarantee equal distribution) until all students are allocated to a team leader.

The teacher then reads out the teams, with the leaders, and they are published on a chart. It is explained that each team will later sit and work together. They need to elect a noise monitor and a materials monitor. The leader's job is to help the group to co-operate, work by the fair rules published on a card and do their best work. Each group can work towards BOEs— behaviour outcome enhancements. The more cynical call them rewards!

BOEs ranging from ten points to one hundred can be written up on a chart. Ten equals an energy enhancer (jelly bean, shared packet of crisps or some other delicacy!) for each member of the team. Thirty equals a canteen voucher. Fifty equals a time-release BOE which allows the team to play a board game at the teacher's discretion. One hundred points equals a free activity for a whole timetable slot, negotiated with the teacher.

Points are allocated to each group for on-task work, co-operative behaviour, working by class rules etc. Points are not taken off for poor behaviour. The group simply earns no BOEs. The strength of this approach lies in the initial novelty and the emphasis on group reinforcement. It should be a short-term program of four to six weeks, to be replaced by planned co-operative learning strategies (see Dalton 1985; Hill and Hill 1989).

I have seen very difficult classes, at both junior and senior levels, come out of a self-defeating spiral of low expectation in less than a week, using this approach. Like any strategy, though, it needs to be well-planned, preferably with collegial support in the establishment phase (see Rogers 1990 a; Barrish, Saunders and Wolf 1969; Brown et al 1974; McCarthy et al 1983; Wilkes 1981).

Caveat

Some teachers have a strong philosophical and educational objection to reward technologies, behaviour modification or outcome enhancements. Such objections need to be taken seriously, as they work against successful, short-term, use of such programs. A group-based program such as that outlined here, can be successfully conducted without so-called tangible rewards. I have found, however, that with very difficult classes the BOEs are a positive kick-start for a class that has experienced labelling, a lot of understandable negative comment and a downward spiral of low expectation.

Chapter 7

MANAGING PLAYGROUND BEHAVIOUR /BULLYING

It's cold. There's a brisk southerly nipping at your ears and you're out there with students who are running, yelling and playing. As you cup your hands around the mug of tea and walk and scan the playground:
- you see a student in an out-of-bounds area (What do you say or do?)
- a student is surreptitiously pulling a branch off a tree (What do you say or do?)
- a student comes up, whining, 'Miss, they took my ball, Miss!'
- you see a couple of boys running into the toilet, loudly yelling. It looks suspicious (What should you do?)
- you see a couple of boys karate kicking each other, and grinning, drawing an audience (What should we do about overly testosteronic play?).

And so it goes. Welcome to playground duty! It's harder, of course, on the very hot days when there's a northerly wind, or when it's drizzling but not wet enough for the wet-day timetable.

If you're a Grade 1 teacher, you may feel a little intimidated by the big boys who cast aspersions on your management role, 'You're just a Grade 1 teacher!' If there is one area of management that needs a whole-school approach it's playground management—in fact, any duty-of-care role outside the classroom:
- wet-day supervision when you are required to supervise students you may not know
- corridor duty
- bus duty
- swimming, excursions, school camps.

Playground safety— considering others

In the establishment phase of the year, grade teachers will discuss with their classes what playing safely means:
- playing in assigned areas
- playing in a way that does not harm others
- playing ball games at the right time and in the right place (lunchtime, not 'little play')
- finishing food before going on play equipment
- allowing only Kinder and Prep students on play equipment on assigned days, or having a special playground for Prep students (those students in their first year at school)
- using play equipment only in fine weather.

Duty of care outside the classroom

Duty of care outside the classroom is a crucial area of behaviour management. Once students leave their classrooms, they leave a reasonably ordered, defined, governed structure. There are clear routines and rules and there is always the visible presence of the teacher in the classroom. Once in the playground, students are 'free'—they run, jump and play. We can all remember that sense of release once we hit the exit door and fresh air. Of course, students are more free in the playground to engage in unsafe play, drop litter, play in undesignated areas, spit, tease and swear. Students do not always exhibit the same social probity in the playground as they do in the classroom.

For ordinary members of the community, a duty of care is normally owed to others to refrain from doing things that could reasonably be considered capable of causing injury. The law does not usually attempt to make persons liable for a failure to do something positive, such as going to someone's assistance. It is different, however, if a person is placed in some position of responsibility for another. A duty of care may then be owned, not only to refrain from injury-creating activities, but to take steps to protect that person from injury. Such a responsibility applies in respect of a teacher's duty to a student (Boer and Gleeson 1982, p 124).

This applies even more now, when some schools have had the frightening experience of prowlers, when bullying has become a national issue of debate, when students often arrive at school very early and are involved in after-school programs. It is essential to have a duty-of-care policy that is whole-school—not just for teachers either—there are many support staff in a school who have a right to address student behaviour (cleaners, groundspersons, canteen staff).

Duty of care means just that. We have a duty to care, especially for Infant students in that significant socialising year. It is always a massive social step for a student who is barely five years of age to engage with a mass of seemingly disordered bodies, on asphalt, grass, sand and play equipment. Who goes first on the equipment?—those who are bigger, stronger, older? Who goes first to the drink taps and toilets? Who has access to the games areas? What are the rules 'out here'? Of course, the 'old hands' have worked all this out. Some schools assist this socialising process by using a buddy system for Preparatory, Reception and new students. The buddy shows them around, plays alongside them and shows them the ropes.

If the policy is to involve all staff, then we need to engage all staff in professional development, policy formation, preferred practices and referral procedures. We need to ask whether it matters how students are spoken to and disciplined by support staff. Is it appropriate for a groundsperson or canteen supervisor to utilise consequences for disruptive behaviour? If so, how? Should they walk past disruptive incidents, ignore them, or simply refer the issue to a teacher? If students hear support staff addressing them in the same manner as regular staff, they may think twice about behaving in ways they 'think they can get away with because real teachers aren't here'.

It is important for principals as well as teaching staff to do regular playground duty—the same goes for wet-day duty and bus duty. It gives them the opportunity to have regular first hand experiences of social behaviour in a duty-of-care setting, and gives some collegial empathy and understanding as well. It is also fair.

Many schools introduce support staff to all students at a public assembly in the establishment phase of the year. Name tags are sometimes used to give a visible credibility to their role. Support staff can also be encouraged to use the preferred practice approach (p 30 ff) within their duty-of-care role and work out the typical behaviour they note and how to address it (p 201). Even bus drivers can be more supportive of the school policy by identifying the behavioural issues and coming up with a plan (with staff) that better reflects school aims (p 176).

Increasing consistency

The key emphasis of duty of care is that teachers support students' behaviour in ways that enhance safety, health, and fair treatment. The emphases of discipline planning noted earlier are just as important in the playground and corridors as in the classroom. I have observed the phenomenon of teachers leaving their classroom with an understandable sense of, 'I've finished my management role until the class bell goes!' Then they walk down the corridor unseeing, unhearing. They miss the student pushing another over. They miss the silly play fighting just outside the exit door (after all, they're on their way to the staffroom). They ignore the student pulling a small branch off a tree, and the Grade 6 girls swearing. 'Oh well,' I've heard teachers say, 'why should I get involved? I'm not on duty.'

Once we leave our classroom, there is a sense in which we are always on duty, even if it is simply the word of reminder en route to the cuppa. Most duty-of-care management in this sense is 'least intrusive'—the brief reminder, direction or even nonverbal signal. Where staff have this active commitment to duty of care, even when off duty, it is more likely that students will respond to our reminders about positive behaviour.

During a recent playground supervision, I came back towards the staffroom across a covered concrete area, and observed a couple of male teachers apparently ignoring two Grade 6 boys who were karate kicking. Is it just a case of 'boys will be boys', or will a quiet reminder, regularly made in such circumstances, be appropriate? I called the two boys over, away from their immediate audience, 'Fellas'—this a little louder as I established eye contact from a distance. No response. 'Fellas' (pause). This time they looked across to me. 'See you for a sec,' I said as I beckoned them across with my hand. At this point, I turned aside to chat with a small group of students, giving take-up time to the kung-fu specialists. They came across. It didn't take long. I asked them their names. Initially they appeared confused and a little apprehensive as to why I'd called them over. I had a brief chat about safe play. They replied (how often have I heard this?), 'We were just mucking around.' 'I'm sure you were, Brett and Adam, but I'm reminding you that karate kicking is not on, especially because younger students copy you. They think it's okay when older boys do it.' We parted on pleasant terms.

165

Consequences and consistency

The most substantial duty-of-care role concerns playground supervision. Most of our supervision involves active movement around the grounds: chatting with students, encouraging and acknowledging positive play, checking the use of play equipment, and encouraging a clean, safe environment. Most of our discipline involves reminders or directions about the rule or the responsible behaviour. Most students respond to positive direction. Some display secondary behaviour (p 35). A few blatantly refuse:

- 'You're just a Grade 1 teacher anyway!' (This from a Grade 6 student to an Infants teacher.)
- 'Other teachers let us play here! So!' (Some students argue, challenge and resist teachers' correction.)
- Some just run off, refusing to accept teacher discipline.

Following up students beyond the playground

Students and staff need to know that this kind of behaviour is unacceptable and that if the student refuses a reasonable request from a teacher, there will be follow-up (the certainty principle, p 38). To support this follow-up, some schools use a monitoring book in which duty staff or support staff note refusals and inappropriate behaviour. Any aggressive behaviour, of course, results in immediate time-out. Unacceptale behaviour will be followed up within twenty-four hours. Some schools use the same book to note students who behave in a particularly responsible, supportive way. This information can be linked to merit certificates. Other schools hand out tokens for positive behaviour and give canteen vouchers, community certificates, a special school mug or a small word of approval at assemblies.

Selwyn and O'Donnell (1984) describe a whole-school plan for improving co-operative behaviour in the playground.

- Teachers on playground duty have a book of raffle tickets. When they observe positive behaviour, at their professional discretion, they hand out a raffle ticket with a positive comment, 'You went out of your way to drop that litter in the bin.' 'We appreciate it that you're playing bat tennis co-operatively.' 'You checked before racing around that corner. Good on you.'
- The ticket stubs are collected and a draw is made at selected times, including assembly.
- A teacher co-ordinates the scheme for the staff—organising tickets, prizes, presentation times and guidelines for their consistent use.
- Initially, tickets were given without explanation. After the first 'public' draw there was a rapid motivational response.
- The staff were careful not to reward students who set up positive behaviour, but only the ones whose behaviour was spontaneous. They were also careful not to run the program for too long but to have an ending with a special draw. It can always be re-introduced on an ad hoc basis.
- The program did not rely on the raffle system alone but on a range of activities to enhance positive play, social co-operation and an aesthetic environment.

Many schools have a system in which teachers use a bumbag or small backpack while on playground duty. Each bumbag is coloured and numbered to denote the supervision area. It contains band-aids, spray-on disinfectant, cloths to clean wounds, a small bottle of brandy (joke!), several small laminated green cards, a large laminated red card, a notebook and a pen that works.

The notebook is there to record all refusals to obey reasonable requests from teachers. The details are later logged in a behaviour monitoring book in the staffroom. The small green cards can be given to students who desperately need to go inside to find something important. They present the card to the corridor duty teacher or to someone in the office, and have to report back to the playground duty teacher with their sunhat (or whatever) and the green card.

Wearing sunhats has become an important safety and health issue in some schools. Many schools even include hats in their uniform code. Students and parents forget though, and old habits die hard. Some schools have used reward schemes to increase the habit, especially during hot months. Each grade teacher keeps a weekly record of who is wearing a hat at recess time. A consistent weekly score means a canteen voucher for an iceblock. Some schools use a balance of prevention and consequence. Students who haven't brought a hat for a week have to play in the shaded areas until they turn up with their hats. This policy, of course, only operates in the summer months. Many schools now have over ninety per cent success with students wearing hats and appropriate play clothes.

If a student presents at the office or exit door without a green card, unless it is a clear emergency, they are requested to check with the duty teacher. This slows down those students who pester office staff.

The large red card is used as a signal to be sent to the office in an emergency for:
• the student who does a 'runner'
• the student who is up on the roof or up a tree refusing to come down (The teacher can walk away and remove the attention-giving audience or make the choice clear to the student in the light of deferred consequences and then walk away.)
• a serious fight.

The card is given to a trusted student who races to the office and is directed to the staffroom by office staff. Breathless, the student explains, 'Down by the sandpit, there's a fight!' One of the teachers looks up from reheated leftovers and sighs, 'I'll go.' The support of an extra pair of hands is crucial in a crisis. Staff need to discuss how to monitor use of the card in terms of follow up, whether teachers should go on a roster for red-card support, and when parents will be contacted. Most socioeconomically disadvantaged schools have some cue-card support system in place as part of their overall playground plan.

The simple use of a 'bumbag system' reminds staff of their need to consciously aim for reasonable consistency. Students, too, know very early in Term 1 that if duty teachers say they will follow up, they will do so.

Roxanne, a teacher, remarked:

> I've really worked on smiling, making comments and greeting students by name, and I'm finding that I am actually enjoying duty! The highlight was one of the toughest and roughest boys greeting me with 'Gooday' last week—unprompted. Made my day, I can tell you! Developing a discipline plan for playground duty has enabled me to remove associated stress. I realise how powerful using a plan can be—especially having witnessed numerous win/lose battles between kids and duty teachers . . . when I reflect on my career over the last three years I have moved from a cynical, stressed, even disinterested teacher (at times) to a far more enthusiastic, far more effective, less stressed teacher. I know the use of a discipline plan (for classroom and duty-of-care management) has been a key factor.

Time-out in the play-ground

Some students are caught up in heated exchanges and trade blows. Some throw missiles—rocks, sticks, tan bark and sand. Some display aggression at the drop of a hat. It is essential that students know that this kind of behaviour will always result in time-out (and why). For a time-out plan to be effective, staff need to explore the key questions:

- What sorts of behaviour result in time-out in the playground?
- Will we have a graded time-out system?—for example, partial exclusion through to being sent to a withdrawal room.

Many schools have a time-out bench situated near the office (in view), as well as seats nominated for cool-off time in other key areas of the playground. Students may be sent there for five minutes, ten minutes, or at teacher discretion. All time-out consequences are recorded in the monitoring book and followed up. Students are familiar with the notion of time-out benches used in sport. It is wise, though, not to use names such as 'sin-bin' (the name used for temporary exclusion of a recalcitrant member in the House of Representatives!). 'Sin-bin' is poor theology as well as poor psychology.

For more serious behaviour, students are sent inside to be supervised. Staff need to discuss:

- Do we set up a time-out or withdrawal room? Will the time-out room be used for cooling off as well as for deferred consequences? Some schools use the time-out room for a later punishment so that a lunchtime play is forfeited in the room because of a previous offence. In this case, strict records need to be kept of offences and punishments, as well as notification of parents. The normal protocol of time-out should apply.
- Where will we have the withdrawal area? Should all staff be rostered?
- Will the room operate at each playtime or only lunch play?
- How long does a student stay there?
- How does the use of time-out link with specialist behaviour management programs for recidivist students?
- What should happen in the time-out room?
- Should there be other consequences following the use of time-out itself—apology, reparation, restitution? How will such follow-up be administered?

- Should parents be contacted after the first occasion of time-out, or after the second or third? It is important to stress to all members of the school community that time-out is part of a total school policy that is primarily preventive, focusing on the right of all students to a safe environment.

The ideal person to follow up playground incidents (unless the incidents are particularly serious) is the duty-of-care teacher. If possible, release time should be given for that teacher to follow up with a deferred consequence. A student who thinks herself clever enough to tell the Grade 1 teacher, 'You can't tell me what to do' is often shocked when the teacher turns up at the classroom door to ask if she can 'see Jessica to follow up a playground incident'.

It is also important that grade teachers are not penalised for the behaviour of their students when they are in the playground. That annoying line, 'You know what *your* Jessica did in the playground' needs to be replaced by the phrase: 'When Jessica is in the playground or corridor or on an excursion, she is everybody's Jessica.'

It is essential to keep good records of playground behaviour to pick up trends, check if our plans are working (especially to note if there is a change in frequency and seriousness of disruptive behaviour relative to our plans) and, most of all, to ensure that within the bounds of human fallibility, all staff are supporting the policy and plan.

Key steps in forming a management plan for duty of care beyond the classroom

1 Ascertain what is happening

Ascertain from the students and staff what the concerns are about behaviour in the playground, on excursions and while travelling on school buses. Classroom meetings, surveys, and staff discussions can then be used to find out what is currently happening as perceived by teachers and students and, where appropriate, parents (see also key questions in Chapter 1, p 26 ff).

For example, when addressing bullying as a school-wide issue, each grade teacher can run a classroom meeting in the same week to focus on the issue using questions that clarify:
- what students perceive bullying to be
- why students bully
- what they get out of it
- how people feel when bullied
- what we can and should do to address it (p 178 ff).

There are always several stakeholders when problems or issues arise in a school. For example, if there are concerns about bus duty provision, students, teachers and drivers can share their concerns at ad hoc meetings. The difficulties experienced by drivers and bus duty teachers can be addressed more easily when a collaborative model is employed (see case example p 176).

2 Clarify issues

As information on key issues is gathered, it is important to clarify the picture as much as possible.

- How is litter managed? Is the litter residual? blown in by the wind? Is there a lot of old litter under bushes? in the far-flung corners of the playground? Are our litter bins serviceable? Are there enough of them?
- Is there any particular age group or particular students or any ringleaders that cause a problem with respect to playground behaviour?
- Are there blind spots, trouble spots or areas which are hard to supervise in the playground?
- Is there any particular time of day which is a problem in playground supervision?
- How frequent and serious is the common disruptive behaviour relevant to duty of care? What are the most frequent behaviour problems encountered in the corridor, playground or on bus duty? How serious is the disruptive behaviour in the eyes of staff and students? There may be some disagreement on this one, so it is important to bring people's attention back to the fundamental rights (p 31) as the focus for what is serious.

When analysing frequency and seriousness, what normally emerges is that there is a variety of behaviour that is annoying but 'low serious', for example, litter, teasing, students forgetting or not playing by the rules, playing in some out-of-bounds areas (for example, no ball areas). However, some of these issues can be potentially serious. Some of the behaviour is low in frequency but serious regarding rights such as safety and fair treatment: racism, ostracising of students, unsafe play practices and games, aggressive behaviour and bullying.

ANALYSIS OF PLAYGROUND BEHAVIOUR

High Percentage	
High Frequency	Low Serious

Low Percentage	
Low Frequency	High Serious

Figure 8

3 Current practices and plans

Clarifying the shape, frequency and degree of seriousness of the problem(s) puts our current practices into sharper focus. How do teachers and support staff currently deal with litter, teasing, students who tell tales, play fighting, being out of bounds, unsafe play, swearing? Does it matter what we do? Do we just leave management to the idiosyncratic practice of whoever is on duty? Are our rules clear? Are they known and published? What consequences are appropriate? How can we utilise time out? O'Rourke and Glynn (1978) demonstrated that:

marked improvement in students' playground behaviour, and marked reduction in playground fighting occurred when teachers and other adults moved about starting up games and activities to engage more and more students, instead of merely patrolling and supervising. This study also found that the number of fights varied according to which teams of teachers were on playground duty. These findings strongly support the case for a consistent school-wide approach to behaviour management (in Wheldhall 1992, p 24).

Glynn also notes an interesting study by Presland (1978) regarding litter in the school playground. A team of students monitored residual litter, by zoning the playground and recording a daily litter count on large display graphs. The feedback itself was beneficial, showing a subsequent drop in litter. What is intriguing about this study is the power of student feedback to motivate attention, concern and change in behaviour.

It is important that staff (using small-group problem-solving approaches) give their responses to these identified issues and begin to assess more workable solutions in the light of aims and preferred practices (p 30 ff). Then workable plans consistent with aims and practices can be developed. If what we are currently doing is not reflecting our aims and preferred practices, we need to challenge current practice.

It often becomes apparent that there are widely differing responses to litter, dobbing, play fighting, out of bounds play etc. Play fighting, for example karate kicking, exuberant punching and jumping on top of each other, is accepted as just 'boys being boys'. If girls were to exhibit the same behaviour, I suspect there would not be the same acceptance. Some teachers ignore students who report that they are being hassled or excluded from a game or being 'picked on'. Other teachers respond to such students by telling them:
• to 'go play somewhere else!'
• to 'grow up' and not be 'cissies'
• 'No wonder no-one wants to play with you when you whine like that!'
• to 'stand up for yourself and go and snatch the ball back if it's yours'
• to 'Go away. Don't bother me. I'm trying to drink my cup of tea!'

Others overindulge the student, give too much pity and take responsibility for students' problems.

At the very least, a consistent approach:
• acknowledges students' perception ('Thanks for telling me . . .') and is supportive without owning their problems
• encourages students to think about what they can do to deal with it
• offers reasonable help when necessary.

Staff will consider options for assisting students in such circumstances, based on the common reportings in their playground and how they can balance immediate help with long-term strategies.

I was doing my playground duty last year and a Preparatory Grade student came up to me, frowning and jaded, and in a sheepish voice said, 'Mr, Mr'. Realising he didn't know my name I told him. 'Mr Rogers, someone just did do this to me.' He held up his second finger as a vertical salute. 'Did he? What do you think that means?' I asked. He walked alongside me. 'It means a very bad thing,' he sighed. 'What do you think you can do when people do rude signs like that?' 'I don't know,' he said. Then, thinking a bit, he suggested, 'Come and tell you!' He was smiling now. 'Yes, you could tell me, but I won't always be here when people do that (or say rude, mean or unfair things). What else could you do?' 'I can tell another teacher.' 'Yes, you could. But there won't always be a teacher here when . . .' 'Anything else?' 'Yes! I could go and play somewhere else,' and he ran off happily. I think all this boy wanted was someone to listen to him for a while and give reassurance. It took only a few minutes.

Teachers have to use their professional judgment frequently to determine how intrusive to be in support or correction. However, by discussing common scenarios as a whole staff, we can re-appraise the utility of the sorts of response we can make. Students who complain of having their ball taken are helped if encouraged to go and ask for it. Ask the student to practise with you first to increase confidence. We can then stand some distance away, obliquely watching this little act of assertion. The person having taken the ball (seeing the teacher nearby) may give it back. In other circumstances, it may be appropriate to ask both parties to meet each other away from the main group and check out what the problem is. Use the 4Ws approach (p 27) and encourage them to come up with a plan.

Teachers will increase the level of co-operation in dealing with residual litter, if they preface their direction to pick up litter by a relaxed chat and then pick up the litter with students—some schools have teachers taking out plastic bags and pairs of disposable gloves.

Teacher: 'G'day, how's it going?'

The teacher eyeballs the four boys who have residual litter at their feet.

Students: 'Okay.'

Teacher: 'There's a fair bit of litter here.'

Students: 'It's not ours.'

Teacher: 'I want you to give me a hand to pick it up, thanks' or 'Let's do the playground a favour (or let's do the cleaner a favour, eh?). Give me a hand.'

By making the civic-duty move, the teacher has made it easier for the students to co-operate. They grumble a bit. The teacher cajoles and it's soon in the bin. If students are seen dropping litter, then a direct question (p 116) or rule reminder is appropriate.

There are times when a direct and assertive command is required, as when students are running in and out of toilets, coming into corridors for no good reason during recess. 'Okay, out now!' 'But miss!' 'Out now!' She won't accede to procrastinating whines.

Using the skills noted earlier (language of discipline and a least-to-most-intrusive model of management), teachers can develop preferred responses to common playground issues. For the more serious matters such as aggression, fights and bullying, unambiguous consequences must be applied immediately with back-up procedures for duty teachers. This will involve a time-out plan that may need to include a staffed area inside the school.

4 Solutions: developing workable plans

Solutions often fall into several categories:
• managerial
• structural
• educational
• social
• procedural.

To achieve better management practice, the following will require some consideration: our language of management, our degree of intrusiveness, what strategies we will use when addressing low-level issues such as silly and inappropriate play, litter, students pushing others over, sand throwing, aggressive play. On these occasions a clear, firm, 'Stop!' followed by a decisive direction to play somewhere else, or 'take five minutes on the time out bench', or a deferred consequence is appropriate. These discretionary procedures need to be discussed by all staff because we all have to face these issues in our duty-of-care management (p 88).

Structural solutions involve basics such as checking if there are enough rubbish bins. Although it is no excuse, some students drop litter rather than walk a hundred metres. Windproof bins help the residual litter problem as will an educational focus on 'Keep this part of our country beautiful!' With cutbacks on cleaning staff in schools, staff may need to consider how practical litter patrols can work. We also need to educate students about safe play, fair play, and considering others. This will mean a discussion in the establishment phase of the year on the playground rules and the right to feel safe, be safe, play fair, and care for each other and the environment. Using the preventive focus (p 22), staff will work through several basic playground rules with all their classes during the establishment phase.

These rules covering key rights and responsibilities can be pictorially represented. One picture, for example, illustrates a student playing on a slide but another student up a tree. The words, written by a class member and typed on the sheet, say, 'There are good places to play, but some unsafe places we shouldn't play.' At the bottom of the picture is the statement, 'Consequence: we miss out on playing time.' Another picture shows a student spitting on the asphalt.

The words at the top say, 'No spitting. It's unhealthy.' At the bottom, the consequence reads, 'We clean up our own mess.' Another picture shows two older students playing bat tennis. One half of the picture shows safe play, the other unsafe. The words say, 'We play safely so that no-one gets hurt.' 'Consequence: we miss out on playing time.'

These A3-sized pictures are displayed for several weeks in the foyer under the heading Play Safe, Play Fair, Care For Others And Our Playground. An A4-sized book of selected pictures from all grades is then published and made available to all classes and interested parents. It is the students' contribution to the playground policy. The pictorial representations can form a policy book, 'Our safe playground' or 'Our playground is a great place to be because . . .' It can be produced in community languages where appropriate. This approach is more effective because:

- the students are involved from the outset
- the focus for playground behaviour is the fundamental rights of safe and fair treatment/play and the responsibility of caring for *our* environment
- discussion and pictorial representation make the focus more appropriate for students and more user-friendly
- publishing it as policy, gives a clear signal to the community about the way this school manages playground behaviour.

When developing rules, it is important that they are expressed behaviourally, are few in number and are as positively expressed as possible. It's hard to express 'no spitting' positively. We tried—'If you have to spit, do it with your mouth closed!'

It is also important to publish the rules and discuss with students and staff how the rules and consequences will be enforced.

Social/ educational solutions

There are many areas within the school environment that contribute to the positive or negative tone of the school and which can even affect behaviour:

- graffiti left up for some period of time sends a message that the school doesn't care if it's there, making repeat offences more tempting
- broken or damaged seating, inadequate or too few rubbish bins, damaged drinking fountains, long cracks or holes in concrete/asphalt pathways (The problem is that broken and damaged structures are easily overlooked when one lives with them all the time.)
- rubbish bins so far apart that students sometimes can't be bothered to walk to them
- few shaded areas on very hot days
- inadequate drinking fountains and toilet facilities
- inadequate signs, especially for visitors to the school. It is worth doing a 'visit' tour around the school, as if one were a total stranger, to get that impression of 'welcome' in the language on the signs. How directional are the signs? Do the signs have pictorial emphasis for non-readers or non-English speakers, especially for location of toilets?

Environmental conditions can enhance wellbeing, safety and positive social exchange. Many schools are now more thoughtfully planning their playground environment along with their behaviour management plan. There are often parents and members of staff, with special talents in environmental aesthetics whose skills can be used.

While some structural changes are obviously costly—large scale grassed areas, play equipment, toilet reconstruction—most require time and effort with relatively low cost.

Seating: Those old seats or benches along the walls of buildings can be removed and repaired. Fix up the dangerous exposed bolts and nail heads (it's amazing what some schools accept in their 'public' seating!), replace broken splintered timbers, and then paint them. The seats can be relocated in curved and circular arrangements preferably near shaded areas. Special seating areas can be set up with railway sleepers on grassed areas with some tan bark and plants for students who may not want to play on the equipment or run around. These areas are to be just a quiet haven, explained to all students as such.

Signs: What do the signs say about this school? Are they legible? Are they large enough? A broken, damaged sign, unfortunately, makes a statement. Are there signs at all key entrances to the school? Could outsiders find the office purely from signs? Are they colourful without being overbearing? Can some signs be enhanced with simple cartoon figures? Note how signs are used, pictorially, in public places these days. Seek advice from the many service providers in this area. In these days of 'selling our school'—crass as it sounds—it is important to promote a positive image and also to seek to practise it.

It is also worth considering how welcome the entrance and administration areas appear. Is there comfortable seating, regular and attractive display of student work, a framed gallery of current staff (all staff—not just teachers), a framed mission statement with student illustrations, dried flowers on the coffee table with photo albums of school activities, attractively published policies, welcoming staff?

Toilets, drinking fountains: Even if we can't fully update the equipment, we can make sure all broken equipment is fixed, paint the walls, put up a new splashback to the rapidly fading chrome drinking taps. New taps, a tiled splashback and paint (with a bright sign) can really give a new lease of life to an old building.

Aesthetically green: Many inner city schools now sport thoughtfully arranged, potted flowering shrubs and small trees to give a sense of 'green life' to an otherwise drab slab of asphalt.

Movement: A few bags of cement and screenings will fix up those holes and cracks which are tripped over. At one inner city school, teachers were constantly reminding students not to run out of exit doors, as some students tended to slip easily on the hard asphalt. A speed hump was formed near each exit door with several attractively arranged large pots of plants, three metres from the door. Students soon changed their exit behaviour, and it looked nice too (said the students whose role it was to care for the plants). Rails and signs at the canteen can encourage orderly queuing. As noted earlier, it is necessary to discuss with students why queues are important (and teachers may need to discuss the poor modelling of pushing past a line of students to grab a meat pie and Diet Coke!). Canteen supervision 'staff' also need to discuss how they will manage group behaviour—pushing/shoving in line, yelling out orders from the back of the line, and swearing (p 142). They too need a management discipline plan supported by administration.

Shade areas: In schools with limited shade areas, shade structures of timber and nylon shade cloth can be erected over seating arrangements. When balanced by shrubs and potted plants, such areas can give an aesthetic lift to the unrelieved, harsh asphalt.

Gardens: Many schools have students engaged in garden upkeep. Grades are rostered to plant, weed, water, and nurture their spot. Even grotty old portable classrooms can be enhanced by curtains, signs, a bit of paint and a welcoming garden patch.

These are basic structural solutions which need to be balanced by the credo: If it's broken, fix it quickly, and let's make sure we make the best of the environment we have.

Improving bus duty

Bus duty, especially in a large school, is not the most enjoyable duty role—especially on hot, windy days and those wet, miserable days. One school program tackled the issue of bus duty, deciding to go for a whole-school approach that involved students, bus drivers, the bus company and duty teachers.

1 The deputy principal made sure that all the key groups had an opportunity to register their concerns. Some of the issues that arose were:
   • the students felt they were not being given nice buses like some of the other schools
   • one group of students seemed to be regularly late for the bus
   • drivers were concerned about noise, swearing, litter, calling out through windows, changing seats on the bus. How could they manage these matters more effectively—especially, rude and argumentative students? What should they do in extreme situations such as a silly fight, or moving between seats when the bus is in motion?
   • buses would arrive anywhere in the car park and the four student groups had to go looking for their bus
   • the bus drivers on the school route were changed frequently
   • duty teachers found their role taxing.

2 The problems were defined in terms of frequency and seriousness—the bottom line being the right to travel safely and the right to fair treatment for all.

3 A workable solution evolved at a meeting with key students, senior staff and the bus company. It included:

- painting clear lines on the asphalt for the bus bays in the parking area, a large letter denoting each bus for each destination (basic, but it hadn't been done before)
- better quality buses to that school route (the bus company clearly listened and co-operated with the school)
- music on the buses (at reasonable volume selected by a student committee from student requests)
- educational and social approaches—students and bus drivers met to share concerns, students visited the bus depot for afternoon tea to see where their drivers worked—'the other side of the fence'
- bus drivers being promoted as part of the school's support staff, not merely bus drivers
- formation of a committee of students for each bus, elected by students who travelled on the bus (this was developed by the senior staff in the school)
- regular bus drivers being assigned to the school and, in their own time, having discussion and professional development with teachers, relevant to their management role on the buses. This training involved basics in crowd-control, personal relations skills (such as using students' first names, being positive, greetings/goodbyes) and using a 'least-to-most' management style (p 103). Without the goodwill and support of the bus company and its drivers, the program would not have worked. It is a tribute to the school's communicative skills that such willingness was forthcoming and sustained. The committees for each bus (known as the bus groups)—student representatives, bus driver, a senior staff member known as the bus group—discussed acceptable and unacceptable behaviour on buses and what could be done to ensure safety and fair treatment for all on the buses. A positive behaviour code for bus travel was drawn up with a focus on four key rules:
  - find a seat and stay in it
  - keep your hands and feet to yourself
  - use positive language
  - eat it, bin it.

These rules were published on a laminated card and displayed at the front of the bus at the beginning of each trip by a bus monitor, an elected student. Parents were made aware of these rules and the consequences for flouting them. No aggression was allowed on the buses at all. Disruptive behaviour was always followed up and, in severe cases, students were denied access to school bus travel, after due process with parents.

Basically the school followed the four key questions noted earlier (p 22 ff), and using a problem-solving approach (p 26) came up with a duty-of-care plan that reduced working stress of all parties by:

- allowing the students to own their part of the problem
- involving all stakeholders (especially the bus drivers who made a real effort to see things from the students' perspective and to see the value in positive management practices)

- emphasising rights and responsibilities
- monitoring, evaluation and celebration of successes.

BULLYING IN SCHOOLS— AN ABUSE OF RELATIONAL POWER

The popular view of the bully is that of a large boy, threatening to hit a weaker, smaller, insecure student. Is it bullying when several girls repeatedly pick on another girl and call her names? or when a student's bag is taken, urinated on and thrown in the bushes as he tries fearfully to make his way home from school?

Is persistent name calling defined as bullying? What about squabbles, quarrels, pushing, shoving and that annoying male testosteronic play? How many times do we, as teachers, see boys 'playing' by pushing, shoving or jumping on top of one another? All students, and most adults, squabble from time to time and hassle one another. Ahmed, Whitney and Smith note, 'It is not bullying when two students of about the same strength have the fight or quarrel' (Smith and Thompson 1991, p 105).

Definitions of bullying need to consider the intention and provocation in the exhibited behaviour. Most bullying is not physical. It is psychological. In this sense, it is intentional, selective, unprovoked and repetitive behaviour towards another person by one who is stronger physically and psychologically. While physical bullying is to be deplored, so is behaviour such as spitting on someone or on personal property; defacing property (for example writing derogatory or racist names on a pencil case) or repeatedly hiding another's property; persistent teasing, name calling and racist taunts (for example, fatty, *shit*-head, slant-eyes, slut, slag, moll); repeatedly picking on someone because they are small, or fat; even extortion and threats: 'You can't use the toilet cos you're a Preppie!'

Some people in the community (including some parents and teachers) say that schools are making too much of the bullying issue. They say that teasing, hassling and name calling are normal in childhood and this kind of behaviour has always been with us. Students need to learn to cope with it. Our acceptance of, or acquiescence in, such behaviour does not naturally follow. Having worked with many schools on bullying issues, it surprises me how lightly some teachers regard persistent teasing, name calling, racist and sexist slurs, students being excluded from games, or the magpie-gang teasing of some girls towards a victim until the victim is psychologically bloodied.

Bullying is, essentially, an abuse—an intentional abuse—of relational power. (Rogers, 1994 c). Everybody has relational power. Some students are capable of bullying adults as well as each other and some adults bully other adults as well as students. I can remember having to stand under a cold shower on several occasions when I forgot my PE kit at school in the 1950s. Along with many of my generation, I was slapped, pushed, pulled, poked and hit under the guise of discipline. My teachers, the ones who did it, would never have seen their behaviour as an abuse of relational power.

Bullying behaviour is a learnt behaviour that will be tolerated by students and teachers depending on:
* the degree of acceptance in the school of such behaviour
* the educational messages generated about safe, fair, behaviour (implicit and explicit)
* the policy imperatives of the school. Ken Rigby, whose institute has surveyed more than sixty schools in the past four years, has found that 'the extent of bullying varies, depending on the degree to which it is tolerated' (*Age*, 13/3/1994)
* the support given to victims of bullying
* the consequences and due processes applied to bullying behaviour.

Australian research has indicated that:
* one student in twenty engages in bullying behaviour
* one in eight is the victim of significant bullying (Rigby 1994, Slee and Rigby 1991). This finding is very close to that of European research on bullying
* most bullying occurs in the playground, but bullying can occur in classrooms
* in studies of absenteeism, just over five per cent of students judged to be victims of school bullying said it made them feel that they did not want to go to school. Just over fifteen per cent said it had led them to stay at home (*Age*, 13/3/1994).

We say a student is BEING BULLIED, or picked on, when another student, or a group of students, say nasty or unpleasant things to him or her. It is also bullying when a student is hit, kicked, threatened, locked inside a room, sent nasty notes, when no-one ever talks to them and things like that. These things can happen frequently and it is difficult for the student being bullied to defend himself or herself. It is also bullying when a student is teased repeatedly in a nasty way (Smith and Thompson 1990, p 105).

Victims and bullies

Victims tend to be students with low self-esteem whose experiences at the hands of bullies exacerbate their low sense of social and personal value. When coupled with a belief that there is little they can do to stop it, school becomes quite an unhappy, even frightening, place.

As the South Australian Research Institute (Rigby et al) noted in the *Age*, 'We needed only to see the loneliness, the isolation and the general unhappiness of the victims to confirm our belief that adults do need to consider school bullying to be a serious matter, and that we need to find ways to address it' (*Age*, 13/3/1994).

Smith and Thompson (1991) point out that when a school has knowledge about bullying it has a 'moral obligation to act on it. Put simply, we know that unnecessary suffering can be avoided'. Bullying lies within the range of normal, social behaviour encountered by most students. Students know what it is and who does it—though few admit to doing it themselves. While teacher nominations of victims correlate with questionnaire responses, agreement for bullies is not so high. Peer nominations by students show better agreement and generally show high consistency (Smith and Thompson 1991, p 3).

Students need to know that all kinds of bullying are wrong because they affect the rights of others. Even if a bully's sense of relational power and personal esteem is enhanced by bullying behaviour—'This is how I get my sense of personal worth and prestige'—they have to know their behaviour is wrong. Schools need to point out to parents of bullies, who may trivialise their offspring's behaviour, that bullying is wrong, will not be tolerated and 'this is our school's policy', backed up by Education Department policies on protective behaviour and harassment.

Bullies often display aggressive behaviour (Olweus 1978 in Robertson 1989), are easily provoked and tend to blame their victims. ('It's their fault they look different, speak different, have different clothes. They deserve it!') Studies show that over twenty per cent of confirmed bullies go on to adult delinquent behaviour and engage the criminal justice system (Eron et al 1987).

Bullying is learnt behaviour

Home background is a significant and influential factor in bullying behaviour and aggressive conflict resolution in general (Olweus 1989, Rutter et al 1979, Rutter 1985, Patterson et al 1989). Bullies have parents who are, or have been, bullies in the sense of the definition noted (p 179) and who use aggressive means in order to establish needs, to deal with frustration or gain relational control. They characteristically abuse relational power.

It is in the privacy of dysfunctional homes that school bullies are witness to acts of incredible emotional and, sometimes, physical abuse. Instead of the home being a place of emotional security, a place where the inevitable conflicts of life can be worked through, their home is a laboratory where the abuses of relational power are learnt. Guilt and fear are induced from the way the male abuses the female, and from the frequent yelling and even screaming. Home is a place where discipline or behaviour management arises from reactive frustration rather than preventive thought. Siblings frequently punch and hit each other. Violent, aggressive hitting is used by people to get their way or resolve a problem. In an essay on private violence Time magazine (1983) makes the point that, 'the worst thing about family violence is its natural reproduction of itself, like a poisonous plant sending out spores . . . Violence committed there, especially by somebody understood to be a guardian . . . is a special betrayal' (p 33).

Bullies are usually boys, although girl bullies do exist. Like bullying boys, they are impulsive and dominant, but rather than attacking their victims physically, they are apt to harass them verbally or simply exclude them from the group (Olweus ibid). For the most part, they bully other girls, he says. Aggressive girls have been 'socialised like boys', says psychologist Leonard Eron of the University of Illinios. These girls might not face the same bleak futures as their male counterparts, Eron (1987) adds, but as adults, they do tend to have psychological problems and to punish their children harshly, thus contributing to a new generation of bullies (see Roberts 1988).

Replication of aggression, bullying and violence is not inevitable outside of such homes, but likely. Even without replication, a home like the one described above tends to create a desensitising to aggression and bullying and a lack of social awareness about how people ought to behave towards each other (Rogers, 1994 a). This is especially acute when such students have to relate to adults in positions of authority—teachers, parents, caregivers.

When students come into a school, whatever their home environment, they have to learn that the right to feel safe is central. A school cannot afford to tolerate or accept bullying, even at a tacit level based on the opinion that it is 'real world' behaviour or is character building or just a case of 'boys will be boys'.

Bullying: a whole-school approach to creating a safe environment

If the issue of bullying is to be taken seriously, the school must work with its community on a long-term basis so that they know:
- what the school means by bullying
- why bullying is totally unacceptable (it's no wink-wink-nudge-nudge matter)
- that bullying is wrong because it infringes fundamental rights to safety and fair treatment
- that this is our educational program for rights-enhancing behaviour
- how our school policy addresses bullying from the perspective of fundamental rights.

In 1983, the Norwegian Ministry of Education began a nationwide campaign against bullying, largely under the guidance of Professor Olweus. 'There is a network of action,' he says, 'that includes teachers, parents and students.' At school, his plan requires close supervision of students and clearly laid-out rules against bullying that are consistently enforced. The program also involves parents in discussion groups on the subject, and it entreats adults and classmates to support and protect victims (Roberts 1988, op cit, pp 56). As Smith and Thompson (1991) note, 'If you get it out in the open, you've got more chance of solving it.'

High/low bullying schools

There are several identifiable features which distinguish schools as high or low in respect to the amount and kind of bullying that occurs in them.
- In low-bullying schools, victims are likely to be taken seriously, to be listened to, and a due process entered into to support them. Most importantly, action is taken to stop the bullying. I can recall at school in the 1950s, the unwritten code that, 'worse things will happen if you report the bullying'. Bullies trade on secrecy, threat, anxiety and fear. Creating an open climate where students know it is okay and safe to report, will decrease the bully's abuse of relational power. As Ian Warden noted: '. . . to report the bully for his bullying was to multiply his wrath and to be even more comprehensively bullied next time'. 'Bullying is a practice that flourishes in secrecy like other forms of personal violence that stem from an abuse of power. Therefore, schools need to consider strategies that increase student–staff contact' (Hyndman and Thorsborne 1990, p 3).

181

- Reporting is different from telling tales. When students tell tales they may be after revenge, wanting to get someone into trouble, even to get attention for themselves. Reporting needs to be seen by students, teachers and parents as a legitimate way of telling people who need to know about this behaviour so that they can do something to stop it. Such reporting is important even on so-called minor bullying—repeated teasing, taking and hiding bags, hassling on the way home from school. As one boy recently said in an interview, 'I finally went to my teacher and he made it stop.'

> If the students get support on the minor incidents from staff, then they begin to believe that the support is also available for the major ones . . . If the senior members of staff are seen as giving up their time to be involved, it is therefore serious in the students' eyes (Smith and Thompson op cit, p 21).

The Elton Report (1989), a major report on discipline in schools in Great Britain, suggests that bullying, both physical and psychological intimidation as well as racial and sexual harassment, is widespread and tends to be ignored by teachers. They recommend that, 'head teachers and staff be alert to signs of bullying and racial harassment, deal firmly with such behaviour; take action based on clear rules which are backed by appropriate sanctions and systems to protect and support victims' and that staff make clear to students that it is their responsibility to share this knowledge with staff in confidence (pp 102-103). Unravelling the truth of the matter is not easy, especially when the victim has teased others and ended up on the receiving end of similar behaviour (p 185).

- A whole-school approach to bullying contains clear policy guidelines and due support processes for victims of bullying, as well as unambiguous consequences for bullies. Most of all, schools that can be termed low or high bullying, exhibit clear differences in attitudes and ethos. Low bullying schools see teachers, backed up by administrators, as having clear views regarding the unacceptability of bullying, a preparedness to be alert to its signs and having clearly stated policies for dealing with it.
- One of the other differences between low and high bullying schools is seen in the kinds of discipline practice in force in the school. Where the school endorses, or at least ignores, punitive practices that rely on embarrassment, ridicule, put-downs and verbal aggression 'it is not surprising that most bullies are generally confident and quite convinced that violence and coercion are legitimate means of establishing social dominance in the group' (Bjorkquvist et al 1982 in Smith and Thompson 1991, p 38).

A whole-school approach

Developing a whole-school approach to bullying will take time, effort, education, attitude change and behaviour change by all members of the school community.

1 Awareness raising

Using surveys, discussion and classroom meetings, a school can assess what its teachers, students and parents think and believe about bullying. Questions can focus on issues such as:

- What do you think bullying is?

- What do we mean when we say someone is being bullied?
- Why do people bully?
- What do they get out of it?
- How does bullying (from repeated teasing through to physical forms of control) make people feel?
- What kind of bullying goes on at our school?
- What can, and should, we do about bullying? What do you do when you know a fellow student is being bullied? (see Rogers, 1994c)

A good discussion starter for schools on the bullying issue is *Bullying in School*: a video and instructional manual based on the Australian research of Ken Rigby and Phillip Slee (1994).

Using a survey approach

Confidential surveys can address questions such as:
- Have you been bullied in the last term? How often? In what way? By one or more students?
- What do you do when you know bullying is going on, or see a student your age being bullied? Give examples of non-physical bullying with this question.
- Have you taken part in bullying others at school this term? How?

These supplementary questions are taken from a modified questionnaire designed by Dan Olweus from the University of Bergen (see Smith and Thompson 1991, Chapter 10).

One positive way to raise awareness about the nature of bullying is to use drama to illustrate the variety of bullying incidents. Drama helps clarify how repeated teasing, name calling, and exclusion make people feel. The self-talk of victims can be dramatised: 'Should I tell? Who? My best friend? My teacher? What will happen if I tell? Will they believe me? Will they make it stop?'

Advice can be role-played using dramatic formats, especially how to stand up to a bully or teaser using assertive approaches. Students in one school had this advice, 'If you are getting bullied by a teacher, you should write it down, and tell your friend to write it down so you have evidence. If one teacher doesn't believe you, you try another' (Smith and Thompson 1991, p 74). The few teachers who bully, tend to use quite punitive measures in discipline and punishment and employ similar strategies to those used by student bullies— secrecy, threat, and abuse of relational power.

2 Develop a policy process and action plan

Define bullying to the school community. Stress particularly that school should be a safe place where the emphasis is on mutual respect, regardless of perceived or real differences.
- See the anti-bullying process as an integral part of a positive pro-active behaviour emphasis, not merely an anti-focus for example, anti-bullying, anti-harassment, anti-racism policies.
- Outline the support process for victims. Let students know it is acceptable

to report to grade or duty teachers; and most of all, that something will be done to make it stop.

- Clarify the rules for safe behaviour in the playground, for example, 'Keep hands and feet to yourself' and 'Use to help not to hurt.' Emphasise what safe play means. It isn't fun to enjoy yourself by purposely and intentionally hurting others physically or emotionally.
- Explain what harassment means. Clarify the consequences for harassment and for totally unacceptable aggression.
- Outline and explain the consequences for aggressive behaviour and physical bullying. In extreme cases, this will involve partial exclusion from social play, staggered home times if the bullying is occurring on the way home from school, and even partial enrolment.
- Outline what time-out is used for, in and out of class, relative to such behaviour.
- Educate staff in positive discipline practices and use of applied consequences (p 99).
- Be sure to inform parents of the school's policy and action plan.

3 Supporting victims of bullying

When communicating with victims it is important to consider their feelings, their natural anxiety about reporting bullying, their low self-esteem, their feelings of inadequacy and perceived powerlessness. Whenever students share their concern about safety at school, they need an adult to listen non-judgmentally, supportively and with understanding: 'I'm glad you felt you could tell me about what's happening.' If the victim is female and the supporting teacher is male, it helps to have a female colleague sitting in or alongside for ethical probity and physical reassurance where appropriate (p 119).

> The calm, non-judgmental demeanour of the adult in a non-threatening encounter with a victim of bullying helps to forestall any resistance the victim may initially have to expressing and exploring feelings about being bullied (Knox 1992, pp 160).

- No-one *deserves* to be bullied. Students who display ambiguous victimising (Rogers 1994 c) through 'crying wolf' or provoking an incident and then appearing to be the object of others' psychological or physical machinations, may need to be reminded that if they keep doing this, they'll continue to be hassled. Teach them other ways to gain attention and to belong and use a problem-solving approach that increases behavioural ownership:

> What happened? What did you do? What can you do:
> - when people call you names?
> - when they won't let you play or join in their games?
> - when they threaten you?
> What do you think you need to do to make it stop?

It is important for parents and teachers to:
- listen to, and talk with, victims
- emphasise that it is not their fault this is happening

- look for signs of possible bullying:
    - someone who is normally happy, displaying uncharacteristic unhappiness
    - deterioration of school work
    - not wanting to go to school
    - unexplained bruises, cuts or injuries
    - sudden increase in anxiety about going to school
    - an uncharacteristic desire to be with an adult all the time
    - extra requests for pocket money
    - loss of, or damaged, personal property
- It is essential that parent(s) work with the school on any suspicions they may have of bullying. Communication is the essential key. Parents can initiate a special time at home or school and talk generally about school—what's going well, what's not going well, what the parent has noticed. Concerns about bullying often come out during a supportive general discussion.

Assisting victims

Tatum et al (1989, 1990) has emphasised the importance of recording, in writing, a bully's behaviour, or getting the student to write down what has happened. The same should occur for the victim. Discussions and contractual outcomes should also be recorded and the parents of both parties notified. This is to invite their support and also keep them aware and informed. The report and any agreed behaviour contract are included on the student's file and used as a basis for follow-up and evaluation.

It can be helpful to bring victim and bully together to work on restitution. This should be encouraged (especially in the case of the victim), not forced and should always be after ample cool-off time. The aim is to encourage each side to tell their story and then agree to act (behave) within the school's rights and responsibilities and to express such agreement behaviourally: 'This is what I will do to make this bullying (be specific about the behaviour) stop.' The contract is then monitored and evaluated weekly.

Give skills to victims

While a teacher can, and should, take whatever measures are possible to stop bullying, it is also important not to overprotect the victim. There will not always be an adult protector around to help them.

Teachers and parents can teach students how to stand up to bullies in an assertive way. Assertion is a skill and needs to be practised, emphasising:
- how to look assertive rather than aggressive
- how to think strong
- specific words and phrases to use to convey one's rights. These can be practised by having a script, 'I don't like it when you (here the student is specific about the bullying behaviour). Stop it now.' (see Rogers 1994c)
- how and when to walk away
- that it's all right to answer bullies' threats of 'I'll get you if you tell!' by saying something like, 'I've told Mr or Ms . . . that if you do this to me, if you hit me or take my bag, I'll tell.' In the worst case scenario, if they are hurt,

185

at least they've told and it will be followed up, but the disclosure and warning often makes bullies think twice.

When students start to talk, look, think and act assertively, they often feel better as they convey strength of intent and purpose. I've noticed as an adult, that when I've stood up to bullyish behaviour in the workplace as an adult, it rarely reappears! Bullies find satisfaction in the acquiescence and displays of postural and verbal weakness. Don't give it to them.

Many schools now teach assertiveness through classroom meetings, co-operative group activities and confidence-building activities (see the excellent text by McGrath and Francey, *Friendly Kids, Friendly Classrooms* 1993; see also Kafer 1984).

Because victims are sometimes loners, they are easy targets for bullies. It can be helpful to point out the value of playing in groups and invite some of their peers to do just that. For students new to the school and 'Preppies', grade teachers can set up buddy systems for the first few weeks or more until they've settled in.

Most of all, victims need to know:
• they are not bad for having been victimised; they are not to blame for being bullied
• that it is okay to tell. The response is likely to be, 'Thank you for telling me. I'm glad you felt it was okay to tell me.'
• that they will be supported, but that part of the support includes some action by them:
  What have you done to stop it?
  What do you want me to do?
  Are you willing to face the bully with me there to help, to tell them how it feels, when they say or do these things, and that you want this to stop?
• their help is required to make the bullying stop (Explain how.)
• point out that the problem will not go away by itself. Report it. Take action.

4 Supporting parents

Victims, and parents of victims, need to know they can in confidence share their needs, concerns and feelings about bullying.

Encourage parents to talk with their children, if they are willing. This is a crucial step. Also give the assurance that the bullying won't go away by itself. It will help if, 'you (or we) tell your teacher'. Explain how bullies threaten and demand secrecy. Most of all, when students talk take them seriously.
• Co-operate with the school. On the few occasions I've had to deal with concerns about our daughter's emotional and physical safety at school, I've initially felt like coming to school with six guns ablazing!—a natural parent reaction. Supportive, co-operative parents are a powerful deterrent and they have a right to be involved in solving and fixing the problem.
• Supporting parents of bullies.
If you are like me, you will not feel like giving support to such parents, but we need to talk to them. Explain why bullying is totally unacceptable and

how, in some instances, it may be tantamount to assault. It may be difficult for them to appreciate this. We can further explain the co-operative emphasis of our school, the problem-solving approaches we use, and the consequences given for bullying. Invite their support in a plan to modify their offspring's behaviour and share the approaches being used at school.

Working with parents of bullies is difficult because of their attitude to aggression generally. What the school has to convey is that, 'In our school we . . .' I've had parents tell me to hit their son: 'That'll teach him! It didn't do me no harm!' We have to point out again what we mean by discipline and punishment; what we are trying to achieve in the school and that we need their co-operation to achieve it in their offspring's case.

- Where possible and necessary, encourage professional help from psychologists, ethnic liaison workers and social welfare officers/staff.
- Schools can also run parent education and information nights on issues related to behaviour management, to pick up conflict management generally and the bullying issue in particular. Visual learning through role playing of bullying is effective.
- Without threatening them, they may need to consider the fact that bullying has incurred litigation in some schools.

5 Dealing with bullies

As noted earlier, it is tempting for teachers to want to get back at the bully, to make them feel what it's like to be hurt. Our modelling will convey a lot about how we deal with our frustration or anger at their behaviour.

Because most bullying occurs out of sight of grade or duty teachers, and reportage is through the victim or victim's peers, teachers need to check with the bully before initiating a process of mediation and restitution.

- Refer them to what is known by other students. (This is why getting bully and victim together can be beneficial.)
- Direct them to a plan.
- Target and evaluate the plan.

Pikas (1989) outlines key, structured statements such as:
- I would like to talk with you about Jimmy (a victim of bullying).
- What do you know about it?
- All right, we've talked about it long enough.
- What should we do now? What do you suggest?
- That's good. We shall meet together in a week, then you can tell me how you've been getting on. (Smith and Thompson 1991, p 145)
- Gang bullying requires speaking to each of the gang in turn, checking, referring, directing, targeting a process of restitution. It needs to be firmly explained that no-one deserves being bullied because they speak, look, or act differently or in a way 'you don't like'.
- Make sure all incidents of bullying are recorded when reported by students and staff, and followed-up as soon as possible.
- It is important to have unambiguous non-violent sanctions for bullying. Restitution may even be an appropriate consequence in some instances.

The Nottingshire Education Service notes that one in five bullies can be classed as 'anxious bullies' who are suffering major educational difficulties (Smith and Thompson 1991). It is worth considering how support can be given to these students. It may be necessary to help bullies identify what makes them angry and set up a program where they can learn some anger-management skills (see Rogers 1994 cf McGrath and Francey 1993).

The difficulty is that our emotions as adults can be quite strong when bullying and safety are involved—we don't feel like actually helping the bully. Not all teachers have had training in this area, so we may need to refer students to key personnel or enlist their support in the school's due process for bullies and victims. It may be helpful for the bully to work with a counsellor who can help to identify useful strengths and develop them by giving some peer-monitoring roles and cross-age tutoring roles to work with the bully.

6 Utilising the support of the student's peers

Classroom meetings can be used to build support for victims and illustrate to bullies what their peers really think about bullying. It is important for bullies to hear what their peers say about bully behaviour. Feedback should be shared and given in a non-aggressive, but not unemotional, way. Hearing their peers discuss their behaviour can have a powerful effect on bullies (Rogers 1994 c).

Discuss with students the difference between reporting and telling tales/dobbing and why it is okay to report to those who need to know and who can make it stop. Students and teachers who watch a bullying incident—or know it's going on—are tacitly supporting bullying, if they do not report it. When it is observed, a victim's peers can powerfully model peer displeasure at a bullying act. It is this social displeasure that will eventually change the school's ethos. A crucial factor in dealing with bullying is the process of changing the attitude of all members of the school community.

- Emphasise and publicly reward positive and non-violent behaviour, in and out of class. This kind of behaviour can be included in records of achievement. Public acknowledgment of positive, supportive behaviour puts a sharper focus on unacceptable behaviour.
- Develop educational processes to counteract bullying attitudes and enhance positive attitudes and behaviour through story, drama, role-play, projects, positive signs, peer support and buddy systems. An excellent book to initiate discussion in junior and middle school is *No More Bullying* by Rosemary Stones (1992) (see also *Kidscape Training Pack: for use with Primary Students*, Elliot 1986).

Some schools are successfully experimenting with a system which has senior students acting as counsellors on bullying. These students are trained to listen, to advise and refer as appropriate. Some students initially prefer to go to a student rather than an adult.

7 Increase supervision and duty-of-care awareness

There are sometimes areas in a school which are difficult to supervise, such as toilets and corridors—the hot spots. Regular supervision of these areas is an important management responsibility. Staff need to consider how best to tackle this management issue by inviting students to contribute in assessment and problem-solving. A supervision plan is then more easily developed and utilised (p 169 ff). A similar emphasis can be incorporated in the school's playground management plan.

Structured activities and well organised play areas assist in creating a positive playground environment. Teachers can contribute to this by spending time in the playground with students, organising activities, non-competitive games and traditional sports (p 192).

8 Emphasise and promote positive discipline practices among all staff

9 Involve the community in a positive way

The Elton Report (1989) suggests involvement of the community at the educational and intervention level: parent and ethnic liaison groups, community welfare, and the community police.

A rights-enhanced community is both the starting point and the bottom line. Bullying is a feature of social exchange but not an inevitable feature. By developing a whole-school approach, we enable all students to enjoy their right to feel safe at school.

Peer mediation

Many Australian schools have successfully involved senior students in mediation roles—most notably in the playground. Mediators are appropriately trained, particularly in non-aggressive, conflict-resolution skills, and work in pairs with ongoing supervision. Because the peer mediators are chosen by their own peers as well as staff, they have credibility in their role. They do not act as de facto police, or prefects. Their role is to act as a neutral go-between in a problem or dispute, and to enable all parties to come to a non-aggressive solution. Where this is not possible, they refer the problem to a duty teacher. In schools where mediation has been set up, staff report that:

- it fosters a climate of problem solving generally, in and out of classrooms
- the benefits and skills of peaceful resolution are shared widely because the training often involves all senior students
- fewer problems need to be referred to teachers
- positive leadership skills are increased in senior students (see Hoffmeister 1993).

1 If a need has been ascertained through staff and student discussion, the school needs to decide on:
  - a workable training program, considering what elements and skills need to be included
  - how parent support can be garnered and how parents can be involved As with any school-wide program, it is important to inform parents in a user-friendly text with student contributions, and invite their suppor and appropriate involvement.)
  - who will lead the training, and supervise the mediation

• how grade teachers can support the program. Some schools run mediation and problem-solving programs for all senior students so that there is a school-wide focus on the program and peaceful conflict resolution.

Mediators are then chosen through teacher selection and student nomination. All the mediators are then trained and work within a rostered system on playground duty. They work in pairs and report to their post at recess to liaise with the duty teacher.

2 Through training, students learn:
• how to intervene—whether simply to offer help; model playing a game properly; give a reminder of the rule or offer problem-solving mediation
• basic assertion skills
• how to mediate with neutrality
• how to take disputants through basic problem solving
• how to distract disputants away from the main group for cool-off time
• when to intervene
• when to refer a problem to the duty teacher. Mediators do not attempt to solve fighting, chase students who've 'done a runner' or are climbing on the roof, or mediate in any serious behaviour issue.

Many schools use role-play in mediation training to develop the necessary language skills. I'm always impressed at how skilful students are in their mediation role, and how effective their input is. Our politicians could learn a lot from them.

Some school programs have students doing their duty, complete with a clipboard to help mediators cue in their language, for example:
Is there a problem here? If so, what is the problem?

• What can we do to solve it?

• Do you want some assistance?

• How did you feel when . . .?

• What is our rule for . . .?

They encourage the disputants to take turns without controlling the outcome. If it seems likely that mediation will not work, the disputants are reminded of the relevant playground rule(s) and possible referral to a duty teacher.

When mediation is used during classroom time, grade teachers can call on a mediator to help students work through a problem. A quiet time is set aside for one-to-one conferencing and the mediator takes the respective students through the problem-solving steps.

3 The program is enhanced if mediators:
• are introduced to the whole student body at a special assembly
• wear special hats or badges to identify them as mediators, thus increasing their visible presence which helps duty teachers to spot them in a busy playground.

In one junior school, the trained mediators wear hats with the logo: Special Eyes.

> Classroom squabbles? Trouble in the playground? Never fear, the Special Eyes are here. Forget old-fashioned milk monitors and bullying prefects: today's Special Eyes sport trendy baseball caps and have assertiveness training for resolving playground disputes. The techniques stress a positive approach, encouraging praise instead of criticism, and tackle issues such as bullying.
>
> 'We won't be asking the students to jump in like Superman but just to use the new rules to help diffuse confrontations.'
>
> 'We want to develop a feeling of citizenship and say to the students that if they have a problem, then these people may be able to help them out.'
>
> The specially designed baseball caps were chosen for their kudos, and the team of six seven-year-olds was selected after teachers' recommendations.
>
> The new rules encourage the 240 students to face up to the consequences of their actions and be assertive rather than aggressive.' (Bill Russell and staff, St Andrews First School, Great Yarmouth, November 1993, from a local newspaper report.)

- Grade 5 students work as deputies with Grade 6 students. Mediators always work in pairs.
- Students receive certificates upon completion of training.

The program is regularly evaluated through weekly meetings with mediation supervisors. Mediators take turns to chair these meetings which are supported by the mediation supervisors. Such meetings allow for problems and issues to be aired, and plans to be finetuned. Surveys with students, teachers and parents are taken yearly to reassess the program's effectiveness.

Before setting up a program of peer mediation, it is worth networking with schools who already run programs so that their knowledge and skills can be utilised.

Peer mediation and productive play

Some students find productive play difficult. They roam aimlessly, they annoy others, some don't know how to initiate play, or play positively. Some students lack the basic knowledge, and skills, for activities such as down-ball, skipping games, hopscotch, ball-to-wall games and tennis. One Tasmanian school, Mayfield Primary, aware that problematic behaviour was often linked to playground time, decided to develop a peer-assisted approach to playground play.

Students were selected to participate in a training program that taught them how to initiate play, encourage play, lead specific games in planned areas of the playground and to mediate in inappropriate play activity. The physical education teacher trained the peer mediators in a range of activities and games. Each class in the school then had sessions with the PE teacher to introduce peer leaders to each grade group and teach the same games and activities, appropriate for the playground, so that all students had the same input. This gave the lower and middle school students an opportunity to meet the peer leaders and understand their role in the playground.

The peer leaders have access to appropriate equipment and are rostered in pairs for lunch play. The playground is organised to accommodate a range of activities and games and the peer leaders work in the areas within their roster. At the beginning of lunchtime they are called up to plan equipment needs. An announcement is made over the intercom system that particular peer leaders are responsible for down-ball, bat tennis or football during each lunch play. They wear coloured baseball caps with Peer Support written on them. When they need to mediate, the focus is on reminding disruptive students of the rules for safety, fair play and fair treatment. Consequences include the time-out bench or direction to a teachers' aide who supervises alternative activities for students who choose not to play within the set games. All serious behaviour is referred to a duty teacher. Fighting results in withdrawal inside.

The success of the program lies in the training of students chosen for their peer acceptance, their relational skills and their commitment. A special feature of this program is the PE teacher's whole-school involvement in teaching appropriate games for the playground to all classes with the peer leaders. Once the program is established, peer mediators are involved in training the next group of mediators.

Chapter 8

SUPPORTING COLLEAGUES IN A UNITED WHOLE-SCHOOL PLAN

'Everybody hurts . . . sometimes' (REM).

Collegial support

I take demonstration lessons as part of my consultancy role. Several teachers watching you take a lesson with a challenging Grade 6, or even Grade 1, is a nerve-racking experience I can assure you! It took me a while to get used to teaching while colleagues observe. Like many teachers from my generation, I grew up believing my class was totally my class, *my* private domain.

Although teachers work with others (minors) all day, they are often isolated from peers and from positive, informed observation and support. Some teachers like that state of affairs—that strange sense of security where one can teach without having one's 'fallibility' exposed. I understand that. However, this long-term and physical isolation makes it more difficult for teachers to learn from the methods and practices of other teachers.

I've taken difficult senior classes, with two or three teachers ensconced down the back, when a painful boy seeks to engage me in power play, or the class is particularly noisy and it takes me several minutes to settle them down or a student chucks a 'wobbly', overturns a desk and swears at me for no apparent reason. I've then had teachers, in debriefing sessions say, 'I'm glad it happened to you.' By this, they mean nothing nasty. It is simply their way of saying, 'You too? Well it's not just me. I'm glad.'

Sharing failure with collegues is therapeutic.

Sharing 'failure' with colleagues is therapeutic. Recognising that we all have similar concerns, issues and problems creates a climate where genuine problem solving can take place. In some of my early schools, I have to say, it was felt that male teachers who shared such concerns were, in effect, weak. Yet, when the culture of the workplace is supportive, staff work better, more happily, and in a more relaxed, productive way.

Social support has been identified as a resource that enables individuals to cope with stress (Kyriacou 1981, 1987; Montgomery 1986; Rogers 1992). 'According to the moderating hypothesis, individuals who have supportive social relationships are able to rely on others to aid them in dealing with stressful situations . . . researchers have consistently found that individuals who possess high levels of social support are in better physical and mental health . . . teachers who were classified as burnt out spent less time with their fellow workers than did other teachers' (Russell, Altmaier and Van Velzen 1987).

I really thought I was getting through to them!

193

Collegial support can operate at several levels in a school, but whatever the level its aim is to create a climate where professional sharing and problem solving is the norm.

1 Moral support

All of us need that general sense of emotional support, the demonstration of empathy and understanding. Strangely, teaching can be a lonely job. The few occasions we meet with colleagues are often in transit (a quick rush to the staffroom to microwave yesterday's dinner, a cuppa, and off to playground duty), or through meetings. This is why it is important to allow time for sharing during our meetings, so that staff can enjoy a sense of teamwork and so that interpersonal support can be promoted. Schools need to consider how they use team meetings and what kinds of team best suit the needs of staff. Senior staff need to consider how to build workable teams. This depends on the skills of team leaders, how often teams meet, the size of the team and how individual teams communicate with and work with the total staff body. Many schools now use year-level teams for curriculum and behaviour management planning and to supplement general staff meetings.

As Johnson and Johnson note (1989), being part of a team can increase confidence and self-esteem, foster opportune and positive communication and be a vehicle for co-operative planning and decision making. Supportive teams can also empower staff through the generation of ideas, and by being orientated towards solutions about curriculum and behaviour management rather than focused on problems. Most of all, collegial teams decrease the sense of isolation and lack of focus or direction that can occur when the bulk of a teacher's professional life occurs in isolation.

The kind of support that comes from colleagues who care needs to be demonstrated in practical ways:

- fair and considerate treatment of staff, including sensitive listening, when they have problems
- basic consideration of the welfare and wellbeing of colleagues, especially when they are sick or having a rough time with their class (It is often shown in small ways through special morning teas, birthdays remembered, even the way the staffroom is set out to consider its role—seating, aesthetics, facilities for tea and coffee making.)
- quality of communication, especially with senior staff (In a study on peer support (Sarros in Bernard 1990) when individuals perceived they had support from their principals, there was, teachers noted, less stress and personal achievement 'burnout'.)
- daily briefings to set the day, shared by staff wherever possible
- recognition by senior staff of the effort and contribution made to the life of the school by teaching staff.

2 Problem-solving support

This can range from the way advice is given, to the opportunity for sharing issues and concerns. In a culture that is supportive, there are both formal and informal ways in which staff can assess concerns and needs, and access workable solutions. This is especially relevant to the development of action plans when assessing staff needs and concerns. It can range from specific task force groups on issues such as playground behaviour through to the use of small, ad hoc, decision-making groups during staff meetings. What is essential is that staff believe their concerns are heard, and that formal and informal processes are in place to translate the communication processes into workable action plans. Later, it is helpful to allow feedback and evaluation of the effectiveness of plans.

3 Structural and instrumental support

There are many areas in a school where stress can be significantly reduced by structural change. Even a flickering neon light, lousy cupboards and inadequate furniture, can induce unnecessary stress, let alone poor time-out provisions and playground management plans. Good, whole-school plans reduce stress by increasing the certainty that help is available when it's needed and by increasing the safety margins. Teaching staff, especially, need the assurance that middle and senior management will listen to them and give necessary and active support, particularly in situations which are difficult to manage.

Professional development is also linked to collegial support when programs that genuinely address staff needs are put in place. How does the school, through its administrative support and policy procedures, care for its front-line teaching staff and how do they, conversely, support their senior colleagues?

4 Collegial feedback and peer appraisal

I have heard countless teachers relate that they are given very little professional feedback. Recognition of one's efforts and specific contributions—feedback— is important. It assists us to understand how effectively we are meeting our aims for teaching and learning. At a more basic level, feedback enhances our self-esteem.

Giving feedback about ineffective teacher practice is much more difficult. Few of us find it easy, and certainly feel uncomfortable that it may be interpreted as judgment. The purpose of professional feedback is:
- to assist staff in ascertaining where their strengths are, and where their ineffective practice is and to have some agreed and documented reference for effective practice. Developing any framework for acceptable management practices raises questions about the value judgments involved in establishing criteria such as: effective, acceptable, ineffective. Developing a common framework of preferred practices (Chapter 2) will go a long way in assisting in the development of a useful appraisal
- to give *descriptive* feedback, not to be judgmental (p 199).

The quality of collegial feedback depends on who gives it, how it is given, and whether the processes set up to engage feedback are elective. As Johnson and Johnson note (1989), productivity suffers when trust is broken by competition, harsh communication, criticism, disrespect and negative comments.

Teachers need, and in good schools receive, support from senior managers (heads and deputies) and in secondary schools middle managers (heads of year or department), as well as peer support. The tradition of classroom isolation makes this difficult in two ways. Good teachers may get little or no recognition from senior staff for their achievements. This is demotivating. Professional etiquette may also leave teachers who are having difficulty, to suffer regular humiliation in the classroom. Teacher appraisal is another way of opening the classroom door. Supportive appraisal should improve standards of classroom management (*The Elton Report* 1989, p 79).

Developing a culture of support

In developing a culture of support it is important to recognise the benefits of collegial support which:

- decreases the sense that, 'It's all my fault. I'm the only one who has a problem like this'
- takes off the pressure of feeling totally responsible for 'your' students
- can reduce structural and professional isolation
- can reduce negative feelings of inadequacy and low self-esteem—a problem shared is a problem halved (Problem resolution by just talking things through is beneficial in itself. It is enhanced when it leads to structural support and structural solutions.)
- can increase interpersonal problem solving (Johnson and Johnson 1989)
- significantly increases individual coping resources and can mitigate burnout (see Russell et al 1987; Kyriacou 1981; Sarros in Bernard 1990)
- can enhance early detection of problems, thus allowing a more effective intervention process.

Determine needs as staff see them

- what kinds of collegial support exist already?
- where and how?
- what kinds of support are people wanting?
- how do we invite and offer collegial support?
- how do we set up processes, based on needs analysis, to enhance a collegially supportive culture.

Appraisal

If appraisal is to be effective in the teaching profession, it needs to be developed by teachers. They are better (often more critical) at rating their practice than people outside the school, and teachers are more likely to act on teacher-initiated and teacher-supported appraisal.

If carried out from outside the profession, appraisal is more likely to be seen as interference or outside judgment linked to tenure or promotion issues. It will work only if teachers see the procedures as legitimate.
Appraisal:

- needs to occur over a period of time, rather than be episodic
- is most effective when it occurs within a trusted peer process, elective wherever possible, always collaborative

- needs to focus on the quality of teaching and management (not merely on outcomes) through review procedures that document changes over time, and that can appraise (praise) quality of life and understanding of students. Most teachers see appraisal at its best when linked to the professional development of staff

- needs to assess whether a teacher's individual values and goals are in congruence with institutional values and goals. If a teacher does not reasonably embrace the institutional values and goals, or if there is a significant mismatch, great difficulty in professional development is created. Senior staff need to consider how to support, and even confront, teachers who are unwilling to support school-wide policy and practice.

> A primary motivation for teachers to take on extra work and other personal costs of attempting change is the belief that they will become better teachers and their students will benefit (McLaughlin and Marsh 1978 in Guskey 1986).

> . . . regardless of teaching level, most teachers define their success in terms of their students' behaviours and activities, rather than in terms of themselves or other criteria (Harootiunian and Yagay 1980 in Guskey 1986).

Developing a culture of support— questions to ask

- What kinds of collegial support exist in the school at the moment?
- What support have you sought to obtain from administrative staff, senior staff, teaching peers?
- In what ways are you supported in your role here?
- Are there areas where collegial support isn't operating but clearly needs to? Where? Where do you think the problems lie?
- How can we improve the quality and kind of collegial support in our school?
- How do you respond to the notion of peer observation and feedback (p 199) as a mechanism for peer-controlled appraisal?
- If senior staff considered that your teaching practice was significantly ineffective and failing to meet professional requirements or institutional aims, how would you want to be approached about it? (This legitimate function which needs to be exercised at times, is one of the most difficult roles undertaken by a senior or head teacher.)
- Do you have any suggestions you would like to offer?

Peer feedback in professional development

A number of Australian reports on stress in the teaching service have highlighted the need for whole-school approaches to address both teacher stress and behaviour management concerns which are a key source of stress.

In the *Education Quarterly* (October 1992), a report researching stress and staff morale highlighted the understandable factors contributing to negative stress such as: authoritarian leadership (students, too, become stressed out on characteristically authoritarian, rather than authoritative, leadership), inflexible procedures, poor staff relations and student behaviour, excessive work demands and Department of Education demands (so what's new?).

However, there were two factors which emerged from the report that are crucial to the theme of whole-school approaches to behaviour management.

Goal congruence

A set of objectives easily understood and shared by all staff was the single strongest predictor of staff morale. Another major stress survey, *Teacher Stress in Victoria* 1989, noted that an 'absence of shared beliefs (or culture) within the school about fit and proper student behaviour . . .' and 'differences (in) underlying views about discipline practices in the same school . . .' were themselves a source of stress for teachers (pp 43–44).

Lack of feedback

Teachers also complained about the lack of feedback more than any other aspect of their role. In some ways, this is a surprising finding in that teachers tend to be wary of collegial feedback that is uninvited or skewed towards assessing performance. However, in common with this report's findings, I've found that teachers respond well to supportive feedback based on team approaches to problem solving—feedback that they have some control of, that isn't imposed but elective. This raises important questions for teacher appraisal. Notwithstanding, it is generally accepted by teachers that supportive feedback is desired and valued. When did a colleague, especially a senior colleague, last give you some supportive, descriptive feedback on your teaching or your contribution to the school? Last week? Well done!

Peer feedback

Peer feedback is an elective feature of collegial support. It is a mutual learning experience between teachers who have a common, professional motivation to improve in key areas of their practice. It is not easy to open one's classroom to even a trusted colleague; our self-esteem, as it were, is on the line. That is why successful collegial feedback has to be invited and supportive. It is a way of professionally decreasing the natural isolation in our profession.

Peer feedback is a professional approach that strengthens self-appraisal by:
• having a trusted colleague observe a number of classes
• having a framework for mutual observation that includes what we will observe, how/when such observation will take place and how the feedback will be given
• being based on mutuality and collegiality, not on superior–inferior relationships. While it can be linked with appraisal schemes, it is more effective if offered as part of a collegial support process with a professional development focus.

When using peer feedback for behaviour management skills, it is important to recognise that teachers vary in their sense of need for skills. Professional development, in-servicing and policy development cannot force skills onto teachers, though it can set up a desired framework for preferred practice (p 30 ff). Using collegial groups and teams (p 194), senior staff, who themselves will need to be able to model good practice, can encourage the practical utility of peer feedback as a way of developing preferred practices and skills. Some state education departments are now advocating teacher appraisal schemes. These will be most beneficial if the schemes are internally developed along collegial lines.

The emphasis is on teacher growth challenged by collaborative planning, shared decision making and collegial work in a framework of experimentation and evaluation (*Lowe and Istance* 1989).

The emphasis is not on controlling and assessing performance, but rather on individual teachers controlling their professional growth by actively using peer observation and feedback in the natural setting of the classroom and in duty-of-care settings.

> An important distinction regarding the appraisal of classroom teaching can be made between formative assessment (feedback aimed at facilitating the improvement of teaching) and summative assessment (a judgment aimed at accrediting a teacher's competence and possibly related to promotion prospects) (Kyriacou 1987, p143).

There has to be a 'here', 'there' understanding between one's present practice and areas where change would be useful, and necessary, if goals are going to be met. A framework for change can be developed using:
- preferred practices (Chapter 2)
- particular skills (Chapter 3 and 5)
- particular emphases in classroom management, such as the beginning and ending of lessons, entry and settling of a class group, gaining and sustaining group attention, crossover of activities, movement routines
- nonverbal behaviour in corrective behaviour management (p 49 ff)
- a particular curriculum focus or new practice such as classroom meetings or co-operative learning.

Giving feedback

When observing in a colleague's class, consideration needs to be given to:
- how a colleague (the observer) is introduced to the host class
- where the colleague sits at key points in the lesson
- how 'intrusive' the observer is
- whether the observer can join in at certain points in the lesson and still observe
- the form in which the feedback (information) is taken and reported later
- how feedback will form the basis for future change in one's practice.

When giving feedback, peers need to have discussed:
- how to give it. It is not easy to note unproductive, poor, inadequate or ineffective practice. While it is enjoyable to give positive feedback on a teacher's practice, should we also give it on negative aspects of their practice?—Yes, if feedback is going to be useful. If collegial feedback is denied when a colleague is not aware of aspects of current practice that are ineffective, then feedback loses its usefulness. One has to know what is happening in classroom practice before knowing how best to address change. It is quite conceivable that one can be in a class day after day and not be aware of one's behaviour—especially when under the normative stress of day-to-day teaching—in the same way as an observer would

- the importance of observation—over time—to obtain a characteristic picture within which colleagues can refer questions such as:
  - Were you aware that . . .?
  - Were you aware of . . .?
  - Did you notice . . .?
  - Did you hear yourself say . . .?
  - How did you feel when . . .?

(All these feedback questions can then focus on specific, remediable behaviour patterns.)

- the tone and its necessity to be respectful of another's feelings (hence the question format above rather than a blunt 'I saw you do this')
- the setting in which feedback needs to take place—over a cuppa, but not in the staffroom
- the use of a mutual journal between observations. Make a plan for change based on mutual observations. Be sure, above all, to balance positive and negative aspects of collegial practice, especially giving weight to the bad-day syndrome
- the focus of the reporting practice. This needs to be understood contractually before embarking on observation and feedback. If feedback is comprehensive, colleagues can then focus on areas for finetuning and change. The emphasis is on honesty without hurt and on giving requested feedback for which mutual permission is healthily granted
- how to make feedback specific. 'Were you aware that when students call out you normally do this?' 'Did you notice Jason rocking back in his chair several times?' 'Did you hear yourself say, "Don't call out" half a dozen times to Fiona?'
- the need for feedback to be non-judgmental—peers are not judging a colleague's practice, but are *reporting aspects of it* (Rogers 1992) by:
  - focusing on behaviour not on another's personality
  - giving specifics: 'Have you considered this?' 'Did you notice that . . when . . . how . . .?'
- the amount of feedback given. Avoid overwhelming. I've been in a number of classes where the loudness of a teacher's voice is so important an element in the dysfunctional mode of the room that we've started to work just on that, then on specific language skills, movement in the room etc
- the best time to give feedback. It may help (if our colleague is willing) to 'mirror' behaviour. 'Can I show you what I heard you say?' 'Can I show you how loud?' 'Can I show you how it looked to me?' 'I'd like you to consider . . .' Of course, this is risky. Feedback always is. That is why it will really only be effective if it is mutual. We've often laughed with each other as we've given each other the polite goods, as it were. It may also be helpful to use a tape recorder or video tape a colleague's class and vice versa . . .
- the need for feedback to remain confidential—except in those rare instances when feedback is linked with performance-related peer review.

SUPPORT STAFF WITHIN A WHOLE-SCHOOL APPROACH

School A

She needs the work. She's made sure her little one is organised with the neighbour. She's managed to get to the school by 8.30 am. 'She' is a supply (relief) teacher.

She goes to the office and asks what class she has. They don't know. The principal comes over. He's not sure either and suggests she check with the DP. She has no idea who the DP is. She goes looking. Nobody has offered her a cup of tea yet. Time is passing and she wants to go to her classroom. She also wanted a chance to use the photocopier. She finds out that she's been given a Grade 5/6 composite class. The DP—she found him—says, 'They'll be a bit of a challenge. They're in the class past the canteen. You'll find a work program there.' At this stage she doesn't even have a class roll or a map of the school and doesn't know the grade teacher's name. She'll need to know that in her chat with the class. She still hasn't done her photocopying. She's not feeling comfortable about today's teaching role.

School B

She arrives at the office and is soon met by the DP who greets her: 'Hi, you must be Denise Smith. Welcome to our school. My name is . . . Would you like a cuppa, and can I run through the details for the day?' The DP gives her a class roll, a sheet that has a summary of the school's behaviour management plan, including the exit time-out policy procedure and who the reference teacher is. 'You'll need this number for photocopying but if it's urgent I can have it done now. Here's a timetable for Linda Wilson's class. I'll introduce you to them at 9:00. Your class is in room 17. Here's a map of the school. I've shaded the classroom.' She's feeling good about today . . .

Supply teachers often say they can tell what a school is going to be like in the first ten minutes of being there. It's often those first impressions—of feeling accepted, valued and secure, that basic uncertainties have been taken care of—that influence the day.

Supply teachers are not mere babysitters. It is important to convey the message that they are valued members of staff by:

• the way we welcome and receive them
• making sure they know where the toilets are, where the photocopier is and how to use it
• letting them know the protocol for tea and coffee
• having a legible map of the school marked with the classrooms where the teacher will be working
• providing a class timetable, particularly for specialist teachers
• knowing the special rules/routines for that class. Each grade/specialist teacher needs to leave these in the front of their work program. It's not helpful to establish with a new class by saying, 'I have no idea what your rules and routines are. I wonder if you would tell me.' It is especially important at Infant level that supply teachers are aware of key routines—for 'little play' and lunch, quiet reading after lunch, who the monitors are—that stabilise the social life of twenty-five plus students. These need to be kept in the room in an accessible form
• providing a user-friendly summary of the behaviour management policy, especially the exit/time-out plan. This is headed by, 'Dear colleague, welcome to our school. You are a valued member of our staff. To support you in your role here, we have prepared this profile. If you need further help, your collegial peer for today is_____(a buddy teacher) in room_____.' This sheet (with bell times etc) could finish with, 'We would appreciate it if you would leave any follow-up messages about behaviour of students, and what you have covered today (worksheets, stories etc) on the teacher's desk. We thank you for your contribution to our school today.'
• giving information about bell times and specialist times. Does the grade teacher walk the class over and stay with them in art, at PE and recess times? While this is all too obvious, many supply teachers have told me that they have to find all this out at the last minute
• saying who the first-aid teacher is and in what room
• introducing the supply teacher to the staff, especially at morning tea, and to the class—this gives the supply teacher status in the students' eyes
• clarify the playground duty roster and plan.

It is helpful if supply teachers also consider their role by:
• coming half an hour early
• leaving the room at least as tidy as they found it—chairs and materials away, board cleaned, work corrected
• leaving a summary of work undertaken and follow-up comments about behaviour management, especially any consequences which have been used
• leave the class with a positive tone, not, 'You're the worst Grade 5 I've ever had. I'm glad you're not my class. If you were, you . . .!'

Support staff are real staff

The groundsman had just laid a large lawn area near a footpath. He'd marked off the area and watered it. A couple of senior students walked across the soil. He called across, 'Boys! I've just spread grass seeds there. Use the path, thanks.' He was annoyed but not nasty. One of the boys said, 'You're just the caretaker. You can't tell us what to do!' No support person in a school—cleaner, gardener, groundsperson, canteen staff, whatever—is *just* an anything. They are part of a team. Students need to know that support staff are legitimate staff. By introducing them at formal assembly time and supporting them through professional development, we communicate collegial value and status. Invite them to come to a staff workshop. The workshop can discuss and consider:

- their concerns about behaviour as they see it (this is crucial)
- clarification of preferred practices of the school on behaviour management
- how these can be applied to their situation
- legitimising their duty-of-care role and indicating how and when they can discipline students as they move around the school
- how they can support teaching staff in the follow-up of behaviour when appropriate, for example, with consequences. Staff need to consider whether support staff have access to the behaviour monitoring book in the staffroom and how communications between teaching staff and support staff can be improved.

Make sure they are paid for their attendance at professional development sessions to show that their presence and support is valued.

SUPPORTING NEW TEACHERS

As a new teacher to a large primary school, many years back, I was naive, uncertain about the school culture and my new profession. I was given a Grade 5 class—'upper grade because you're a male'. All I was told was, 'You've got Grade 5, room 21, you'll get your attendance register later and a specialist timetable. We haven't made that one up yet.' On the student-free day, teachers were given time to set their rooms up. When I saw my room—chalkboard scarred, cupboards with hinges broken, no curtains (on what I could already see would be a hot west wall of windows), and not enough desks, I told the principal. 'Oh just have a look in the bicycle shed for other furniture.' His gesture and tone was dismissive. I searched and found the shed, only to discover its wired gates chained shut. I could see a pile of old desks. I chased up the caretaker for a key and soon found out why the desks had been dumped there. I also found out, being last in, that all the good desks had already been taken for the other senior classes. With screwdriver, nails and glue, I managed to fix up the required number of desks for my students.

A new teacher in a school, especially a first year teacher, has to negotiate the idiosyncratic culture of that school as well as schooling and teaching, generally. Although I was introduced to my colleagues, had a pile of paper policies, a class roll, a work-program file and my room, I felt unsupported and on my own. In time, I made friends, got to know the paper culture as well as the day-to-day culture. I re-painted the blackboard, put up shelves and fixed the cupboards. The hardest part of all was getting the petty cash.

I coped. I also learnt that it was not encouraged to talk too much, or too publicly, about discipline and behaviour management. This applied even more to male teachers. That was the culture in those days—give the upper grades to the males because they'll be able to straighten out the naughty boys—with the strap or cane if necessary.

Rather than leave new teachers, and (more importantly) first year teachers, to come to terms with the school by chance and time alone, it helps if senior staff plan for staff induction for all new teachers to the school. This involves more than, 'Welcome to our school. Take this pile of papers. You're in room 21, Grade 5. Best of luck.'

- How can we enable new staff to feel at home without overwhelming them?
- Do they know how we establish our classes here?
- What are the basic things they need to know about how we run things at our school?
- What routines, procedures and communication processes do they need to know about? (What may seem patently obvious to us may not be so for them.)
- Do they have relevant policy documents?
- Is there a support person we can team them up with for the first four weeks or so?

It will greatly assist new staff to a school if they are:
- in-serviced in the behaviour management policy
- given an administration profile covering basics such as bell/break times, protocol for use of photocopier and the roster for staffroom duty
- given copies of the key policies, especially the behaviour management policy (p 208)
- informed about how to obtain necessary materials for the class, art materials, class furniture, PE equipment, etc
- given a list of staff with a basic professional profile of teachers' skills, talents and specialist subject areas. If we know that a colleague has majored in music, students' literature or art, we can ask for advice. This is more relevant in a big school where it takes time to get to know colleagues. Now that there are large numbers of part-time teachers in schools, it is particularly helpful to know which days they are at the school. The profile can also include what grades a colleague has had, and over how many years. This is particularly helpful if one is struggling with a grade level outside one's direct experience. If staff members agree, their phone numbers might be noted, so that staff can chat outside school. Obviously, this is more relevant to large schools
- told that a collegial reference partner is available—a 'buddy system'
- are able to attend regular team meetings for junior, middle and senior school where staff can plan curriculum matters, discuss management and discipline issues, review policy and action plans and generally appropriate the support of colleagues. Of course, we could leave new staff to discover all this for themselves, or just give them bits of paper but it is more helpful if a support colleague is available during their establishment phase.

New and beginning teachers want to feel that they belong. While there are many ways to learn to belong, the most basic way is through being treated by others as if it is true.

STRESS MANAGE- MENT

One positive way to work on stress management is to identify what the workplace stresses are, as perceived by staff. This exercise can be done yearly—a year is a long time. Things change. No doubt the Directorate of School Education will have some new directive or policy to make our lives more, more what? more functional? more challenging? more burdened? And, of course, staff come and go.

Using a small group, or a combination of survey and small-group approaches, several phases are explored. Staff are encouraged to focus on how stress affects them personally.

- Identify factors in the workplace that cause individuals stress. Note how stressful each factor is perceived on a scale 1–5 (little to a lot). It also helps if staff note down why they regard a particular factor in their school or class as significantly, or particularly, stressful.
- Staff can use the survey data as input on the frequency and seriousness of workplace stressors, and see if any pattern emerges. It can be as basic as deficient fluorescent lighting, and lack of cupboard or shelf space. At the other end of the scale it might be the way communication processes are not working as effectively as they could—for example, lack of input into key decisions. What is important is that staff genuinely feel they can share their perceptions, needs and concerns, and secondly that by working together something can be done about those issues.
- In making decisions about what to do about stressors, staff need to discuss what needs finetuning, modification or a complete change of approach.

Also, thought needs to be given to:

- which issues can be modified or changed in the short-term as opposed to long-term (especially where money is a factor in bringing about change)
- what we can realistically work on and how
- what is achievable regarding change and what issues are actually non-negotiable ('We're stuck with this one, folks. Let's make the best of it, okay?').

Lastly, an action plan needs to assess the issues from the point of view of achievable change. Identifying workplace stressors, only to have little done about them, is itself very stressful. As with all action plans, we will need to nominate who? what? how? and when? Such plans need to be evaluated during and after implementation. Time can be set aside at staff meetings to facilitate staff evaluation on action plans.

Chapter 9

DEVELOPING A BEHAVIOUR MANAGEMENT POLICY

Fundamentally, a policy is a balance between a school's defined aims and objectives, and the procedures, practices and plans for meeting them. A policy may be stated or unstated but will eventually be observed in the characteristic behaviour of staff in the school. In fact, the real policy is the day-to-day practice of behaviour management which may be a far cry from what we say we believe or do, or even from what we have published.

The Departments of Education in all states and territories of Australia have, in recent years, outlined the need for schools to clarify their aims and objectives for discipline and behaviour management, and to express these in a policy document that reflects current educational thought.

One of the recommendations of a major study on teacher stress in Victoria (1989) was that schools develop a collaborative policy process for discipline and behaviour management, that '. . . each school be required to have a published discipline policy (developed in consultation with parents and students) and to ensure that it is applied consistently' (p 44).

Consultation with the wider community

The degree of consultation in policy development is affected by the community the school serves and the willingness and degree of effort applied by the school to engage the community. Surveys, coffee nights, inviting parents onto the steering group (p 210)—most of all, keeping parents informed by user-friendly feedback—are all ways in which parents can be genuinely involved.

It is important to create an open, welcoming environment for parents. After all, they and their children are our 'clients'. As teachers we have a clear, professional obligation and role regarding management, teaching and learning, and social development. We share with parents the same aims and objectives for their children:
• their common welfare and wellbeing
• an attitude to relationships that considers others' rights as well as one's own
• responsibility and accountability for one's behaviour
• basic values such as honesty, caring and co-operation.

When developing policy, it is important to have parent representatives on the steering group. Throughout the draft process, results of surveys, recommendations, trial practices (for example, playground management) should be communicated to the wider parent community.

Developing a draft policy

A policy takes some time to develop. Even if there is already a policy in place, from time to time, it will need finetuning or adapting.

1 The prime mover for a policy review is often community awareness, which can be triggered by need, crisis, Education Department policy imperatives or change in clientele. Professional development programs in behaviour management can also refocus a school's thinking and practice. In a whole-school approach, policy development focuses on the need to work and act collaboratively with reasonable consistency within a supportive framework. No-one writes up a document as if a written document is the answer. It is, rather, a process—a journey—during which all staff have the opportunity to reassess and affirm:

- the community's values and assumptions about discipline, behaviour management and student welfare as it relates to the students' overall education
- the best arrangements, practices and plans to achieve the school's aims.

DEVELOPING A POLICY OF BEHAVIOUR MANAGEMENT

ISSUES

| Playground behaviour | The 'hard-class' syndrome | The 'hard-case' student | Consistency of practice |

'HERE'   the journey of change   **'THERE'**

'Here' is where we are, what we believe and characteristically do regarding behaviour management

'There' is the direction we want to go; not an arrived at point

| Awareness raising | Professional development | Collegial 'team building' | Policy development | Regular evaluation |

POLICY
Entry points into the journey

Figure 9 © B Rogers 1995.

There is never a perfect 'there' to which a school directs its journey. Here to there is determined by current beliefs, practices and needs, and assessment of those in light of what we want to achieve in behaviour management terms. There are many entry points (*Figure 7*) along this journey for raising awareness. Time needs to be given for staff to come to terms with changing circumstances, new or improved practices, changes in plans and even the risk of working collaboratively.

2 Research and assessment is essential (key questions and process formats are discussed on p 22 ff). Careful thought needs to be given to survey questions, especially when conveyed to parents. There is little point in asking parents 'What kind of discipline would you like to see in our school?' when we are properly bound by law not to use corporal punishment, and current educational philosophy and practice encourages appropriate uses of negotiation and dialogue within a context of mutual respect. *Positive School Discipline: A Guide to Developing Policy* by Cowin et al (1985) is an excellent resource for developing the survey and research process.

A framework for a policy is developed on page 18 of this text. It is essential that the key areas of behaviour management noted there are addressed in the policy process.

3 Formulating a draft policy. A policy is both a school's expression of its values, beliefs and practices as well as a quasi-legal document. Achieving the right balance isn't easy. It needs to be both accessible and reasonably comprehensive. Some schools have opted for a policy with a separate parent summary and a separate students' version with illustrations. Other schools have one document with user-friendly language, student illustrations, and appropriate appendixes for more complex issues. Some schools have a separate playground management plan consistent with the overall policy on behaviour management. In the drafting process, it is helpful to use published documents from other schools as a guide.

A boring caveat—I've seen marvellous published policies which are the result of hours of drafting, redrafting, and collaboration—reproduced in part or whole in another school's document without permission or even acknowledgment of the source. It is important that the school goes through the *process* of review, rather than borrowing from the labour of others.

A behaviour management policy normally includes:

- a policy statement, sometimes termed a mission statement—a concise, one-page statement of the school's beliefs and aims, regarding behaviour in the school (p 212 and appendix)
- a user-friendly definition of the terms used in the document—discipline, behaviour management, rights, consequences, punishment
- the preventive aspects of behaviour management. Acknowledgment will be made that the policy aims to create a safe, secure environment for learning

and behaviour and that the school emphasises principles of mutual respect, co-operation and fair treatment in its discipline practice

- concise definition of the rights and responsibilities of all members of the school community (see examples in appendix). An important note for parents is the emphasis on the shared responsibility of parents and teachers in the discipline and management of students in schools
- an explanation of corrective practices and problem-solving procedures. Disruptive behaviour and rule breaking will not be excused but dealt with from a positive corrective stance, and appropriate uses of problem-solving procedures. It is helpful to include illustration of the step-wise levels of corrective management outlining the degree of seriousness at each level (see appendix)
- an outline of the fundamental school rules and a framework for classroom rules (p 79)
- explanation of any specific due process for significantly disruptive behaviour in terms of rationale and practice (for example, time-out policy, harassment and bullying policy, suspension policy)
- an outline showing how repairing and rebuilding procedures take place in the school (parent conferencing, contracting, welfare and counselling provisions, and how external resources can be contacted and utilised in solving behaviour problems)
- Education Department guidelines and relevant documentation for policy implementation, (often included in an appendix to the policy document).

The final document should present the policy in a form that is easy to read, with clear sections, imaginative use of headings, sufficient white space and illustrations. The length of the document is also important—fifteen to twenty pages are ample to comfortably contain the necessary information.

Trial the document

A draft document, published and circulated, can be given a reasonable trial over a couple of school terms. Students and parents can evaluate the document's accessibility and practical utility. Evaluation can be made through general feedback from staff and students (via classroom meetings), staff discussions, teacher checklists noting whether the adopted practices and plans have affected behaviour in and out of class, data from the playground behaviour-monitoring book (have numbers dropped?), usage of time-out, referrals and detentions.

After appropriate finetuning of the document, the school council can ratify it for publication as its official behaviour management policy. Even then, cyclical review will be necessary so that additions or extensions can be made as needs arise or circumstances change.

Once the policy is formed it ought to be the basis for regular staff in-servicing for behaviour management, especially at the establishment phase of the year and for incoming teachers. It can be quite stressful if a teacher who is new to a school, has to arrange exit of a disruptive student from a classroom. The teacher might be uncertain about the procedure at

this school and wanting to know answers to questions such as:
- Is this acceptable here?
- To whom do I send a persistently disruptive student?
- Will I be treated as a failure if I do so?
- How will I use detention?
- What are the lines of authority?
- How are the roles of team leader and deputy principal exercised with respect to behaviour management?

Degrees of responsibility and accountability need to be clarified for all staff in a supportive way. What is the role of team leader and deputy principal— for time-out? follow-up? counselling procedures? parent conferences? setting up contracts for behaviour change? using sanctions such as suspension? A good policy enables and ensures that all staff can exercise individual and corporate responsibility. As the report *Teacher Stress in Victoria* (1989) notes, each school should, 'ensure that the lines of authority, responsibility and accountability be clearly defined so as to ensure that leadership can be exercised, policy made and implemented and shortfalls in performance detected and corrected' (p 44). In this sense, a policy is also a magnifying glass for what happens in a school and can be used diagnostically to review current practice.

Role of the policy steering group

Most schools when reviewing behaviour management and discipline policy keep track of the process by electing a steering group or working party, whose brief is to steer the staff through awareness raising, issue clarification, problem solving, professional development, action planning and policy writing.

The steering group sets out a timeline for the key issues involved in the policy process. Consideration is given to priority issues. These are decided through survey, needs analysis (p 24 ff) and staff discussion.

All issues relevant to behaviour management and the policy itself, are referred to the framework for behaviour management in the school (p 18). A key step in the policy process is gaining staff agreement on the framework for behaviour management policy. This process involves small-group collaboration, awareness raising and professional development on management concerns.

The steering group gives ongoing feedback to staff and parents (when appropriate) through survey results, draft guidelines, action plans and publication of staff decisions. They aim to develop a behaviour management policy within a set timeline. Twelve months is reasonable. During that process, trial action plans are utilised by staff and evaluated (for example, common class rules and consequences on key issues) and common skills are practised and reviewed. Corridor and playground supervision and duty-of-care schemes are reviewed and modified or new plans developed.

It is the process that is important, with key groups having input and contribution to the outcomes.

The published policy is finetuned from the draft process and becomes the basis for behaviour management in the school.

Questions to consider during and after the policy process

- How old is the current policy (published or unpublished)?
- Have we explained crucial terms like discipline, welfare, consequences, rights? Are the explanations given in user-friendly terms? (especially for parents)
- Have we explained what we discipline for? (Basic as it sounds, the goals of discipline and behaviour management need to go well beyond a punishment focus.)
- Does the policy outline the consequences for severe behaviour such as harassment and bullying—verbal, physical, sexual—or do we define all such behaviour as bullying?
- How collaborative is the policy process? Who will write it?—preferably key people on the policy steering group with feedback from staff on key sections en route. Were parents/students involved in any way? How?
- Have the guiding principles and preferred practices been included? (p 30 ff).
- Does the policy include school-wide rights/rules and a common framework for classroom rules?
- Has the exit/time out process and policy been explained? (p 83).
- Does the policy outline support mechanisms for classroom teachers in their behaviour-management role?
- Has the policy addressed how/when parents are to be contacted regarding discipline/behaviour concerns? Have their rights and responsibilities been noted? (cf Rogers 1990, pp 89–95).
- How will we write it all down? What are the essentials to include? Do we have a separate policy for parents—a summary policy, as it were? Do we need a separate, mini-policy for students, illustrated by them?
- Will we make a copy available to all parents on enrolment?
- Have all staff been in-serviced in the policy?
- It is important to note that Education Departments require schools to have a published policy on behaviour management. It is a quasi-legal document interfacing with issues and public legislation, such as:
  - workplace health and safety
  - anti-discrimination
  - students' rights
  - equal opportunity, gender equity, educational provision for students with disabilities, anti-racism, sexual harassment and grievance procedures (due process)
  - child abuse legislation.

It may be appropriate to make mention of this in the appendix to the policy.

Here is an example of a mission statement and statement of aims:

Spring Gully Primary School
Student Welfare and Discipline Policy

1   PURPOSE:

1.1 To enhance the development of positive relationships between students, teachers, parents and other members of the school community.

2   GUIDELINES:

2.1 All individuals are to be valued and treated with respect.

2.2 The rights and responsibilities of students, parents and school staff are to be clearly communicated and then honoured.

2.3 The physical and emotional environment for teaching and learning is to be safe and secure and appropriate for the stage of development of the students.

2.4 School decision-making processes are to be collaborative.

2.5 The school's policies and procedures are to be fair, logical and implemented consistently. (Key sections of this policy are included in the appendix.)

This policy has several key sections:

RIGHTS (of students, teachers and parents)

RESPONSIBILITIES

RULES

CONSEQUENCES

REVISING AND REVIEWING THE SCHOOL DISCIPLINE
   AND WELFARE PLAN

SUPPORTIVE ACTION (time-out, parent support, contracts, behaviour agreements, administration and Education Department support)

A framework for a CLASSROOM DISCIPLINE PLAN.

Here is another example of a belief statement (or mission statement) from a Tasmanian Primary School.

Figure 10

OUR BELIEFS

At Mayfield we believe that there is nothing more important than strong positive working relationships within a community. Positive relationships allow everyone to achieve maximum potential and growth.

Our belief is that a co-operative school is a happy, secure place where everybody's needs are met and all have the opportunity to succeed.

At Mayfield there is a variety of strategies and programs in place that foster the co-operative school ethos. The Supportive School Environment Program operating throughout the school is not an isolated program but an integral part of every aspect of school life. The program endeavours to promote the wellbeing of all those who work within the school community.

Through this program, students, in particular, learn skills in behaviour management and conflict resolution. They learn mutual respect and co-operation. By meeting success, students gain confidence and feel positive about themselves and others.

Developing a whole school policy

The policy will address key areas in the school's beliefs and practice:

- What do we fundamentally believe about discipline? What do we mean when we say we discipline students? Do we have preferred management styles. Why?
- What are we trying to achieve in behaviour management and discipline? Is the policy educationally sound? Thomas McDaniel has noted (1989) that a discipline program should be pedagogically defensible. Discipline is always a learnt behaviour; discipline techniques should be based on what we know about learning theory and instructional methods. Teachers should understand how [their] program [discipline program] relates to educational needs of students (p 82).

- What does our behaviour management approach teach the students about behaviour ownership? accountability? respect of others' rights?
- Is the policy psychologically appropriate? What do our punishments teach, affect?
- Does the policy cater for community welfare—the welfare of teachers, students and parents?
- How does behaviour management policy affect student welfare? Does the policy consider the welfare of teachers, especially in stressful situations with behaviourally disordered and hostile, aggressive students?
- Does the policy demonstrate practical utility?

The policy should be able to answer the important 'What . . .?', 'What are . . .?' and 'When . . .?' questions.

- When a student refuses reasonable teacher requests in class, and is persistent we . . .
- When students need to be kept back for consequences, our preferred practice is . . .
- What are our preferred classroom rules?
- What are our school-wide rules, especially about playground behaviour?
- What is our preferred practice for bullying behaviour?

A policy is an attempt to gain some congruence between stated beliefs and preferred practices, and to enhance consistency of behaviour management across the school.

Conclusion

Joint undertakings stand a better chance . . . when they benefit both sides (Euripedes, *Iphigeneia in Taurus*).

No plan or policy for behaviour management can hope to address all the issues raised by human fallibility and disobedience. Yet there has to be a policy, a common framework within which teachers can legitimately and professionally exercise their responsibility of leading and teaching students to own their own behaviour in ways that respect the rights of others.

A teacher's professional obligation and skill to do this is called into question many times each day. In the wider society and through the media, schools and teachers are made into a 'whipping boy' for society's problems. Schools need to work with their local communities to clarify what their role and function is, regarding behaviour management. They need to clarify what they mean by discipline and corrective management, how behaviour management issues fit in with teaching and learning generally and with the development of respect, tolerance, determination to give one's best, honesty, co-operation, accountability and communal goodwill. It's a lot to ask of a school.

Schools play a very powerful role in transmitting society's values, customs and expectations about interpersonal behaviour. If a policy has been genuinely collaborative and whole-school, if it has allowed concerns and needs to be expressed, and has pursued common plans based on shared values, then there is likely to be more clarity, certainty and consistency in our practice of behaviour management. When such a policy has had community input and feedback, and seen it expressed in daily practice, then the school can expect community support.

Students spend upwards of a third of their five-day week at school. Certainly, teachers spend a third of their day ensconced in classrooms dealing with the widest range of human behaviour, from the irritations of students' calling out through to lying, stealing and bullying. Questions such as:
• What can we do when . . .? (utility)
• What should we do when . . .? (value)
• How shall we do it? (approach, technique)
have to be addressed and answered individually and collegially.

A school simply cannot afford to have several plans for behaviour management, plans that simply rely on each teacher's idiosyncratic approach. Effective schools and effective teachers, have always emphasised:

• unity over isolation
• reflection over impulse
• communication over mere expectation
• collaboration over private practice.

It is my hope that this book will add to the tradition of good behaviour management practice in schools.

Appendixes

Examples of school

behaviour management

policies

Appendix 1   At Spring Gully Primary School EVERYBODY has: RIGHTS

STUDENTS

We all have a right to work, play and learn in a friendly, safe and helpful school.

TEACHERS

We all have a right to teach in a friendly, safe and satisfying school which is supported by the school community.

PARENTS

We all have a right to feel welcome and to know that our children work, play and learn in a friendly, safe and helpful school.

At Spring Gully Primary School EVERYBODY has:

RESPONSIBILITIES

We all need to **care** about ourselves, other students, parents, teachers, belongings, our school and equipment. Here are some examples:

- to listen
- to help
- to try our best
- to discuss
- to encourage
- to be polite
- to make time for others
- to be on time
- to help others understand
- to help others belong
- to try and work out problems in a fair manner

- to be honest
- to look after each other
- to try and understand each other
- to respect others
- to work and play safely
- to share attention
- to share equipment
- to share time
- to co-operate
- to ask for help
- to ask for opinions and ideas
- to have a go

Appendix 3   At Spring Gully Primary School, EVERYBODY has:

RULES

To help protect our *rights* and to encourage *responsibility*, we have basic rules for our classrooms and for times when we are out of class.

Talking or communication rule

Covers • hands up
   • working noise
   • hurtful language
   • assemblies
   • moving between rooms
   • lining up.

Learning rule

Covers • the way we learn and play in our room and out of class
   • how to get attention or help
   • co-operation
   • behaviour on camps and excursions.

Movement rule

Covers • the way we move about
   • equipment
   • being on time.

Treatment rule

Covers • the way we treat each other (no sexism, no put-downs, no racism)
   • manners.

Problem rule

Covers • the way we fix up problems between each other.

Safety rule

Covers • safe behaviour
   • use of equipment
   • camps and excursions.

Appendix 4   CONSEQUENCES

These are the planned consequences for **out of class** rules. Depending on circumstances, they can be used in any sequence.

- Rule reminder

- Verbal apology

- Written apology

- Sit down together, work it out using problem-solving steps which are consistent and common throughout the school.

    – The problem is . . .

    – Some ways to fix it are . . .

    – We plan to . . .

    – We will check with . . . to see if our plan is working.

- Walk with teacher and/or fill in a simple sheet.

    – What did I do against the rules?

    – What rules did I break?

    – Why did I do it?(optional)

    – What else can I do to fix it? Not just 'sorry' but strategies to use when a similar problem arises.

- Withdrawal from playground, other staff involved in **supportive action**, parents involved if necessary, loss of privileges, behaviour agreements.

- Outside personnel, suspension

Appendix 5 REVISING AND REVIEWING THE WELFARE AND DISCIPLINE PLAN

1 At the beginning of each school year and term, the staff will discuss with students the rules and consequences for classroom and out of classroom activities.

2 Younger students and new students to the school may need extra time for discussion.

3 The school welfare and discipline plans will be reviewed early in Term 1 at a staff meeting and at meetings throughout the year where necessary.

4 The Junior School Council will be utilised in promoting and evaluating the welfare and discipline plans.

Appendix 6   BEHAVIOUR MANAGEMENT IN THE PLAYGROUND

Conference staff

- With the child or children. Stop and calm the child.
- Questioning based on: What is the school rule?
- Listen to both sides of a problem. Each child giving his/her account with no interruptions.
- Reflect back on the rule.
- Discuss what children are going to do about it.
- The solutions suggested by both parties.
- Children then choose the solution that is acceptable to them.
- Children then put solution into effect.

Time-out outside

- If further problems occur or child/children need to be removed from the area—go to time-out bench.
- Children placed on time-out bench until duty teachers feel they can put the solution into operation.
- Name of the child/children is written in area duty book with comment about the problem.
- Monitoring of children listed in book.

Time-out inside

- Children move to time-out area inside, located near the principal's office.
- Supervised by staff. Record problem in time-out book.

Immediate withdrawal from playground

- Endangering others by throwing stones.
- Physical aggression making others unsafe.

Parent involvement

Major problem or continual disregard of school rules, parent/s will be contacted. Discussion includes parents, senior staff and class teacher.

Adult conference

Problem still occurring—need to discuss other methods that could be implemented to modify behaviour. Involve senior staff, class teacher, guidance officer, etc.

General comments

These procedures have been set in specific order, understood and articulated by staff and children. The steps will bring about interaction between children and teachers in consistent behaviour management.

Methods determining incidents will be decided by the following guidelines:

1. Minor incident

Work through each step of the Behaviour Management process. Examples: spitting, pushing, not playing in the right areas.

2. Major incident

From Mayfield Primary School, Tasmania.

Related to safety aspect. Children to go straight to inside time-out. Examples: fighting, throwing stones.

Appendix 7   EXCERPT FROM LETTER TO PARENTS AT HARE STREET INFANT SCHOOL, UK

Dear Parents,

This booklet is designed to outline the behaviour policy which we operate at Hare Street Infant School.

Through this booklet we aim to show you how we approach behaviour management both in the classroom and on the playground and to offer you strategies for making the hard job of discipline at home easier.

Our behaviour policy reflects the overall positive approach we have in our school towards all aspects of the child's learning and development.

Thanks for putting your hand up . . .

What do we mean by discipline?

Discipline is **not** control of children—many children are not easily controlled.

We believe that discipline is leading, guiding, encouraging and instructing children within a framework of rights, responsibilities and rules.

The 3Rs (rights, rules and responsibilities)

These **three** strands of discipline should work together to create a caring community atmosphere.

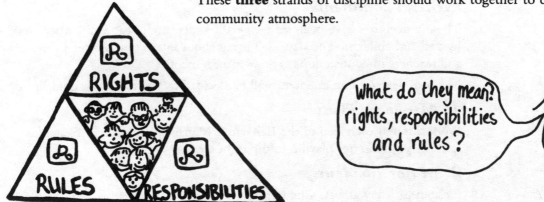

Let's start with the rule . . .

Every society, organisation, club, family and school operates on a set of rules.

In our school these rules are made by discussion between each teacher and their class.

The rules are

—written in a positive way

—owned by teachers *and* children

—fair

—certain.

The rules set reasonable limits to children's behaviour and make expected behaviour clear in advance.

A copy of the rules can be found in each classroom.

The rules are based on the rights of each person in our school community.

Appendix 8 EXAMPLES OF CONSEQUENCES

These are immediate and short-term.

RIGHT	ACTION	CONSEQUENCE
Safety	Using scissors inappropriately.	Children lose the right to use the scissors until they can use them safely. Children will need to fix anything that has been ruined.
Learning	Disturbing other children who are working.	Children lose the right to learn and work in a group, and may be isolated.
Treatment	Hurting somebody on purpose, eg kicking name calling.	Watch them being fixed up in the office. Do two things for the hurt child to make them feel better. eg Write a letter to say sorry. Make something for them. Do their tidying up. The hurt child makes the decision about this.
Movement	Running.	Go back and walk.
Communication	Calling out.	Children will be ignored at first and if they continue to call out they may be isolated to think about the rule that they chose to break.

Appendix 9 IMPLEMENTATION and REVIEW

- This document is to be reviewed and revised thoroughly each year. It will be necessary for all new staff members to be totally familiar with the document in order for there to be effective implementation of the strategies and processes involved.

- It is essential for teachers to plan for behaviour, just as they plan for any other area of the curriculum. The children must see that our rules and responsibilities permeate all that they do.

- General rules should be displayed (in a format suitable to age level) in classrooms, as well as specific safety rules for particular areas (eg music, art).

- Children need to be involved in the making of a list of classroom rules.

- Rules will be consistent throughout the school.

- Rules should be stated in the positive, and the logical consequences made known to the children.

- Parents should be involved where possible (eg parent awareness groups, etc).

STUDENTS' BEHAVIOUR AND APPROPRIATE ACTIONS

In deciding how to manage student behaviour, we may find it useful to imagine five stages from self-discipline to enforced discipline.

The following chart provides a guide which will assist us to explain how teachers can respond to these levels of student behaviour.

Appendix 10 LEVELS OF BEHAVIOUR MANAGEMENT IN THE SCHOOL POLICY

Mayfield Primary School, Tasmania.

Adapted from Rogers, B (1989) *Making a Discipline Plan*. Nelson, Melbourne.

LEVEL	STUDENT BEHAVIOUR	TEACHER ACTION	EXTRA SUPPORT
1	Student respects the rights of self and others—is co-operative and self-controlled.	Positively reinforce behaviour, with appropriate comments and specific feedback (pat on the back, acknowledgment, sharing success, giving responsibility etc).	Involve colleagues in the celebration of children's achievements.
2	Basically respects the rights of others but has difficulties which affect self-esteem. Some degree of frustration, low concentration levels. **Minor disruptions** eg rudeness and annoying others, no homework, punctuality a problem, incorrect equipment.	Supportive teachers seek solution to problem with student. Consultation with other colleagues, support staff, guidance officer and parents. Reinforce success, behaviour contracts between home and school, documentation given to support staff describing problem, class meetings.	If necessary gain collegial help from staff and principal in defining problem and applying solution.
3	Persistently violates the rights of others in a minor way. **Has continuing but minor problems,** eg violates rights of others, continues Level 2 behaviour, poor attitude to learning and work, rude and unresponsive in class.	Teacher consults with colleagues and support staff who may contact parents. Actions may include detention, consultation with appropriate support staff (guidance, welfare, etc). Place on behaviour contract, withdraw from playground or school functions.	Involve support from colleagues, support staff, principal, welfare officer etc.
4	Continually breaches the rights of others. Regular and serious infringements of the rights of others, eg verbal or physical assault, intimidation, vandalism, defiance, disruption, etc. Isolated serious breaking of rules, continued deterioration in behaviour, ignoring any attempts to help.	Teacher consults with colleagues, and support staff who contact parents. Documentation recorded and filed. Information passed to all staff. Actions include child being banned from school functions, internal suspension (followed by counselling and contract), no playground privileges—time-out, daily behaviour report.	Must involve support staff, principal, guidance officer and parent. Case conference a suggested option.
5	Seriously violates the rights of others and shows no signs of wanting to change, eg abusive, poor effect on peers, dangerous, uncontrollable and unco-operative.	Teacher refers problem directly to principal. After discussion with parents student may be suspended.	Must involve principal, parent, guidance officer and District Education Office.

Bibliography

Applied Psychology Research Group, Ministry of Education, Melbourne (1989) *Teacher Stress in Victoria: A Survey of Teachers' Views*.

Axworthy, D, Olney, H and Hamilton P (1989) 'Managing Student Behaviour: A Whole-School Approach' in Szaday, C, *Addressing Behaviour Problems in Australian Schools*. ACER, Camberwell, Vic.

Balson, M (1990) *Understanding Classroom Behaviour*. ACER, Hawthorn, Vic.

Barrish, H H, Saunders, M and Wolf, M M (1969) 'Good Behaviour Game: Effects of Individual Contingencies for Group Consequences on Disruptive Behaviour in the Classroom', *Journal of Applied Behaviour Analysis*, Vol 2 pp 119–124.

Bernard, M (1990) *Taking the Stress Out of Teaching*. CollinsDove, Melbourne.

Bjorkquist, K, Ekman, K, and Lagerspetz, K (1982) 'Bullies and Victims: Their Ego Picture and Normative Ego Picture', *Scandinavian Journal of Psychology*, 23, pp 307–313.

Boer, B and Gleeson, V (1982) *The Law of Education*. Butterworths, Sydney.

Borba, M and Borba, C (1980) *Self-Esteem: A Classroom Affair*, Vols 1 and 2. Winston Press, Minneapolis.

Brown, D, Reschly, D and Sabes, D (1974) 'Using Group Contingencies with Punishment and Positive Reinforcement to Modify Aggressive Behaviours in a "Head Start" Classroom', *Psychological Record*, Vol 24, pp 291–496.

Colby, D and Harper, T (1985) *Preventing Classroom Disruption*. Croon Helm, London.

Cornett, C E (1986) *Learning Through Laughter: Humour in the Classroom*. Phi Delta Kappa Educational Foundation, Indiana.

Cowin, M et al (1985) *Positive School Discipline: A Practical Guide to Developing Policy*. Parents and Friends of Monnington Publications.

Cranfield, J and Wells, H C (1976) *100 Ways to Enhance Self-Concept in Your Classroom*. Prentice-Hall, New Jersey.

Dalton, J (1985) *Adventures in Thinking: Creative Thinking and Co-operative Talk in Small Groups*. Nelson, Melbourne.

Deci, E L (1985) 'The Well-Tempered Classroom', *Psychology Today*. March pp 52–53.

Department of Education and the Arts, Tasmania (1990) *Positive Discipline: Improving Behaviour in Your Classroom*.

Department of Education and the Arts, Students Services Branch, Tasmania (1990) *Student Behaviour of Serious Concern*.

Dobson, J and Gale, R (1990) 'Best of Set Discipline'. 'Item 5 Discipline'. *Corporal Punishment: Help for Teachers*. ACER, Camberwell, Vic.

Doyle, W (1986) 'Classroom Organization and Management' in Whitrock M C (ed) *Handbook of Research on Teaching*. Macmillan, New York.

Dreikurs, R (1968) *Psychology in the Classroom: A Manual for Teachers*. Harper & Row, New York.

Dreikurs, R, Grunwald, B and Pepper, F (1982) *Maintaining Sanity in the Classroom*. Harper & Row, New York.

Elliott, M (1986) *Kidscape Training Pack: for Use with Primary Children*. Kidscape, London.

Elton et al (1989) (*The Elton Report*) *Discipline in Schools: Report of the Committee of Enquiry*. Her Majesty's Stationery Office, London.

Eron, L D, et al (1987) 'Aggression and Its Correlates Over 22 Years' in Crowell, D H, Evans, L M and O'Donnell C E (eds) *Childhood Aggression and Violence*. Plenum Press, New York.

Faber, A and Mazlish, E (1982) *How to Talk So Kids Will Listen and Listen So Kids Will Talk*. Avon Books, New York.

Fullan, M (with Stieyelbauer, S) (1991) *The New Meaning of Educational Change*. New York Teachers College Press, Toronto.

Fullan, M G and Hargreaves, A (1991) *Working Together for Your School*. ACER, Hawthorn, Vic.

Gillborn, D, Nixon, J and Ruddick, J (1992) *Dimensions of Discipline: Rethinking Practice in Secondary Schools*. Department for Education, London.

Glasser, W (1991) *The Quality School: Managing Students Without Coercion*. Harper & Row, New York.

Glasser, W (1986) *Control Theory in The Classroom*. Harper & Row, New York.

Gossen, D (1992) *Restitution*. New View Publications, North Carolina.

Grinder, M (1993) *Your Personal Guide to Classroom Management*. ENVOY. M Grinder & Assoc 16303 NE, 259th St, Battle Ground, WA 98604.

Guskey, T R (1986) 'Staff Development and the Process of Teacher Change', *Educational Researcher*, Vol 15 (5) May.

Hamilton, P (1986) Study noted in Szaday, C (ed) 1989 *Addressing Behaviour Problems in Australian Schools*. ACER, Hawthorn, Vic.

Harris, S J (1973) *Winners and Losers*. Argus Communications, Illinois.

Hill, S and Hill, T (1989) *The Collaborative Classroom: A Guide to Co-operative Learning*. Eleanor-Curtain Publishing.

Hoffmeister, P (1993) 'The Peace-Keeper Programme. Behaviour Problems', *Network Newsletter* No 16 June, pp 3-5. ACER, Hawthorn,Vic.

Hyndman M, and Thorsborne, M (1992) 'Bullying: A school Focus', a paper presented to the Queensland Guidance and Counselling Conference, Surfers Paradise.

Johnson, D W and Johnson, B T (1989) *Leading the Co-operative School*. Interaction Book Co, Minnesota.

Johnson, L (1992) *My Possee Don't Do Homework*. St. Martin's Press, New York.

Kafer, N (1984) *The Skills of Friendship* SET No 1. ACER, Hawthorn, Vic.

Knox, J (1992) 'Bullying in Schools: Communicating with the Victim', *Support for Learning* Vol 7, No 4, Nov 1992, pp 159–162.

Kohlberg, L (1976) 'Moral Stages and Moralization: The Cognitive-Developmental Approach' in Licona, T (ed) *Moral Development and Behaviour: Theory, Research and Issues*. Holt Rinehart & Winston, New York.

Kounin, J (1971) *Discipline and Group Management in the Classroom*. Holt Rinehart and Winston, New York.

Kyriacou, C (1986) *Effective Teaching in Schools*. Basil Blackwell, Oxford.

Kyriacou, C (1987) 'Teacher Appraisal in the Classroom: Can it Be Done Successfully?' *School Organization*, 1987, Vol 7, No 2, pp 139–144.

Kyriacou, C (1981) 'Social Support and Occupational Stress among School Teachers', *Educational Studies* Vol. 7, pp 55–60.

Kyriacou, C (1991) *Essential Teaching Skills*. Basil Blackwell, Oxford.

Lemin, M, Potts, H and Welsford, P (1994) *Values Strategies for Classroom Teachers*. ACER, Camberwell, Vic.

Lowe, J and Istance, D (1989) *Schools and Quality* (an international report). OECD, Paris.

McCarthy, P, Freeman, L, Rothwell, C and Arnheim, B (1983) 'Is There Life After 8D? Group Reinforcement at the Post Primary Level', *Interview*, No 11. Ministry of Education, Victoria.

McDaniel, T (1989) 'The Discipline Debate: A Road Through the Thicket', *Educational Leadership*, March pp 81-82.

McFadden, J, Flynn, C and Bazzo, B (1985) *Junior Life Science: A Positive Approach to Successful Behaviour*. Martin Educational.

McGrath, H and Francey, S (1993) *Friendly Kids, Friendly Classrooms*. Longman Cheshire, Melbourne.

Montgomery, B (1986) *Coping With Stress*. Pitman Health Information Series, Melbourne.

Morgan, D P and Jenson, W R (1988) *Teaching Behaviourally Disordered Students: Preferred Practices*. Merrill Publishing Co, Toronto.

Nelsen, J (1981) *Positive Discipline*. Ballantyne Books, New York.

Oates, S (1991) 'School Principals and Discipline' in Lewis, R and Loregrove, M, *Classroom Discipline*. Longman Cheshire, Melbourne.

Olweus, D (1978) *Aggression in the Schools: Bullies and Whipping Boys*. Hemisphere, Washington DC.

Olweus, D (1989) 'Bully/Victim Problems Among School Children: Basic Facts and Effects of a School Based Intervention Program' in Rubin, K, and Pepler, D (eds). *The Development and Treatment of Childhood Aggression*. Erlbaum, Hillsdale New Jersey.

Patterson, G R, DeBarshye, D and Ramsey, E (1989) 'A Developmental Perspective on Antisocial Behaviour', *American Psychologist*, 44, pp 329–335.

Piaget, J (1932) *The Moral Judgement of the Child*. Routledge & Kegan Paul, London.

Rigby, K and Slee, P (1993) *Bullying in Schools*. (video) ACER, Hawthorn, Vic.

Roberts, M (1988) 'School Yard Menace', *Psychology Today*, Feb pp 53–56.

Robertson, J (1989) *Effective Classroom Control: Understanding Teacher–Pupil Relationships*. Hodder & Stoughton, London.

Rogers, B (1990) *You Know The Fair Rule*. ACER, Camberwell, Vic.

Rogers, B (1992) *Supporting Teachers in the Workplace*. Jacaranda Press, Milton, Qld.

Rogers, B (1992) 'Peer Support. Peers Supporting Peers', Topic 1, Issue 7. National Foundation for Educational Research, UK (Harlow).

Rogers, B (1993) 'Taming Bullies: A Whole-School Focus' *Classroom*. pp 12–15.

Rogers, B (1993) 'The World of Cue: Nonverbal Behaviour in Teacher–Student Management', paper delivered to the 1993 National Conference on Student Behaviour Problems in Perth.

Rogers, B (1994) *The Language of Discipline: A Practical Approach to Effective Classroom Management*. Northcote House, Plymouth, UK.

Rogers, B (1994) 'Classroom Discipline: A Planned Approach', Topic 1, Spring, Issue 11, National Foundation for Educational Research, UK.

Rogers, B (1994) *Behavior Recovery: A Whole School Programme for Mainstream Schools*. ACER, Camberwell, Vic.

Russell, D W, Altmaier E and Van Velzen, D (1987). 'Job Related Stress: Social Support and Burnout Among Classroom Teachers' in *Journal of Applied Psychology*. May, Vol 72, No 2, pp 269–274.

Rutter, M (1983) 'School Effects on Pupil Progress: Research Findings and Policy Implications', *Child Development* 54, pp 1-29.

Rutter, M (1985) 'Family and Social Influences on Behavioural Development', *Journal of Child Psychology* 26, No 3, pp 349–368.

Rutter, M, Maughan, B, Mortimer, P and Ouston, J (1979) *Fifteen Thousand Hours: Secondary Schools and Their Effects on Children*. Open Books, London.

Scottish Council for Research in Education, Edinburgh (1993) *Supporting Schools Against Bullying* (pack). *Bullying and How to Fight It*. (book)

Selwyn, T, O'Donnel, D (1984) 'Chance Encounters of a Useful Kind (or Taking the "Arr" Out of Yard Duty)', *Interview* No 14, ACGCS Bulletin, pp 30–31. Student Services Branch, Education Department, Vic.

Serfontein, G (1990) *The Hidden Handicap: How to Help Children Who Suffer from Dyslexia, Hyperactivity and Learning Difficulties*. Simon & Schuster, Sydney.

Slee, P and Rigby, K (1991) 'Bullying Among Australian School Children: Reported Behaviour and Attitude Towards Victims', *Journal of Social Psychology*, No 131, pp 615–627.

Smith, P K and Thompson, P (1991) *Practical Approaches to Bullying*. David Fulton, London.

Stephenson, P and Smith, D (1989) 'Bullying in the Junior School' in Tattum, D P and Lane, D A (eds) *Bullying in Schools*. Trentham Books, Stoke on Trent.

Stones, R (1992). *No More Bullying!* Dinosaur Publications, HarperCollins, London.

Time, September 5 (1983), 'Private Violence', pp 32–45.

Wheldhall, K (1992) *Discipline in Schools. Psychological Perspectives on the Elton Report*. Routledge, London.

Wheldall, K, Bevan, K and Shortall, K (1986) 'A Touch of Reinforcement: The Effects of Continent Teacher Touch on the Classroom Behaviour of Young Children, *Educational Review*, 38: 207–16.

Wilkes, R (1981) 'Fly Me to the Moon: A Classroom Behaviour Management Program to Enhance Learning.' *Interview*, No 3. Ministry of Education, Vic.

Wolfgang, C and Glickman, C (1986) Solving Discipline Problems: *Strategies for Classroom Teachers* (2nd Edition) Allyn & Bacon, Boston.

Wragg, J (1989) *Talk Sense to Yourself: A Program for Children and Adolescents*. ACER, Camberwell, Vic.

Index

abuse 92
  physical 89
  verbal 39, 82, 89, 91, 133, 140-5
acknowledgment of desired behaviour 40, 62
action planning 16, 19, 28, 43, 45
aggression 16, 20, 32, 57, 65, 69, 82-3, 88-9, 91-2, 98, 105, 140-1, 145
  see also violence
  aggressive play 10
anger 12, 26, 39, 47, 82, 91-2, 104, 129, 138
apology 39, 89, 126, 141
argumentative students 12, 24, 29, 32, 48, 104, 128-9, 133
arguments 9-10, 35, 84, 94, 120, 125, 137, 139
  avoiding 119
assembly 9, 85-6

bad-day syndrome 32, 80, 92, 123, 132-3
behaviourally disordered (BD) students 11-12, 16, 44-5, 149-158
  behaviour management plan 151-8
  collegial support 150
  parent support 151
  see also parents
behaviour management policy *see* policy
behaviour outcome enhancers (BOEs) 162
blind-eye syndrome 45
body language 35, 38, 48-50, 118, 122, 124, 129-130, 133
  see also language
  postural cues 102, 109
'broken record' technique 120
bullying 10-11, 20, 24, 26, 29, 65, 69, 112, 163, 169, 178-89
bumbag system 166-7
bus duty 19, 22, 46, 163, 169, 176-8

camps 19
cane 11
canteen 19, 22, 69, 89, 94, 144

card system 89
   see also exit
case study
   Ms Davis 52
   Veronica 124
certainty principle 39, 43, 91, 93, 96, 99, 122
   certainty rather than severity 38, 84, 90, 101, 127
change 14-15
changeover of teachers 75-6
choice 57, 94, 117-118, 121
class meetings 21, 41, 52, 58, 63-6, 74, 140-1, 148, 159-60
code of conduct 19, 66, 98
cognitive rehearsal 121
colleagues 43, 69, 96
   as a group 11-12
collegial support 160, 193-197
commands 121
communication 15-17, 41, 73
   staff 14
community involvement 206
conditioned distracters 114
conferences 37, 68, 123, 128
conflict resolution 138
consequences 12, 18-21, 23-5, 30, 37-9, 43-6, 69, 71, 82, 84, 89-94,
   97, 99-100, 128, 136
   consistency 166
   deferred 38-9, 119-120, 131
   directed 117
   immediate 119, 131
   related 38, 101
   targeted 57
consistency 12, 19, 44, 58, 90, 165
'continent touch' 119
   see also touch
contracts 18, 20, 37, 68-9, 85, 90, 98, 100, 123, 136, 146-9

cool-off time (COT) 38-9, 42, 70, 82-4, 96, 98, 103, 105, 121-2, 128, 138, 141
corporal punishment *see* punishment
correction 17-19, 23, 33, 35, 39, 44, 46-8, 50, 61, 64, 74, 104
   plan 122
   private 37, 49, 113
   using questions 116
counselling 18, 20, 37, 87, 97, 128

decision making 14
degree of seriousness 20, 90, 92
denial and mistargeting 120
detention 20, 27, 38, 42, 69, 95
direction 108, 115
   across the room 110
   conditional 104
   group 114
directional language 104, 109, 119
   see also language
discipline 11, 16-17, 19, 21-22, 42, 48, 58, 62, 75, 84, 90-91, 96
   classroom 10, 18
   context of 121
   language 103
   plan 47, 100, 122-3
   playground 10-11
      see also playground
   positive 46, 51, 59, 189
discursive approach 134
disruptive behaviour 43, 46, 57, 69, 83, 85, 92-3, 101, 113, 115, 120
distracting students aside 113-114
duty of care 18-19, 30, 47, 76, 105, 121, 122, 163-4, 188
   plan for management beyond classroom 169-174

emotional moment 48, 89, 97, 136

encouragement 23-4, 33, 40-1, 47, 51, 55, 61-2, 64, 74, 148

    balance with correction 104

    language 101

    tone 63

environment

    home 13, 68, 180

    school 12-13, 20, 22, 29, 40, 44, 68, 78, 174-6

establishment phase 22, 30, 41, 50, 57-8, 70, 72, 77, 83-5, 89, 91, 93, 95-6, 108, 136

    of lesson 115

    reminders during 105

      see also reminders

    Figure 2, 23

exclusion from classroom 82

    removal of student 16

excursions 1, 42

exit plan 72, 85-6

    card system 86, 89

eye contact 10, 50, 110, 114, 119, 125, 129, 135

eye level 55

face losing 39, 129

face saving 36, 49, 51, 55, 109, 136

feedback 16, 40, 46, 195-6

    in professional development 197-200

fights 11, 22, 26-7, 29, 34, 43-4, 55, 88, 105, 121, 165

follow through 88, 97, 128

follow up 42-3, 50, 81, 88-9, 93, 95-6, 123, 126, 128, 166

    after class 124

4Rs 18, 31

4Ws 27, 87, 95, 172

gaining attention 107-8

gender equity 17

global behaviour 121
global set 48–51, 131
goal disclosure 125, 148
good practice 81
guilt 13

harassment 17, 19–20
hard–class syndrome 16, 44, 80, 159–160
Hare Street Infant School, UK 20–22
hats 22, 49
humour 58–61, 76, 81, 133

'I' statements 114
ignoring
    tactical 36, 54, 56, 87, 110–113, 115, 122, 124, 134–5
incentives 41
    see also rewards
isolation of teachers 16, 43, 193

language 49, 78s
    see also body language
    directional 104, 107, 109
    nonverbal 34–8, 49–51, 55, 102, 105, 107, 112
    of correction 47, 58, 122, 123
    of discipline 21, 100–102, 121
    of encouragement 101
    planning 33
least-to-most-intrusive correction 18, 24, 33–5, 83, 94, 101–2, 133
    see also correction
litter 10, 11, 22, 39, 79, 93, 116, 172
losing face
    see face losing

manners 36–7, 40, 69, 71–2, 106
mentor system 58
mirroring 125, 152–155
mixed ability 12, 46, 72, 74

modelling 14, 17, 32, 36, 40, 44, 62, 72, 81, 91, 125, 138, 155-6
monitors 21, 55, 57, 63, 73
morale 13

negotiation 17
new-start syndrome 76
new teachers 44
noise 12, 21, 27, 55, 72, 79-80, 104, 107, 122
   talking over 114
noise meter 79-80, 115
non-teaching staff 20
   see also support staff
nonverbal language
   see language

1, 3, 6 method 160
over-servicing 41
owning behaviour 117
   see also YOYOB

parents 20-21, 41-2, 88, 89, 95, 97-8
   interviews with 11
   support 17, 67-8, 186-7
passing notes 60
pause 107, 114
peer
   appraisal 195-6
   mediation 189-92
   mentoring 114
   support 21, 74, 188
phrasing 62
physical restraint 120
playground 20, 26, 46, 67, 76, 88-90
   duty 9-10, 18, 29, 58, 96, 121, 131
   duty-of-care role 105
   management 10, 12, 16, 19, 22, 44, 99, 163

policy of behaviour management 10, 14, 15-19, 22, 27, 37, 42, 83, 86,
    165, 183-4, 206-213
    role of policy steering group 210-11
positive behaviour 21, 40-41
positive language 121, 144-5
    see also language
positive reinforcement 44
preferred practices 17, 19, 24, 27, 29-30, 37, 44-5, 165
preventive approaches 17, 130, 140
'primary' behaviour 35, 62, 104, 112, 129-131, 133-4
principal 14, 16, 84, 97, 164-5
    see also senior management
private correction
    see correction
problem solving 16-17, 24, 37, 42-3, 64, 97, 137, 139, 161, 193-4
professional development 45
put-downs 10, 29, 32, 39, 112, 120, 140-1
    racial 11
    verbal 12
punishment 32, 37, 39, 43, 83, 90-91, 93, 100
    corporal 11, 29, 75, 90-91

qualifiers 64
questions 116, 121

reconciliation 25, 39
redirecting 120, 135
re-establishment of relationship 24, 33, 37, 47, 55, 104, 110, 136
refocusing 135, 137
relocation 38-9, 82, 118, 140
reminders 35-6, 46, 48, 50, 54, 56, 58, 104
    group 114
    positive tone 106
repair and rebuild 101, 128
reprimands 37, 81
reputation class 158-162

respect 31, 37, 55, 62, 79, 92-3, 120, 125-7, 131

responsibilities 11-12, 18, 29-31, 40, 44-6, 58, 64, 66, 68, 72-3, 92, 136, 139

restitution 27, 38-8, 66, 88-9, 95, 99-100

review 16, 21, 24

rewards 21, 41, 89-90, 162

rights 11-12, 18-19, 27, 29-31, 44, 46, 57-8, 68, 72, 78, 82, 84, 90-92, 100, 136, 139

routines 18-19, 22, 31, 46, 57-8, 72, 74, 76, 78, 92-3, 105, 139

rule reminders 111, 114-5, 117, 121, 172

rules 12, 18, 22, 27, 29-31, 36, 39, 54-5, 57, 68, 71-2, 76-79, 90, 92, 100, 105, 120, 139, 174

safety 19-20, 31, 37, 43, 69, 78-9, 84, 88, 92, 94, 112, 133, 163, 164-5

saving face
   see face saving

'secondary behaviour' 35-6, 101, 104, 112, 124-5, 129-132, 136
   low level 133

self-esteem 32, 41, 61

senior staff 20, 86, 90, 97-9
   see also principal

sharing with colleagues 43

signals 114
   nonverbal 138
   privately understood 51, 56, 105-7

staff meeting 10, 43, 70

stress 12, 15-16, 47, 72, 131, 193
   management 205

supervision 18, 22
   wet-day 19, 22, 72, 97, 163

support 16, 30, 43-4, 57, 96-9, 184-5
   see also collegial support
   culture of 196-198
   for new teachers 203-4
   staff 301-203
   teachers by principal 11

support staff 20–21, 164
  see also non-teaching staff
suspension 16, 20, 42, 69, 97–8, 100, 123
swearing 10, 24, 29, 101, 120, 141–5

tactical ignoring
  see ignoring
take-up time 35–6, 49, 51, 55, 57, 83, 94, 104, 109–110, 118, 135–6
talkative students 9
talking out of turn 115
task avoidance 27, 57
teasing 10–12, 22, 24, 26–7, 29, 65
time-out 11, 18–21, 25, 27, 37–9, 42–3, 45, 57, 69, 72, 82, 84–6, 88–9,
  94, 96–8, 100, 140
  area 105
  in the playground 168–9
tone of classroom 80
touch 119–120

united approach 43–5
  individual disagreement with 45

values clarification 66
verbal abuse
  see abuse
violence 16

welfare of teachers 44
whole-school approach 12–13
wounded silence 50

YOYOB (You Own Your Own Behaviour) 39, 57, 66, 94–5, 117